The Sharp Edge
of Wisdom

Devotional readings for serious young and older adults who want to grow with God's wisdom using Bridges' 200-year-old *Proverbs* commentary, translated and illustrated for today

Rick Horne

© Rick Horne, 2019

Cover Art by Brandon McLean of MercuryGraphix.com

Dedication

This is dedicated as an inheritance to: Lesley, Shaun, Becca, Katie, Nathan, Tyler, Cami, Nicole, Luke, Evan, Silas, Marcus, Simeon, Julissa, Jed, Jr., Jaydn, Joey, Jamison, and other grandkids and great-grandkids who make their appearance along life's way.

"A good man leaves an inheritance to his children's children..."
Proverbs 13:22

May you all drink deeply from
the wells of God's wise counsel
and live!

"Blessed is the one who finds wisdom...she is a tree of life to those
who lay hold of her..." (Proverbs 3:13,18)

Acknowledgements

In every sense of the word, God's providence has led this project—more than 200 years in the making. The chief Parent in the Bible, the Lord, raised up pastor Charles Bridges in the 19th century to shepherd his people with godly wisdom from Proverbs for Christ-centered living. I've sought to translate 52 selections from his commentary into modern language for 21 century teens, parents and others. I hope my 40-plus years as a teacher, school and family counselor, husband and parent, and bi-vocational pastor have enabled me to do justice to Bridges' wise counsel for the needs of teens and families today.

On a practical level, author, co-pastor, professional colleague, and friend for more than 40 years, Bob Walton, edited and made suggestions about the content for *The Sharp Edge of Wisdom.*

More personally, my wife, Betty, our kids' mom and their kids' grandmother, persisted in proofing and suggesting improvements to these messages all along the way. "She opens her mouth with wisdom...a woman who fears the LORD is to be praised. Give her of the fruit of her hands, and let her works praise her in the gates."

Proverbs 31:26,30,31

Any lasting value of these pages, of course, has its source in my Father's goodness. I'm hoping *The Sharp Edge of Wisdom* yields some of what the Psalmist said would be true of the righteous who would "still bear fruit in old age" because of being "full of sap and green" (Psalm 92:14).

Soli Deo Gloria

Other Books by Rick Horne

Life-Shaping Decisions, Applying God's Word to Career Planning
(A Teacher's Edition is also available)
Association of Christian Schools International,
Purposeful Design Bible Curriculum, 2002

Scorners and Mockers: How to Dampen Their Influence in Your School
Purposeful Design Publications, 2005

Get Outta My Face!: How to Reach Angry Unmotivated Teens with Biblical Counsel
Shepherd Press, 2009

Get Offa My Case: Godly Parenting of an Angry Teen
Shepherd Press, 2012

How Change Happens: An Introductory Pastoral Counseling Course (Part I)
(Adaptation, by permission, of The Christian Counseling
and Educational Foundation's course, "The Dynamics of Biblical Change")
CreateSpace Independent Publishing Platform, 2018
Kindle version, 2019

*What Change Looks Like: Applying the Model to the Heat that Invites Suffering, Depression,
Anxiety, Frustration, Guilt, Oppression, Spiritual Warfare and Other Challenges*
(Adaptation, by permission, of The Christian Counseling
and Educational Foundation's course, "The Dynamics of Biblical Change")
Planned for Publication in 2020

The Sharp Edge of Wisdom
Table of Contents

The Sharp Edge of Wisdom
What This Book Is About and How to Use It

He's running full speed, swinging his sword. Evan jumped out of the way to avoid Luke's slashing moves, but alas, Luke was able to slap Evan's backside with his plastic sword. They both fell on the floor laughing. No harm done!

In this fictional scene, no harm was done because the swords were plastic.

The book of Proverbs isn't plastic. It contains *The Sharp Edge of Wisdom* in over 900 verses. It can cut deeply into one's life. It won't draw blood, but it will draw out lots of other ugly, destructive stuff from our insides—what Proverbs calls "folly" or "foolishness." At the same time, each proverb points us to *wisdom*: living life as God designed it—with a heart of love for him and his ways.

Charles Bridges, a 19th century pastor, earnestly counsels us about wisdom and folly in his commentary on Proverbs. I'm hoping these devotional meditations will make his comments even more helpful to today's young people and adults by putting them into modern English.

What are proverbs?

Proverbs are *sharp*, terse, compact statements. They are the *edges* of big truths about how God planned life to work. The Hebrew word for "proverb" basically means a comparison. It's a "sharp simile" or an expanded "full-grown allegory"[1] or illustration.

"In Proverbs, terseness [brief, pithy, concise sayings] becomes... the hallmark of its lines."[2]   The edge of a sharp sword begins cutting upon contact. The proverbs are like that. They make an impact on us as soon as we begin to think about them, but there are even deeper effects, rich depths of wisdom, when we meditate upon them.

Who is Proverbs for?

Solomon wrote the proverbs for young adults and anyone else who wants to be wise and enjoy the benefits of wisdom (Proverbs 1:4,5). Though they are short, the sharp edges of Proverbs' wisdom are life-changing, but they are especially designed for the challenges, temptations, fears, relationships, and hopes of youth.

How can we get the wisdom of Proverbs?

Wisdom is decision-making that respects God's law. It submits to his will. It seeks his glory and honor in every decision. It includes knowledge and understanding, but it is especially connected to a humble desire to *do* God's will. "The fear of the

---

[1] Kidner, D., 1964, *Proverbs: An Introduction and Commentary*, Vol. 17, p. 55, Downers Grove, IL: InterVarsity Press.
[2] Waltke, B. K., 2004, *The Book of Proverbs, Chapters 1–15*, p. 38, Grand Rapids, MI: Wm. B. Eerdmans Publishing Co.

LORD" is the concept that captures all these thoughts and more. It is "the beginning of wisdom" according to Proverbs 9:10. This wisdom marks one's life by desires and character qualities that look like Jesus' (1 Corinthians 1:30; James 3:17,18).

The more we humbly think about each short, pithy saying in Proverbs, the more God will work his wisdom into us. The proverbs cut very deeply!! The writer of Hebrews, in the New Testament, said the same thing about God's word, in general: "For the word of God is living and active, sharper than any two-edged sword, piercing to the division of soul and spirit, of joints and marrow, and discerning the thoughts and intentions of the heart" (Hebrews 4:12). The proverbs concentrate on only a slice of the meaning of each truth they teach and "...by their nature cannot express the whole truth about a topic."[3] But you can unpack the fuller, richer wisdom in each of these bundles of truth by looking up other cross-references connected to each proverb and meditating upon them. You will find lots of these references in the "Bridges' Comments" section for each proverb.

Handle these *sharp edges* with care. They will cut deeply if you let them. That's a very good thing and it will make you wise! Wisdom says,

> Blessed is the one who listens to me, watching daily at my gates, waiting beside my doors.
> For whoever finds me finds life and obtains favor from the LORD,
> but he who fails to find me injures himself; all who hate me love death.
> Proverbs 8:34-36

How To Get The Most Out of These Meditations

1. Pray to unpack the riches

Proverbs "is not a portrait-album or a book of manners: it offers a key to life."[4] In other words, it's not a child's story book. It's for young adults who want to be wise and older adults who ought to be wise and want to be wiser still.

"The fear of the Lord" is that key to the door of wisdom (Proverbs 9:10). That is the attitude that says, "I want your wise counsel about everything in life." The proverbs are short, sharp, pithy statements of God's law—broken down into small, bite-size, practical pieces. No one proverb says all there is to say about any single topic, but each does reveal an element of wisdom God wants you to practice.

As you think about each proverb, pray that God will teach you more and more deeply what he is saying. Your understanding will expand and your wisdom will mature.

2. Use one selection per week

---

[3] Waltke, B. K., p. 38.

[4] Kidner, D., p. 13.

There are 52 selections in *The Sharp Edge of Wisdom. They will last you a year if you do one selection per week.* These cover about 20% of the verses in the book of Proverbs.

You don't have to do any selection in one day. In fact, it is better to allow the thoughts in each selection to roll around in your mind and heart for a couple of days. That is called meditation. Psalm 1 says that such an exercise is the way to ensure spiritual and life fruitfulness. Don't hurry. It's not the *amount* you read and think about each day, it's daily investment that matters--consistency. "Wealth gained hastily will dwindle, but whoever gathers little by little will increase it" (Proverbs 13:11). Gather the wealth of the Word of God each day.

3. Use one of the four main parts of each selection on different days of the week

Each selection includes the verse or verses for that selection and four additional parts: *Wisdom Lived Out Today*, a *Prayer*, and *Bridges' Comments*, and *To Help You Meditate*. Most selections focus on one or two verses. The parts of each selection are:

The verses

This book uses the English Standard Version (ESV) and the New International Version (NIV84) to present each proverb. Most often they are similar, but the differences may help you to get a bit more of the sense of some of the terms that Solomon and others used when composing the proverbs in the original language. Throughout the *Wisdom Lived Out Today* and *Bridges' Comments* sections, whenever a word or phrase is actually cited from the ESV version of the proverb, that word or phrase appears in *italics.*

Wisdom Lived Out Today

In this section, my grandfather identity comes out a bit. I relate life experiences of some of our grandkids and others that illustrate a key thought in the proverb. There is always more to be gained from a proverb than the focus of the *Wisdom Lived Out Today* section, but this section is my attempt to show how the wisdom of God is right up to date in a specific way for all of us, young and old, though written about 3,000 years ago.

Prayer

The prayer suggests a brief request to the Father that captures the central thought of *Wisdom Lived Out Today* from the verse. Wisdom, you recall, is wanting God's will in every part of your life. These prayers may help you focus your request for the wisdom that each selection urges.

They are not magic words. They are suggestions about the kind of help God says we all need in order to live in this troubled world.

Bridges' Comments

Charles Bridges was a brilliant and wise pastor. I've tried to "translate" what he wrote almost 200 years ago into 21st-century language and style. I've paraphrased some of his comments, illustrations, and quotations of others to whom he refered. I've used today's words and expressions to replace some that he used which have changed meaning since the time he wrote his commentary. I have tried to remain faithful to his meaning and pastoral care in each selection.

Suggestion for reading *Bridges' Comments*: Bridges referred to many verses in the Bible in each of his comment sections. I've included most of them in parentheses ( ). To help you keep in mind the flow of Bridges' thoughts, however, I recommend that you skip over these sections in parentheses the first time you are reading his comments. Go back to the verses later for more depth and understanding. They are well worth the time and effort.

To Help You Meditate

There are three questions at the end of each selection to help you drill down the message of each passage more deeply in your life. Think about each question, maybe in a discussion with others. You'll be able to immediately apply the wisdom God is relating to you in these verses by giving meaningful thought to each (See Psalm 1:1-3).

"Blessed is the one who finds wisdom, and the one who gets understanding,
For the gain from her is better than gain from silver and her profit better than gold.
She is more precious than jewels, and nothing you desire can compare with her.
Long life is in her right hand; in her left hand are riches and honor.
Her ways are ways of pleasantness, and all her paths are peace.
She is a tree of life to those who lay hold of her; those who hold her fast are called blessed."

Proverbs 3:13-18

1:1-4   "Think" About It!

ESV
1 The proverbs of Solomon, son of David, king of Israel:
2 To know wisdom and instruction, to understand words of insight,
3 to receive instruction in wise dealing, in righteousness, justice, and equity;
4 to give prudence to the simple, knowledge and discretion to the youth—

NIV
1 The proverbs of Solomon son of David, king of Israel:
2 for attaining wisdom and discipline; for understanding words of insight;
3 for acquiring a disciplined and prudent life, doing what is right and just and fair;
4 for giving prudence to the simple, knowledge and discretion to the young--

Wisdom Lived Out Today:

"That's not fair!"

Have you ever said that? Who hasn't?

Proverbs was written for anyone, *youth* especially, who wants to understand what fair is. Proverbs is written for anyone who wants to make wise, just, and fair choices.

When Aunt Jen was a sophomore in high school, she had a teacher who, in her classroom, made a sarcastic comment about homosexuals. Aunt Jen knew that homosexuality was wrong, but she also knew something about *wisdom* and *righteousness, discretion* and *justice*. This teacher, in her judgment, stepped over the line.

Soon a couple of the kids in her class took the teacher's comment further and added mocking comments they thought were funny.

Aunt Jen began to boil on the inside. She finally spoke up with an angry look that they couldn't ignore. The gist of what she said was, "You people think these people are to be made fun of? They are troubled. They are sinners like us. I have a non-Christian friend who is a homosexual and she would never want to talk to you about anything serious like salvation with your mocking, disrespectful attitudes." The teacher apologized to her and the class and acknowledged that they were wrong to speak the way they did.

Proverbs was written to give young adults, called *youth* in verse 4, the ability to think with *understanding, fairness, equity, wisdom* and *justice.* Aunt Jen's classmates and teacher showed the opposite of all of these. She sensed that and boldly spoke up.

Look at these verses again. Do you notice anything about why the book of Proverbs was written? We can't get these personal character traits on our own. They must be received from someone who is wise and understanding. Proverbs is for young adults who want to *know*, to *understand*, to *receive*, and to be *given* these qualities of *wisdom, understanding, instruction, prudence, knowledge* and *discretion.*

The word "*youth*" in the Hebrew language means young adult. Anyone from about age 13 to 30 was considered to be a young adult. Youth are not second-class citizens or children. They can think, *understand*, make decisions, and have influence. They can have a good, *just*, wise, and fair influence, or the opposite kind of impact. But what makes the difference is that the young adults about whom Solomon is writing are open to receiving the *instruction* and counsel that leads in a good direction. It doesn't come naturally. What comes naturally is what Aunt Jen's classmates and even her teacher slipped into—foolishness and injustice.

How can you get to be *wise* and know the difference between *just* and *unjust* choices? Make the wisdom of Proverbs a part of your daily spiritual diet. That's why the book was written. Drink deeply at this well of good counsel. There are hundreds of nuggets of wise principles for living in Solomon's book. They have been tested for 3,000 years and have never been found to be faulty. And if you want to see these principles lived out in real life, be sure to include an orderly reading of the Gospels (Matthew, Mark, Luke, and John) in your private quiet time too. Watch Jesus live. He is wisdom in human form.

Make a plan to begin reading in Proverbs each day. Since there are 31 chapters and there are 31 days in most months, read a few verses from the chapter that corresponds to the date of the month on that day. On the first of the month, read from Proverbs 1. On the 21st, read from Proverbs 21, and so on. Read just a few verses and put a little dot beside the verse you finish with. Read and meditate. Roll the ideas in the verses around in your mind. Ask yourself what it would mean to live out these wise words at home, at school, with your family, friends, or enemies. Then next month, on that day of the month, start with where you left off. If you miss a day or even a week, don't worry about it. Skip it for

> **Prayer:**
> Father, I need your wisdom. I can be really foolish sometimes. Thank you for making a way for me to learn to live wisely and justly. Thank you for Jesus' example of living wisdom. Please teach me to be a wise young adult through this book for the rest of my life. Help me develop a consistent pattern of reading and thinking about your wise counsel every day. In Jesus' name, Amen.

now and get it next month. Proverbs will be here next month. Of course, you should read other passages of Scripture, too, but make this young adult's book your book—at least until age 30. After that, keep it as a steady part of your spiritual diet. God will bless your faithfulness and grow your wisdom, justice, and discernment.

Bridges' Comments:

Solomon is the author of Proverbs, according to Proverbs 1:1. He is identified as the son of David and King of Israel. He's had privileges, education, and experiences that, combined with his keen ability to observe, think and draw conclusions (Proverbs 24:30-34), give us access to wisdom beyond the scope of our own life experiences (Proverbs 1:2).

The wisdom Solomon gives us, as you will see, is rooted in "the fear of the Lord" (Proverbs 1:7; 9:10). That is the attitude of submission and openness to the way God wants us to look at life and respond to every situation we face. Wisdom is connected to the painfulness of self-discipline, which is often related to living in just and fair relationships and making good decisions (Proverbs 1:3).

Wisdom is for all kinds of people: *wise* and *discerning* people, more easily swayed and less committed people (the *simple),* and especially *young adults* (whom the Hebrew term *na'ar* identifies as young people from the age of puberty until age 30). *Young adults* have not had a personal long-life history to help them see, on their own, what is *wise* and foolish in most life situations (Proverbs 1:4). Proverbs gives them that wider and *wiser* perspective.

Proverbs opens with a short account of its author. Solomon is recorded as the *wisest* of men; a man of *wisdom*, because he was a man of prayer (1 Kings 3:12; compare Proverbs 2:1-9). The whole world of that day admired his *wisdom* (1 Kings 3:28; 4:34). If he had been the son of Jeroboam, he would have commanded respect. But, much more, he is to be respected as the *son of David* because of his godly prayers (Psalm 72:1) and counsels (Psalm 4:1-4; 1 Kings 2:1-4; 1 Chronicles 28:9). And if a king's sayings are respected, even when they do not have the inherent value of being God's Word, how much more should we give special attention to the *wise teaching* of this king of Israel (Ecclesiastes

---

Wisdom is rooted in the "fear of the Lord."

1:1,11; 2:9,10) who is speaking the Word of God.

Solomon's maxims or proverbs are of great value in and of themselves. They are worth far more than any counsel from the sages of his own or other times (1 Kings 4:29-31). They claim our reverence because they rest on infinitely higher ground. "…behold, something greater than Solomon is here" (Matthew 12:42). Solomon speaks as the inspired "wisdom of God" itself. *Wisdom* is given its own human personality (Proverbs 1:20; all of chapters 8 and 9; and 23:26) so that Solomon's sayings are truly "an oracle (a divine sentence, KJV[5]) on the lips of a king" (Proverbs 16:10).

The great purpose of this invaluable book is not to teach secular or political *wisdom*, though many excellent rules of each are woven throughout the book. But, rather, it is to teach the knowledge of God (Proverbs 1:7) which is "…able to make you wise for salvation…" (2 Timothy 3:15) and equips "…the man of God…for every good work" (2 Timothy 3:17; Titus 2:11,12).

Here, Solomon sets forth the glowing privileges of *wisdom*. He urges us to "get" it with intense earnestness as the "principal thing" (Proverbs 4:5-9, KJV[5]). It is our very "life" (Proverbs 4:13). *Instruction* is the means by which we gain it. We are directed to *receive instruction* (Proverbs 1:3). Further, we are *to know wisdom and instruction*; to perceive the words of *understanding*; we are to receive *instruction* to get the complete package *of wisdom, justice, judgment, and equity* (Proverbs 1:2,3; compare 2:9). Solomon also shows us the outcome of the practical application of all of these qualities throughout Proverbs.

In Proverbs, the "simple," or naïve, who are so easily deluded (see Proverbs 14:15; 21:11), can learn *prudence* (Proverbs 1:4). They need this in order to tell the difference

---

[5] KJV refers to the King James Version of the Holy Bible from 1611, which Bridges cited regularly in his commentary. Occasionally, his use of an old King James Version word is especially vivid and this author includes it.

between truth and error (Philippians 1:10; 1 Thessalonians 5:21), to guard them from false teachers (Psalm 17:4; 1 John 4:1; and compare Acts 17:11), to "give *instruction in* sound doctrine..." and to "...rebuke those who contradict it" (Titus 1:9; 2:8; compare Matthew 22:15-46).

Youth are especially directed to this book (Proverbs 1:4b). Their undisciplined passions and energy produce waste. Their thinking fluctuates wildly at the mercy of the winds of opinion in the world around them. They urgently need settled master-principles to help them live with sound purpose, choices, and behavior. Here, then, they find *knowledge and discretion* (Proverbs 1:4b). This is not a religion of imagination, impulsiveness, or emotionalism. This is the sound, practical energy of Scriptural truth.

To Help You Meditate:

1. What situations seem to show up most commonly where you think something unfair or unjust happens? What first steps do these introductory verses in Proverbs urge you to take before you make a response?

2. What time of the day would work best for you to be alert and focused on a few verses from Proverbs? Would a daily journal of your thoughts help you to think about the concepts of wise counsel that you read?

3. What value can Proverbs be for a young person (or any person) approaching life's important decisions?

1:5,6   Know the Ropes or Go in Circles

ESV
5 Let the wise hear and increase in learning, and the one who understands obtain guidance,
6 to understand a proverb and a saying, the words of the wise and their riddles.

NIV
5 let the wise listen and add to their learning, and let the discerning get guidance—
6 for understanding proverbs and parables, the sayings and riddles of the wise.

Wisdom Lived Out Today:

When I was in college, I had the opportunity to go to Charleston, South Carolina, to get a summer job with the Merchant Marines. A friend in college set me up with the opportunity. On a Saturday while we were there, our host offered to allow us to use his sailboat in the Charleston Bay. It sounded like fun. And what could be so hard about sailing a boat in a bay? Though we knew nothing about handling sails and sailboats, we decided to take him up on his offer.

The next day, Sunday, at the church that our host and we attended, a man came up and asked how we were doing and what we did over the weekend. We mentioned our sailing efforts. "Oh, was that you guys I saw out in the Bay going around and around in circles?" Yes, it was us! We didn't know how to handle the ropes. The boom and main sail just kept swinging back and forth; we kept ducking to not get hit by it, and the boat kept going in circles. It must have been hilarious to watch from the shore.

Solomon says that the book of Proverbs is to help young adults "know the ropes" about life. In verse five he says this wise book is to help people *obtain guidance*; literally, to know the ropes. Throughout the book of Proverbs, Solomon composes short, catchy proverbial statements that capture wise desires, thoughts, decisions, and actions that God says will make life work well. A little later on, in verse seven, he'll show that the most solid and rewarding desires, thoughts, decisions, and actions begin with an attitude of submission to the LORD. He calls that attitude of submission "the fear of the LORD" (Proverbs 1:7). But in verse 5, he's just introducing all of us to the fact that we can "know the ropes" about life and not just go in circles—with lots of wasted motion and exhausting and dangerous and even self-destructive effort, going nowhere.

Solomon urges everyone, even those with a measure of wisdom, to give their attention to the wisdom in this book. No one is beyond the need for more wise guidance about life because life doesn't stand still. It always progresses with lots of moving parts. Wise people will be open to learn more wisdom and how to manage those parts well. Solomon adds another benefit to knowing this wise counsel: someone with this wisdom will be able to help others unravel troubles that mystify them about life. Solomon calls these wise sayings proverbs, *sayings, words of the wise,* and *riddles* (Proverbs 1:6).

Many things that wise people say are easily ignored or labeled "old fashioned" or "out of date" by simple and foolish people. Proverbs 12:1 compares such closed-minded

Prayer:

Father, help me to have the attitudes of humility and eagerness as I read *Proverbs*. Make me the wise person you want me to be, knowing how to handle the many ropes of life in ways that please you. Please give me the wisdom and understanding that you've designed to work in this life for your glory and my good. Please give me the humble attitude with which all this *guidance* begins: the fear of the LORD. In Jesus' name, Amen.

people to a dumb beast. "Stupid" is the English translation. But the word is really related to someone acting like a dumb animal. Wise young adults, though, will listen and benefit by receiving skillful direction, *guidance*, from people with a track record of wisdom behind them. Of course, Jesus himself is such a person. Let the spiritually wise guides in Proverbs, and the Lord Jesus himself, God's wisdom in human form (1 Corinthians 1:30), help you to "know the ropes" about wise fruitful living.

Bridges' Comments:

Proverbs is certainly a book for people who do not have much common sense and who can be swayed easily, but it is also for young adults (Proverbs 1:4) and for those who already have some measure of *wisdom* and *understanding* (Proverbs 1:5). One of the marks of such a wise person, in Proverbs, is that he knows he has not arrived! He knows he has not "already obtained" it, but, as Paul said, presses "...on to make it my own" (Philippians 3:12; compare 1 Corinthians 3:18; 8:2).

David, Solomon's father, was conscious of his kingdom and spiritual privileges, but still sought more enlightenment from God (Psalm 119:98-100 and see also Psalm 119:18, 33, and 34). He knew that the most carefully stored wealth and other kingdom resources would soon be used up if he didn't add to them every day. Godly leaders have always known that they must continue to grow, or they will waste away. No one stays the same. We either grow or deteriorate. Jethro instructed Moses (Exodus 18:17-26). Our Lord taught his disciples (Matthew 13:11-16 and John 16:12). Peter enlightened his fellow apostles (Acts 11:2-18). Priscilla and Aquila "explained...." to Apollos "...the way of God more accurately" (Acts 18:24-26). For sure, we must all be hearers if we hope to be teachers. One church leader in Bridges' era said, "He gathers that hears; he spends that teaches. If we spend before we gather, we shall soon prove to be bankrupt."[6] The longer we learn, the more we know that we need to learn, and the more ready we are to *hear*, the more we may *increase in learning* (See also Proverbs 9:9; 18:15).

In our world's crises, both the church and the world should crave every form of God's wise instruction to become people of "understanding of the times, to know what [God's people] ought to do..." (1 Chronicles 12:31). Solomon himself explained wise words and mysterious sayings to the delight and benefit of his royal servants (1 Kings 10:1-5). To a teachable *hearer,* even "the depths of God" (1 Corinthians 2:9,10) become accessible. Hence, the value of God's pastors. Such a one is "a mediator" [go-between], one of

[6] Bishop Hall, cited by Bridges.

a thousand (Job 33:23; compare Acts 8:27-35). He is the God-appointed instrument to announce the "truth in love" (Ephesians 4:11-15; 1 Thessalonians 3:10). The church might have been spared much disorder and many heresies if, instead of getting side-tracked with twisted teachings and weak-based opinions, it sought out "messenger[s] of the LORD of hosts" (Malachi 2:7). These would be honored leaders who had "...the lips of a priest..." who "... should guard knowledge..." and from whom "...people should seek instruction"

"If we spend before we gather, we shall soon prove to be bankrupt."

(Compare Hebrews 13:17 and 1 Corinthians 3:2-4).

The posture to have is a humble subjection to the LORD of the Word and the Word of the LORD. This will cause one to "...be strengthened by grace...and not led away by diverse and strange teachings..." (Hebrews 13:9). All of us need to come to the wise to learn and not first of all to teach. I must not come to have my curiosity fed, but to grow in confidence in the grace of God.

To Help You Meditate:

1. What is there about the nature of Proverbs, as short, catchy statements, that makes them invaluable to young adults and people facing many challenges of life?

2. What is the "fear of the Lord" and why is it so important in a person who wants to "know the ropes" about life?

3. Have you ever known someone content to *not* grow in knowledge or wise counsel? What are some likely consequences of that attitude if they don't change it?

1:7; 9:10   "Knowing" How to Get a Worm on a Hook

ESV

1:7 The fear of the LORD is the beginning of knowledge; fools despise wisdom and instruction.

9:10 The fear of the LORD is the beginning of wisdom, and the knowledge of the Holy One is insight.

NIV

1:7 The fear of the LORD is the beginning of knowledge, but fools despise wisdom and discipline.

9:10 The fear of the LORD is the beginning of wisdom, and knowledge of the Holy One is understanding.

Wisdom Lived Out Today:

"Eeooo! I'm not touching that!" Lesley declared when we were on one of our earliest fishing outings with seven or eight of her cousins. She was talking about the dirty, wiggly, slimy worms that I was trying to get her to pick up and thread onto a fishhook. Eventually, on the next year's fishing trip, she did touch them, bait her own hook, and even hold the slimy fish she caught for a picture. At first she *knew about* getting a worm on a hook. But after some time, she gained the *wisdom* or skill to actually bait a hook on her own.

Proverbs is about *knowledge* and *wisdom*. They are related, but different. *Knowledge* has to do with information; knowing things about living my life as God has designed my life to be lived. But this *knowledge*, in the way the Bible uses it about life, is never just some list of facts. It grows out of a relationship with the God of *knowledge*. "The fear of the LORD" is a description of that relationship in Proverbs 1:7. This is the source of both true *knowledge* and *wisdom* or skill for living. Proverbs 9:10 says that *wisdom* also grows out of the soil of *fear of the LORD*. Lesley was willing to follow my instructions, eventually, and touch the wiggly, slimy worm, because I'm her grandpa and I kept coaxing her to do it. Because of our relationship she gave in and touched the worm and even tried to get it on a hook. Not too successfully at first. But then the skill came. She trusted me and my instruction and gained *knowledge* because of our relationship. Then, because of her trust and willingness to use her new *knowledge*, she gained the *wisdom* or skill to use her *knowledge*. She not only handled worms, but also, in time, slimy fish.

The fear of the LORD component of *knowledge* and *wisdom* is not primarily being afraid of God. Rather, it's respect for him and the desire to please, obey, and listen to his voice above all other voices about living. That's the spirit Solomon wants the young adults to whom he's writing to go after.

As I'm getting to *know* him and what he wants me to *know*, I begin also to acquire *wisdom*. In short, *wisdom* is the skill to put that *knowledge* into practice in my life situation—whenever, whatever, and wherever that situation may be. Wisdom is the humility and skill to live in the situation God has placed me in according to his good plan for me. It's living with God's mind in view. This is the opposite of living with my own feelings about who my friends should be, what music to listen to, how much time to be on my phone, or whether or not to listen to my parents. These choices are all about me and my wants and likes or dislikes. The *fear of the LORD* type of *wisdom* seeks God's mind on all matters of living. *Wisdom* and *knowledge* ask, "How can I now live the way you, LORD, want me to live with the pressures of life coming at me right now? How, Father, can I make decisions (*wisdom*) that line up with the way you want me to see things in my life (*knowledge*)?"

Lesley has become wise in matters of baiting hooks. As she seeks the *fear of the LORD,* she'll be more and more *knowledgeable* and *wise,* as well, in the matters of this life and eternity.

Bridges' Comments:

The preface of the book of Proverbs, verses 1-6, states the purpose of this book—to make people wise. The sentence, in verse 7, lays the foundation of all wisdom--*the fear of the LORD is the beginning of knowledge.* This is a remarkable sentence. One church father said that there are no unbelievers who have given such wise guidance in their books as this statement does at the beginning of Solomon's Proverbs.

This is also the counsel of Job (Job 28:28) and David, Solomon's father (Psalm 111:10). It is

> **Prayer:**
>
> Father, teach me to look more and more to you for all of my learning and all of my living. Help me always to ask, "How does your wise counsel, in your word, direct me to think about whatever I'm facing, decisions I have to make, or, reactions to challenges and temptations that come at me?" Please make me knowledgeable with true *knowledge* and wise with your *wisdom*. In Jesus' name, the One who is God's Wisdom for me, Amen.

so profound an understanding that Solomon repeats related concepts in Proverbs 1:29; 2:5; 3:7; 8:13; 10:27; 14:26; 14:27; 15:16; 15:33; 16:6; 19:23; 22:4; 23:17; 24:21. Later, after surveying all of life, Solomon concluded that the fear of God is the "whole *duty* of man"[7] (Ecclesiastes 12:13); compare this with Job 28:12-14 and verse 28). All man's duty and happiness, from the beginning lessons about life to his last instructions for life, are traceable to *fearing the LORD.*

Therefore, when Solomon is about to teach us about life from the mouth of God, he begins at the *beginning,* with the *fear of the LORD.* To say it's the *beginning* means it's the most important, or principal part of *knowledge* (as the Hebrew word for *beginning* conveys). All so-called *wisdom* and *knowledge* without this starting place are foolishness and

---

[7] Literally, the Hebrew text reads, "Fear God...this is the whole of man!" "Duty" is supplied by translators. But Solomon seems to be saying that all of human identity can be summed up in fearing God. If you fear the Lord, you become fully human, as God intended you to be.

ignorance to one extent or another. *Knowledge* must always be related to God to be most worthwhile and fully accurate (compare Deuteronomy 4:6,7). Otherwise, what I think is *knowledge* is really just some degree of fantasy.

But what is this *fear of the LORD* that creates this connection with *knowledge* and *wisdom?* It is that affectionate reverence, the loving and holy respect, by which the child of God bends or conforms himself humbly and carefully to fit to his Father's law. God's wrath is so bitter and his love so sweet, that from these spring a sincere desire from the believer's heart to please him. And because the believer knows he is in danger of falling short of fulfilling this desire, due to his own weakness and vulnerability to temptations, he exercises a holy self-watchfulness and fear so that he might not sin against him (Hebrews 12:28,29). He bends himself to live out God's wise, holy law.

Knowledge must always be related to God to be most worthwhile and fully accurate.

This passion affects every waking moment (Proverbs 23:17) and every inward and outward part of a wise person's life (Proverbs 3:5,6). The oldest and most mature saint, in God's school of life, seeks more and more to be molded in this way. The godly parent trains up his family with this desire (Genesis 18:19; Ephesians 6:4). The Christian scholar honors this passion as the starting place of all his *knowledge.* He keeps the godly end in sight for his learning and guards himself from being seduced by his own or others' opinions or popular cultural fads.

Why do so many around us *despise wisdom and instruction?* Because *the beginning of wisdom, the fear of the LORD,* is not "before his eyes" (Psalm 36:1). Such people do not know its value. They scorn what it requires. They may be wise in their own sight, but God surely gives them their right name: *fools.* For *fools* they must be because they despise God's blessing (Jeremiah 8:9). They rush into their own ruin (Proverbs 1:22, 24-32; compare 1 Samuel 2:25; 1 Kings 12:13; Jeremiah 36:22-32) and despise correction (Proverbs 5:12,13; 29:1). Father, may the childlike *fear* you require be my *wisdom,* security, and happiness!

To Help You Meditate:

1. What makes wisdom wise? How does this contrast with the world's wisdom?

2. Why must knowledge, to be worthwhile and fully accurate, be related to God?

3. Do the people you hang around with mostly seek God's wisdom about life or are they indifferent to it or despise it? What does your friendship with them mean for your growth in wisdom?

1:10-19   Just Drive—It Will Be Fun!

ESV

10 My son, if sinners entice you, do not consent.
11 If they say, "Come with us, let us lie in wait for blood; let us ambush the innocent without reason;
12 like Sheol let us swallow them alive, and whole, like those who go down to the pit;
13 we shall find all precious goods, we shall fill our houses with plunder;
14 throw in your lot among us; we will all have one purse"—
15 my son, do not walk in the way with them; hold back your foot from their paths,
16 for their feet run to evil, and they make haste to shed blood.
17 For in vain is a net spread in the sight of any bird,
18 but these men lie in wait for their own blood; they set an ambush for their own lives.
19 Such are the ways of everyone who is greedy for unjust gain; it takes away the life of its possessors.

NIV

10 My son, if sinners entice you, do not give in to them.
11 If they say, "Come along with us; let's lie in wait for someone's blood, lets waylay some harmless soul;
12 let's swallow them alive, like the grave, and whole like those who go down to the pit;
13 we will get all sorts of valuable things and fill our houses with plunder;
14 throw in your lot with us, and we will share a common purse"—
15 my son, do not go along with them, do not set foot on their paths;
16 for their feet rush into sin, they are swift to shed blood.
17 How useless to spread a net in full view of all the birds!
18 These men lie in wait for their own blood; they waylay only themselves!
19 Such is the end of all who go after ill-gotten gain; it takes away the lives of those who get it.

Wisdom Lived Out Today:

(A true story.) She was in her early 20s. The group she was hanging around with were about the same age. Her husband was away for a few weeks for his work. She was out for a good time with her friends. They said, "You're our driver!"

"What do you mean?" she asked.

"Just drive. We're going to have a great time."

The leader of the pack led them to a convenience store and told her to keep the car running. They went inside and threatened the store clerk and took the money from the cash register and some other things off the shelves and ran to the car. They got in and the leader hollered, "Beat it! Get out of here now!"

A few hours later the entire group was arrested. All were charged with armed robbery and found guilty. The girl driving was able to show that she really didn't know what was going down, and she got off with a very light sentence. Now many years later, she's not proud of these things at all. They happened before she got serious with the Lord. But they do show how easily young adults can be drawn into foolishness.

Solomon warns about being drawn into the *net* of people who really are only thinking of themselves and are willing to take advantage of others by taking what doesn't belong to them. This could be stealing someone's reputation by giving in to a gossiping group, stealing the trust of a teacher by going along with several in the class in a cheating scheme, robbing someone of his or her peace of mind by going along with a bullying conspiracy online, or actually shoplifting.

> **Prayer:**
>
> Father, please help me to see the dangers of being drawn into foolish and hurtful, even illegal, things. Help me to be wise in my friendships and courageous in my decisions. Deliver me from fearing what others will think of me and from being willing to compromise righteous behavior to be liked or accepted. Instead, help me to live righteously for Jesus who modeled strength in the face of temptation rather than give in to the threats of leaders and invitations to sin. In Jesus' name, Amen.

As it turned out, the girl in our story was able to get through the ordeal with a "slap on the wrist." But that did come back to haunt her a year later when she was denied custody of her young child because of her criminal record. Giving in to such influences can have serious, life-long effects. *"...they set an ambush for their own lives,"* Solomon says. *"Such are the ways of everyone who is greedy for unjust gain; it takes away the life of its possessors"* (Proverbs 1:18,19).

It doesn't matter what form of unjust gain one chases. God has created life usually to work in a way that "whatever one sows, that will he also reap" (Galatians 6:7). That's not always the case in this life. Sometimes bad people get away with their deceptive, hurtful schemes, but eternity will catch up with them.

Proverbs is a book of wisdom—showing how to live in line with God's design. There is much safety in that. The last verses of this chapter underscore that. "...whoever listens to me will dwell secure and will be at ease, without dread of disaster" (Proverbs 1:33). These verses stress the importance of choosing friends wisely and the power some can have over others.

Bridges' Comments:

Young people! Listen to this advice from a godly parent and minister. What youth worker or parent doesn't mourn over the harmful influence of bad relationships? Oh, that the Lord's servants were as energetic in their work as *sinners* are in furthering the seductive desires of their master!

Almost as soon as Satan became a rebel to God he became a tempter to people. He successfully trains his servants in this work too (see Proverbs 16:29; Genesis 11:4; Numbers 31:16; Isaiah 56:12). *If sinners entice you,* Solomon writes, not as though this might or might not happen, but to warn the young adult that such temptations will come. Bridges then quotes one old writer's interpretation of Solomon's warning about temptation: since the temptation will come, "prepare for it." Solomon says there is just one safeguarding rule against all such temptations: *do not consent* or give your approval to the invitation such "friends" present to you (Proverbs 7:6-23; compare Deuteronomy 13:6-8; 1 Chronicles

21:1; 1 Kings 13:15-19).

Consenting or just going along with others is the same as giving in to the temptation. It's the same as the sin itself. Eve *consented* before she took the fruit (Genesis 3:6). David *consented* before he committed his act of sin with Bathsheba (2 Samuel 11:2-4; compare Joshua 7:21). Joseph resisted and was saved (Genesis 39:8,9). Job was severely tempted and "yet in all this Job did not sin..." (Job 1:22; 2:10). Joseph and Job did not *consent* to the temptation.

If the temptation you undergo does capture you, do not blame God or the devil. The worst he can do is tempt you. He cannot force you to sin. When he has used his most forceful influence upon you, his most deceitful strategies, your will is still the final decision-making power for either *consenting* or not *consenting* to a temptation (see James 1:13-15). My battling with temptation, though, seeking to obey God by the Spirit, even if I fall, shows my true nature as a child of God. Such battling shows that such sin is not really coming from who I truly am in Christ—the new me (see Romans 7:14-17,19,20,23). *Consenting* with the temptation, however, even if it is not fully carried out, lays responsibility at my own door.

The temptation in this Proverbs passage is for robbery and injury to another. It was covetousness leading to murder. Their plot was cruel. The *innocent* person was to be *ambushed without reason,* to be *swallowed alive, whole* (Genesis 4:8; Psalm 10:8). They want to *swallow* their unsuspecting friend the way the earth opened up and swallowed Korah and his followers in Numbers 16:33. The invitation to go along may seem harmless at first. *Come with us,* they said to begin with. But later they said, *cast in your lot with us.* The price for taking part with these conspirators just got bigger.

"But we might get caught!"

"No," they reply, *"like Sheol (another name for the grave) let us swallow them alive, and whole, like those who go down to the pit; we shall find all precious goods, we shall fill our houses with plunder; throw in your lot among us; we will all have one purse."*

The price for taking part with these conspirators just got bigger.

They are saying, "There will be no evidence of our attack. It will be as if the earth, itself, swallowed them up (see Matthew 21:38). And think of how rich we'll be afterward. We'll divide everything up equally." This is a big promise! It sounds like the promise the Lord Jesus makes in Matthew 8:11, but it's a counterfeit. How can real treasure be found in a world of shadows (Psalm 39:6), where nothing lasts? Even more so, how can the results of robbery be *precious* when God's curse rests on such behavior (see Proverbs 21:6; Psalm 62:9,10).

Most of the time, a plot like this isn't put forward all at once. But step by step, unless the Lord in his goodness restrains it, the plot thickens—gets more serious and more evil. The cover or façade is taken away and the real nature of what sin is, in its nature and certain ending, is revealed. Who wouldn't be uncomfortable with such an evil plot if it were presented to him when he was by himself? But group peer pressure is hard to go against. Before you know it, you can be deeper into the plot than you ever thought possible.

Satan can use other ways, as well, to tempt people into setting hurtful and hateful traps for others. He's able to seduce us by our ignorance of his plans (2 Corinthians 2:11). He can get us to trust in our own willpower or personal standards to not get caught up with hurtful plots. We may think "This will never happen to me." But Solomon says, the best way to avoid the traps others may set for us by their deceit is to *not walk in the way with them; hold back your foot from their paths* (see also Proverbs 4:14,15; Psalm 1:1). Don't even get into a discussion with them. No one falls into such serious sin all at once. It's by gradual steps. "Bad company ruins good morals" (1 Corinthians 15:33). One's tender conscience can become less sensitive by each small compromise. Who can stop himself easily when going down a steep road? One sin prepares for another. One begins to make excuses for sin and even tries to hide it. David committed murder to hide his adultery. He even used God's providence as his cover (2 Samuel 11:4,17,25).

Again, then, we repeat with all seriousness: *hold back your foot from their paths*. The *path* may be strewn with flowers. It may smell good, look good, and feel good at the outset, but it is a *path* of evil, perhaps life-threatening evil. Every step on Satan's ground denies us the security of God's promises. Often, ruin follows by not resisting or *holding back* from that first step (see Mark 14:54,71). The only safety is in "fleeing" (Genesis 39:10-12). Run to your "hiding place" and "shield" and command your tempter to leave you (Psalm 119:114,115; Matthew 4:10). It is terrifying, but true: be aware that the most holy person can commit any sin if only trusting in himself. "...you stand fast through faith. So do not become proud, but fear" (Romans 11:20; see also 1 Corinthians 10:12).

In the next verses, Solomon explains how anyone who is pressured to hurt others opens himself or herself up to serious consequences.

For in vain is a net spread in the sight of any bird. The sight of danger usually leads people to avoid it. Even animals often have enough sense to stay away from traps. Yet young people can often be so obsessed with their sinful desire that they will not take the precautions that even an animal will instinctively take. The animal shuns the *net,* but the foolish person runs into it. These people *lie in wait* for their neighbor's *blood,* but in the end they pay the price with their own *blood.* They *set an ambush* for their unsuspecting neighbor, but end up trapping *their own lives* (compare Proverbs 1:11 and 18; Job 18:8; Habakkuk 2:10).

Ahab and Jezebel, his wife, plotted to steal Naboth's vineyard and have him killed. The plot ended up ruining their own lives (1 Kings 21:4-24). Little did Haman know when plotting Mordecai's death (Esther 7:9) or Judas know when seeking an opportunity to betray the Lord Jesus (Matthew 26:14-16; 27:3-5) that they were digging a pit for themselves (Psalm 7:15,16; 9:15,16). But the sinner could see judgment at the end of his path if he would just open his eyes (Matthew 7:13). Sin is self-deceptive and self-destructive. *Such are the ways of everyone who is greedy for unjust gain; it takes away the life of its possessors* (compare Job 31:39,40; Jeremiah 22:17-19; Micah 3:10-12). My son—once more hear your Father's instruction: *flee* these things (Proverbs 1:8; 1 Timothy 6:9-11).

To Help You Meditate:

1. Can you think of a time you or a friend caved in to peer pressure to make a wrong choice? What fears seemed to control you or your friend?

2. How would the "fear of the Lord" have made a difference if it was what controlled your heart or your friend's heart? Why would it have that different effect?

3. What counsel would you give to a friend who was thinking of giving in to the temptation to gossip or bully someone?

2:1-6   Don't Let the Crowd Shake Your Concentration

ESV

1 My son, if you receive my words and treasure up my commandments with you,
2 making your ear attentive to wisdom and inclining your heart to understanding;
3 yes, if you call out for insight and raise your voice for understanding,
4 if you seek it like silver and search for it as for hidden treasures,
5 then you will understand the fear of the LORD and find the knowledge of God.
6 For the LORD gives wisdom; from his mouth come knowledge and understanding;

NIV

1 My Son, if you accept my words and store up my commands within you,
2 turning your ear to wisdom and applying your heart to understanding,
3 and if you call out for insight and cry aloud for understanding,
4 and if you look for it as for silver and search for it as for hidden treasure,
5 then you will understand the fear of the LORD and find the knowledge of God.
6 For the LORD gives wisdom, and from his mouth come knowledge and understanding.

Wisdom Lived Out Today:

As I write this in 2017, a number of you have distinguished yourselves as remarkable athletes, musicians, and scholars. Lesley and Becca have earned regional and national awards in gymnastics, Shaun, Nate, and Ty have earned tournament recognitions in baseball. Katie, Nicole, Julissa, and Jed have won music, academic and other honors. All of you have something in common that has made you successful: you focus your attention on what you are doing. You concentrate! You don't let the crowd rattle you!

It's true that talent is important in achieving things, but Solomon isn't focusing on talent in Proverbs 2. He's identifying a life quality for everyone who wants to do more than drift, have a stagnant life, or just go with the flow of what everyone else is doing. He's telling young adults how to make their lives count for more than the temporary awards and honors in this life.

Throughout Proverbs, Solomon says that *understanding* the *fear of the LORD* and *finding the knowledge of God* are more important than accumulating wealth, enjoying sex, becoming popular, being accepted, having many friends, or being successful in any area. These things aren't wrong when we pursue them God's way. In fact, we can only fully enjoy them when we keep God's priorities in mind. When life ends, so does the worth of these experiences, and all the earthly awards we receive come to nothing then, too. God offers so much more, and that is what Solomon is talking about in chapter 2. What he offers lasts forever.

What are these *treasures* Solomon urges you to focus upon and pursue with extraordinary effort? What are these *treasures* to concentrate on that last? They are *the fear of the Lord* and the *knowledge of God*--two vital, life-determining possessions. They are related to each other, but they differ slightly too.

To *understand the fear of the Lord* is to see God and all he's said about life as the keys to experiencing a full life. *Fearing* him isn't optional equipment or just another app. This young person thinks to himself, "I need to pay attention to what God says. I need to respect his words. I need to want what he wants me to want. His words make life work—in this world and the next."

To *find* the *knowledge of God* means you turn your respect for God and all he says into a love relationship with him. "Knowing" in the Bible is not just an intellectual, mental process. It's like truly knowing your best friend. There's more to that than just knowing his or her name or knowing *about* him or her. *Finding the knowledge of God* is like that. It's becoming best friends with God. I learn to know him and his thoughts by spending time valuing what he values, respecting what he respects, loving what he loves, and hating what he hates. It's saying about every life situation, "We're in this together!"

Understanding the fear of the Lord and *finding the knowledge of God* is a little like handling nuclear material in a lab to produce some life-saving medical device. You want to respect how dangerous it can be if used wrongly and how valuable it can be if applied wisely. You fear it. Not that you are terrified or paralyzed into inaction by it, but your fear is a good thing that helps you keep your head when handling such powerful material.

That's how it is when you interact with the all-powerful, all-knowing, ever-present, all-holy and loving God. He put life together, so living with his view of things makes life work as he intended it to work. *Understanding the fear of the LORD* and *finding the knowledge of God* is like that. You want to be careful. You are handling life-shaping *treasures*. But though you want to be thoughtful about getting to know him, he invites us to know him and live pleasurably with him. He's good (Psalm16:11)!

Prayer:

Father, I need to know what is truly valuable and worth spending my life on and what is not so valuable. I need to *understand the fear of the LORD* and *find the knowledge of God.* These won't come easily. I must be focused if I'm not going to waste my life and my energy in this life. Give me that wisdom and discipline to focus on your Word, to learn greater respect for you, and to love you more and more. In Jesus' name, Amen.

In fact, look at the focused effort Solomon says the wise young adult will exercise to get these *treasures.* He says this young person *receives my word...treasures up...makes his ear attentive...inclines his heart...calls out...raises his voice...seeks it like silver...*and*...searches for it like hidden treasure.* All these action verbs show that this young person is making a concentrated effort like our athletes, musicians, and academic achievers mentioned above. Your focus on what is truly important will yield *the fear of the LORD* and *the knowledge of God.* These are eternal *treasures* that will have great value in this life and in eternity for you and for everyone you touch even after your life on this planet ends. Being casual or indifferent about a sport or activity never has resulted in great achievements. Similarly, it's the one who centers his or her attention on God's goals to *fear* and *know* him who finds the *hidden treasure* that so many never get to enjoy.

Bridges' Comments:

Having spoken to and warned rebellious mockers in the last half of chapter 1, *wisdom* now speaks to those who want to obey her in chapter 2. Solomon answers the age-old question, "Where can I find *wisdom* and *understanding*?" (Job 28:12,20,21). They are found in the *fear* and *knowledge* of God (Proverbs 2:6). The *fear* and *knowledge of God* preserve us from the temptations that plague us (2:10-19). They also guide us into right and safe paths of *wisdom* and *understanding* for life. The impact of receiving these produces security if we are serious about getting them. But the cost of *not* gaining them means a ruined life, or worse, eternal death (see Proverbs 2:22).

The rules for getting this *knowledge and fear of the Lord* are easy to understand. Applying these directions carefully and deeply, though, is the key. The rules to be applied are:

First: *"...receive my words..."*

Let these words of God be as seeds planted in the good soil of an "honest and good heart." This is a heart prepared by God and for God. Jesus said, "As for [the seeds that fell] in the good soil, they are those who, hearing the word, hold it fast in an honest and good heart, and bear fruit with patience" (Luke 8:15).

Read God's Word as one who "sat at the Lord's feet and listened to his teaching" (Luke 10:39). Be like the Bereans who "received the word with all eagerness, examining the Scriptures daily to see if these things were so" (Acts 17:11). Imitate the Thessalonian believers who, when they "received the word of God...accepted it not as the word of men but as what it really is, the word of God..." (1 Thessalonians 2:13).

Second: *"...treasure up my commandments with you..."* (Proverbs 2:1)

Carry them with you to give you security. Make them your favorite treasures (compare Colossians 3:16 and Matthew 13:44). Keep them as tools by your side, always ready for use (Proverbs 4:20,21; 7:3; Job 22:22). Let your heart be the hiding place for this treasure (Luke 2:19-51; Psalm 119:11). Satan can never snatch it from there. But to receive and treasure God's Word like this, you must give focused and planned attention to his Word, so he continues...

Third: *"...making your ear attentive...inclining your heart..."* (Proverbs 2:2)

"Who is sufficient for these things?" Oh, God, please work on me and within me. You alone can create this kind of focus. Make my experience like that of your Beloved Son who said, "...he awakens my ear to hear as those who are taught" (Isaiah 50:4). So, let me live in conscious dependence upon your grace. Help me to heed your counsel to your people to "incline your ear, and come to me; hear, that your soul may live..." (Isaiah 55:3).

Without this spirit of prayer you may be attentive and earnest, but nothing will deeply affect you. Not one ray of God's light will shine in your soul. Earthly wisdom is gained by study; heavenly wisdom is gained by prayer. Study may form a biblical scholar, but prayer is God's tutorial that forms the wise and spiritual Christian. God's Word first comes into our ears, then it enters the heart. The psalmist said, "The unfolding of your words gives light; it imparts understanding to the simple" (Psalm 119:130).

The child of God who wants God's unfolded wisdom needs to get it from him. He keeps the key of this treasure-house in his own hand. "For this he will be inquired of" (Ezekiel 36:37). He is willing to open such wisdom to the one who wants it and seeks it. First and foremost we must look to him for help to see the Word clearly and to have it make an impression upon us. Every verse that we read and meditate upon gives us much fuel for prayer. Every text we pray over opens a mine of "unsearchable riches" with a light from God that is clearer and fuller than the most intelligent writer of Bible commentaries can uncover. David (Psalm 119:18 and the following verses) and his wise son (1 Kings 3:9-12) sought this learning upon their knees.

Yet, what miner is content with the first glimmer of silver or gold?

The most mature believer will follow that pattern and will *call out for insight and raise your voice for understanding.* This is the greater "knowledge of God" (Ephesians 1:17-18) that Paul talked about.

Fourth: to gain the *knowledge and fear of the Lord* means you must *...seek it like silver and search for it as for hidden treasures...* (Proverbs 2:4).

Prayer doesn't take the place of the hard work of thinking, questioning, searching, researching, and meditating upon the Word. Instead it gives energy to those efforts. Bridges sites Bishop Leighton:

We give too little effort in the humble seeking and begging for divine knowledge. That is why we are so shallow and have so little of the skills of wisdom. Solomon says these come when, *...you call out for insight and raise your voice for understanding, if you seek it like silver and search for it as for hidden treasures...* (Proverbs 2:3,4). Therefore, get down on your knees and dig for them. This is the best posture to discover the vein of gold, and to go deeper spiritually to know the mind of God and to be directed and managed by him. This is how to become skillful in ways of honoring and serving him. Neither angels nor man can teach this. Only God can make this our life pattern. (Author's paraphrase of Leighton's quotation.)

This miner's undeterred efforts, in spite of the pains he endures, seeking *it as silver...*and searching *...for it as for hidden treasures...,* is the only way into this storehouse of wealth. Only to read, instead of truly "searching the Scriptures," is to skim the surface and gather only shallow thoughts. The rule of success is "dig up and down the field; and if the search is discouraging, dig again." The patient work of careful study and then more careful study will open this treasure chest. Yet what miner is content with the first glimmer of silver or gold? Wouldn't he "search" deeper and deeper until he gathered all the treasure? So, explore "the breadth and length and height and depth" of the wealth God has laid up for his treasure hunters in order to be "filled with all the fullness of God" (Ephesians 3:18,19).

The conclusion of a search like this is never disappointing. Living in an atmosphere of personal Scripture awareness is invaluable. To be filled with God's wealth, his treasury of wisdom, and to have large portions of the Word passing through my mind daily gives me a firmer grasp and a more realistic sense of how to apply it in my day-to-day life. But we can only reap this kind of harvest in our private times with the Lord. In private we learn to apply ourselves to the Word and the Word to ourselves. One who merely reads the Scripture, in private or as part of the gathered church body, runs the risk of only skimming the surface of the treasure God has for him. Such readers, in contrast to those who meditate, come out with shallow knowledge at best, without the benefit of the Word's deep transforming power.

In the long run, the church suffers from this kind of shallowness. It is vulnerable to heresies and errors. Jesus told religious leaders of his day, "You are wrong, because you know neither the Scriptures nor the power of God" (Matthew 22:29). They were guilty of this kind of scriptural ignorance. Such surface-level reading may produce ideas about spiritual matters that are only based on partial or disjointed statements of Scripture. Truth separated from truth becomes error. But one who prayerfully searches for God's truth (*if you call out for insight and raise your voice for understanding*) will discern both the *fear of the Lord* and the *knowledge of God*. This kind of search will, without a doubt and without disappointment, yield *understanding* and *wisdom*. This kind of effort is not in vain (see Job 32:8; Isaiah 48:17; James 1:5,17; compare these passages also: Genesis 41:38,39; Exodus 4:12; Daniel 1:17). Turning away from the faith has never been connected to a prayerful and diligent study of the Word of God.

To Help You Meditate:

1. How would you advise a person who wants to grow in the knowledge of God and the "fear of the Lord"? What would you counsel him or her to do?

2. How would you describe the intensity of your efforts to know and grow in the Lord? What would the action words in the beginning of this section of verses suggest you do differently if you want to grow in the knowledge and fear of the Lord?

3. If a friend complains of being bored when she reads the Bible, how could these verses offer her a solution? What diagnosis do they offer to her about why she is bored?

2:7-9   That's Not Fair!

ESV

7 he stores up sound wisdom for the upright; he is a shield to those who walk in integrity,
8 guarding the paths of justice and watching over the way of his saints.
9 Then you will understand righteousness and justice and equity, every good path;

NIV

7 He holds victory in store for the upright, he is a shield to those whose walk is blameless,
8 for he guards the course of the just and protects the way of his faithful ones.
9 Then you will understand what is right and just and fair—every good path.

Wisdom Lived Out Today:

"That's not fair! I had it first," Marcus, one of our grandsons, hollered. He was complaining about the toy train car his brother, Silas, took when he put it down to pick up another car.

A tenth grade girl stormed into my guidance office at school declaring, "I'm so mad. She is so unfair. Mrs. Smith took points off my homework just because I didn't do the problem the way she wants it to be done. I got the right answer doing the problem the way we were taught in my old school. But she takes points off if you don't do it HER way! She's so unfair!"

Young children, teens, and older adults can have a very good sense of what is fair and not fair. That doesn't mean they always handle their mistreatment the right way or that the other person was truly unfair, but justice does matter to us.

Solomon says that people who walk in the *wisdom* that God provides are in a unique position to understand justice and fairness for others as well as for themselves. His wise, trusting people *understand* that their loving God is always up to something good in their lives. They have him as their *shield* of protection if they are treated unfairly or unjustly. God will *guard* their *paths* and their *ways*. They know that justice and fairness do not always happen in this life, but God does promise that his children, who look to him for his wisdom and understanding, will be *guarded* in the long run. Mistreatment by others, for the Christian, is never fatal. It is never final. It may hurt, but it is never the end of life for the believer. God has their back—even if it doesn't look or feel like it.

Young Jed, Jr. was just eight years old. He'd just given his life to Jesus the night before this school day. At school he began to tell his third grade classmates about Jesus, his newly found Savior. He was very excited. A number of them laughed at him and mocked him. His feelings were hurt, but he also knew, in his eight-year-old way, that Jesus had his back. He knew that he had a *shield*, even if he didn't know that word from these verses in Proverbs 2. Jed made up his mind to live for Jesus, though, no matter what they said. Their unfair treatment of him hurt his feelings but didn't really hurt him. He had a *shield*. What a *wise* young man! As he grows older, he will come to understand more about fairness and justice and to know that God *guards* and *watches over* him and all of his people when they are mistreated.

Bridges' Comments:

Meaninglessness (Ecclesiastes 1:18) and foolishness (1 Corinthians 3:19) are the marks of the wisdom of this world. Here, however, Solomon talks about sound wisdom. Such wisdom does not look at things and come to conclusions because of the first impressions they make or the feelings they produce. Wisdom gets past these and sees the real nature and character of things. It is truly a "hidden treasure" (Proverbs 2:4). It is so safe that no thief or contaminating influence can reach it, yet it is so free that every sinner may have access to it. Yes, in the Son of God himself are "hidden all the treasures of wisdom and knowledge" (Colossians 2:3; 1 Corinthians 1:30).

Oh, let us draw upon this infinite treasure daily and hourly for light to guide us in an *upright* walk. One saint has said, "To those who are true and upright in heart, God will, in his own good time, reveal...the *sound* spiritual wisdom which shall make them eternally happy." (Author's paraphrase of the quotation.)

> **Prayer:**
>
> Father, please help me not to be afraid of other people's unjust treatment of me. Help me to know how Jesus was treated unjustly and how you used that to bring about salvation for many. Help me to know that you are my shield when I'm not treated fairly as well. Help me to be fair and just in my treatment of others too - the way I'd like to be treated. Help me to be like Jesus and to love those who are unjust toward me. In Jesus' name, Amen.

Our faithful God is *a shield to those who walk in integrity* (see Proverbs 30:5; Psalm 84:11). His *wisdom* protects us from the subtle thief who spreads this world's wisdom that will rob us of our treasure (Proverbs 22:12). The way of God's people, the saints, is full of danger and plagued with temptation. Yet the child of God is safe in it (Proverbs 4:12; 1 Samuel 2:9; Psalm 37:23,24; and 56:9). The Almighty is *guarding...watching over...* his people, even on the very edge of the enemy's ground (see 1 Samuel 25:39 and compare it to 1 Samuel 27:1 and all of 1 Samuel 29; see also 2 Corinthians 12:7-9).

It is a gracious privilege to possess this *sound wisdom.* It affects all of life. It not only expands our "knowledge of God" (Proverbs 2:5), but it also nurtures in us an understanding of every practical responsibility that we have. The mark of *sound wisdom* is that it guides our feet into *every good path.* This *wisdom* makes the "...man of God...competent, equipped for every good work" (2 Timothy 3:15-17). The gracious wisdom that saves the soul, *guards* and transforms one's heart and life (Titus 2:11,12).

To Help You Meditate:

1. What does the truth mean that God is a shield for people who are treated unfairly?

2. If we do not believe that God is a shield to those who trust his sound wisdom, what are some likely ways we will react when we are treated unfairly?

3. How does "sound wisdom" affect one's life if he possesses it?

2:10,11   The Best Gifts Are Not Usually Free

ESV

10 for wisdom will come into your heart, and knowledge will be pleasant to your soul;
11 discretion will watch over you, understanding will guard you,

NIV

10 For wisdom will enter your heart, and knowledge will be pleasant to your soul.
11 Discretion will protect you, and understanding will guard you.

Wisdom Lived Out Today:

Most of us are happy to get something for nothing. That's why advertisers try to make it sound like their products give you more than you are paying for. "But wait," some commercials say, "there's more. If you buy one, we'll give you a second one free."

But very little is "free." That is especially true of *wisdom, knowledge, discretion and understanding.* They come at a cost that the first nine verses of this chapter lay out.

Nate and Shaun and Jaydn may have great curve balls, but they won't be able to develop that pitch more just because they WANT to. More than a "want to" is necessary. Mastery of the pitch comes after lots of concentration, discipline, and probably some pain, some inconvenience, and hours and hours of practice in a pitching cage. In time, the motions of the pitch will become part of them.

That's what Solomon said about the focus and attention that we need in order to make *wisdom, knowledge, discretion and understanding* a part of us. Once they are embedded, though, look at what they do: they will be *pleasant, watch over you* and *guard you.* This is a dangerous world. God has provided a way for safely living in it as a young adult and as an older one.

These qualities are like sentries standing on a wall guarding an ancient city. What Solomon is telling us is that there are enemies wanting to take us down. Some enemies are outside of us in our culture, like peer pressure, and some enemies are inside of us, like the desires of our sinful hearts. We need to be able to identify these enemies before they get in the city and take over. A few verses later, Solomon identifies two of the most serious enemies young adults need to beware of: people who want to take advantage of you by deception and lies (Proverbs 2:12-15) and seductive, immoral people who will use sex and pleasure to fatally attract you (Proverbs 2:16-19).

Solomon tells us these four sentries, *wisdom, knowledge, discretion, and understanding,* have the God-provided benefits of pleasure, alertness, and safety. Paul, in the New Testament, tells us these sentries are found in the Lord Jesus. "Christ Jesus...who became to us wisdom from God..." (1 Corinthians 1:30).

What do these four sentries look like? *Wisdom* says, "Wait a minute, check out this thing you are thinking about. Is it out of sync or in sync with God's law? Am I willing to trust Jesus for the way things will work out if I make an unpopular decision, though it fits with his will (*wisdom*)?"

Knowledge asks, "Are you sure you know everything you need to know about this choice? Are you thinking carefully or with your feelings? Is there anybody you can check with for more information? Don't hurry!"

Discretion urges you to make comparisons among your choices. It asks, "What choice is really the wisest and most in harmony with God's Word? What will be most honoring to Him?" Compare your options honestly. Choices are sometimes between what is good or evil and sometimes between what is good, better, or best.

Understanding asks, "Why is this a wise choice? What reasons can you give that show that you are building your decision on the solid foundation of Jesus' wise Word?" (Proverbs 24:3-5 actually uses a house metaphor or word picture to show how *wisdom, understanding,* and *knowledge* relate to each other. Check those verses out. See if you can explain how they are connected to each other.)

Do you want skillfulness in your decisions and relationships? *Wisdom, knowledge, discretion* and *understanding* will give it to you. They will give you the mastery of life values like practicing the curve ball will give mastery in pitching. These qualities will be *pleasant, watch over*, and *guard* you. Pursue them with the desire and intensity that Solomon is describing in the first nine verses. Meditate on God's Word daily the way the first nine verses of Proverbs 2 emphasize in order to make these a life-long and life-shaping part of you.

> **Prayer**
>
> Father, I want this wisdom in all my decisions, but it doesn't come easily. So help me to pay the price to make wisdom, knowledge, understanding, and discretion a part of me. Help me to be disciplined in reading your Word and meditating upon it. Don't allow me to cave in to the popular opinions of friends who want to live according to this world's acceptable views about anything. Be my safeguard. Help me to see and follow Jesus and not take a popular, easy way to live. In Jesus' name, Amen.

Bridges' Comments:

Earlier in this chapter, in verse 5, we were told that wisdom brings about "...the fear of the Lord and...the knowledge of God." Now we are told that it *will be pleasant, watch over* and *guard* you. But notice first of all where this *wisdom* must be found—in your *heart*. It is only there that it has any light, life, or power (see Proverbs 4:23). Knowledge, floating in one's head, not tied to a heart relationship to God, is deep ignorance. Like glitter, it may seem to sparkle and attract my interest and hold my attention for a while, but if it is only in my head, it is dry, empty of any real substance, and unable to produce anything.

But when *wisdom will come into your heart*, light shines out of it, and our desires for God's will are stirred up. How *pleasant to your soul* its effects will be (See Proverbs 24:13,14; Job 23:12; Psalm 119:103; Jeremiah 15:16)!

Spiritual life is not just an idea. It's not just dreaming about the way I'd like things to be. When we experience and enjoy it in the deepest parts of us, it gives us *discretion* and *understanding* in all of our choices. It affects what goes on inside of us and outside of us. It makes us conscious of our inner life so that we *watch* and *guard* our hearts (Proverbs

4:6,23; 6:22-24; Psalm 17:4; 119:9-11,104). Such *wisdom* acts like the military guard for royalty (1 Samuel 26:15,16; 2 Kings 11:11). Before becoming a believer, the richness of spiritual aliveness is what we were searching for, whether we knew it or not (Proverbs 2:4). It's what God created us for. Now, having found it, it is our *pleasure.*

Until *wisdom* is *pleasant to your soul, wisdom* can have no practical influence in your life. It is the one who "delights in the law of the LORD" who is *guarded* and preserved

---

Knowledge, floating in one's head, not tied to a heart relationship to God, is deep ignorance.

---

from walking "in the counsel of the wicked" (Psalm 1:1,2; compare also Proverbs 7:4,5). Education, strong convictions, and high moral standards are, by themselves, only partially helpful in one's life. The rehabilitated alcoholic may regain some measure of effective life-management by his 12-step program, but if his heart "root of bitterness" (Hebrews 12:15) is left untouched, some other morally and socially acceptable substitute may siphon off his attention and be just as self-destructive. For example, he may be captivated and distracted by environmental concerns, political concerns, or burning social issues and miss the focus he needs on his heart. He's now decent and respectable, but his heart may be unchanged. Roving or distracted desires and passionate interests in "respectable" causes may miss God as the central reason for all choices about life. That is the violation of the very first commandment. This will just as certainly end in emptiness and self-destruction as his former drunkenness (see Proverbs 1:7,32; 9:10; 14:12; Ecclesiastes 1:2; Jonah 2:8).

One's mind may be disciplined to turn away from what is unprofitable, but still be vulnerable to the idolatry of talents, academics, sports or any of scores of other interests. One may resist the folly of the pride of life and yet take pride in other pleasurable fruits that look respectable. A focus in any of these areas will not quiet or eliminate the natural desires of the heart. My forsaken sin only makes way for some more plausible, but no less deadly, passion to take over.

The heart, changed and shaped by the Gospel, is the only safeguard from those snares inside and outside of us (see Romans 6:17,18; 2 Corinthians 3:18). These traps are sneaky, imperceptible, and fatal. They may quietly and slowly separate us from God, but we will never detect their subversive and deceptive destructiveness until we receive a new heart. Only then can the love of God, for which we were created, satisfy our hearts and give us a true resting place.

To Help You Meditate:

1. What temptations come your way from which you can be protected by wisdom, knowledge, discretion, and understanding, if they are part of you?

2. "Wanting" these sentries to guard you isn't enough. What actions can you take to be sure they are in place to actually offer protection to you?

3. How important is wisdom in one's heart or soul? Why?

2:10-15   How to Be Gullible—or Wise

ESV

10 for wisdom will come into your heart, and knowledge will be pleasant to your soul;
11 discretion will watch over you, understanding will guard you,
12 delivering you from the way of evil, from men of perverted speech,
13 who forsake the paths of uprightness to walk in the ways of darkness,
14 who rejoice in doing evil and delight in the perverseness of evil,
15 men whose paths are crooked, and who are devious in their ways.

NIV

10 For wisdom will enter your heart, and knowledge will be pleasant to your soul,
11 Discretion will protect you, and understanding will guard you.
12 Wisdom will save you from the ways of wicked men, from men whose words are perverse,
13 who leave the straight paths to walk in dark ways,
14 who delight in doing wrong and rejoice in the perverseness of evil,
15 whose paths are crooked and who are devious in their ways.

Wisdom Lived Out Today:

There are two main groups of people that Solomon warns his teenage sons and other youth about: deceitful men and immoral women. People can't be trusted! Not all people, anyhow. There are many whom young adults are urged to be wary of.

Uncle Jed bought a car! It looked good. He thought he knew the guy selling it. He knew a friend of a friend who knew the seller. "It's a great deal!" he was told, but it was only when he gave the man his money and drove it home that the problems began to show up. They were major problems—costing more to fix than the car cost him in the first place.

Many young adults haven't lived long enough or been taught to know how to check out advice or suggestions they are given. They often don't know what questions to ask to be sure they are getting good information. You must listen carefully to employers, salespeople, apartment renters, internet merchants, politicians, and even government and military representatives. A common tactic is to overwhelm a prospective customer with technical detail. For example, not all phone plans are easy to understand. Representatives may speak very fast so that you don't calculate what some of the limits or hidden fees are. What salespeople don't say is just as important as what they do say. Separating you from your money is often their bottom line motive, and these people have learned well how to scam young, inexperienced people.

Of course, this makes it difficult for the honest people young adults come across, but honest people don't usually mind being checked out. They explain carefully and clearly, giving you time to think. They have nothing to hide. They will even offer references of other customers or people they've served. Young adults are wise to make the commitment *not* to purchase, agree to, or sign anything for a major item without checking at least one other trusted advisor.

That's what this section of Proverbs 2 is about. Wisdom is that advisor! She is the one who is *delivering* the young adult from danger and deceit. She says safety isn't complicated, but it does require beginning at the beginning. It begins with thinking that begins with the *fear of the LORD*. This would be the young adult who says to himself or herself, "I want all my decisions to be pleasing to God, first and foremost. I will set my radar up to detect anything that is not righteous, just, fair or on a good path" (Proverbs 2:9).

Prayer:

Father, don't allow me to be so impressed by things people say or the way things look that I don't think about them carefully. Help me to look to you first and talk to others who have more life experience. Make me conscious of the need to be wise. This is especially important when it comes to eternal matters. My world wants me to ignore spiritual things or, at least, not take them too seriously. Help me to weigh popular opinions about life against the solid promises and warnings you give in your Word. Help me to pay heed to the truth and the One who is the Truth! In Jesus' name, Amen.

This isn't a guarantee that we will see everything that we need to see before making an important decision. Uncle Jed thought he was making a good deal because his friends vouched for the seller, but they were fooled too. Usually, though, wise and thoughtful steps go a long way toward preventing us from foolishly swallowing something someone tries to "sell" us. Wisdom keeps us from being gullible or naïve.

This caution is especially important for spiritual matters. Lots of people have lots of opinions to "sell" about what is true or not true in relation to God and godly values. Today, ungodly teachings abound about the creation, the existence of God, what a boy or girl is, what marriage is, what sexual practices are okay, what truth is, what success is, how to think about authorities like police, teachers, parents, and many other topics. A discerning young person will be thinking about whether the advice he or she is hearing squares with biblical teachings. Thinking carefully with the Bible as your lens through which to look at all of life is critical. It may mean going to a parent, pastor, or other biblically informed person whom you trust to help you think carefully. But being wise does mean you will be on guard for *perverted speech* and *crooked* and *devious ways* from advisors. Use the wise people in your life to help you guard yourself from *perverted speech* and those who are *devious in their ways.*

Bridges' Comments:

Many snares for young adults are about to be detailed by Solomon in the rest of his book of Proverbs. Here he summarizes the scary picture of the temptations to which young people will be exposed. This should awaken parents to pray earnestly for their children's solid conversion so that *...wisdom will come into your heart and knowledge will be pleasant to your soul* (Proverbs 2:10).

Youth want pleasure. All of us do, but youth are easily distracted by what others present as pleasurable. Young adults must be brought up carefully with the Gospel so that their minds, their convictions, their passions, and their hearts' renewal before God are thorough. Such growth, and nothing less, will preserve them from heartless people who use words to trap immature or thoughtless young adults. Such growth also *delivers* them from the cruelest, most *devious* "adversary" of all, the one who accuses (see Zechariah 3:1-5) and who plots to exploit, steal, kill, and destroy (John 10:10). That one is Satan.

Every town swarms with Satan's representatives. These are people who often carefully study the skills of deception. Look at the terms Solomon uses here to describe their "art": *Perverted speech, ways of darkness, perverseness, devious.*

Solomon warned us in Proverbs 1:10-13 about seductive people. Now he's doing it again with a little different twist. This tempter uses his speech to appeal to and lead young adults from *the paths of uprightness* to walk *in the ways of darkness* (Proverbs 2:13). He speaks proud things against God and his law. He's like a poisonous fountain sending up poisoned waters. These young people and their companions have probably been trained in *the paths of uprightness.* Now they readily *forsake* those paths, which they never seriously loved. Now they *walk in the ways of darkness* (verse 13), which their hearts do love (see Proverbs 4:16,17; John 3:19,20). Having come in contact with the poisonous breath of the plague of deception, they have become contaminated and are eager to spread their infection.

The crooked path these young people choose doesn't allow them to see around the corner to where it leads.

These young adults leave the paths they were brought up in by their parents. They've come to hate them. They were raised in righteous ways, but they have become open and bold with their evil intentions. They *rejoice in doing evil and delight in the perverseness of evil* (Proverbs 2:14) and are *devious in their ways* so as to draw others into their net. They and their victims plunge deeper and deeper into sin until they lose all traces of the straight way and all their *paths are crooked* (Proverbs 2:15), leading them to eternal ruin.

Isn't this an all too common picture of many young people who have godly parents and a church or religious background? Over time they become "hardened through the deceitfulness of sin" (Hebrews 3:13). They are unwilling to listen to serious warnings, and even turn a deaf ear to the Spirit of God's convictions on their conscience.

Young people, be on guard and avoid friendships with those who are turning their backs on God's true instruction. Such people are hardened in their devotedness to their master's work—the one whom Paul called the "god of this world" (2 Corinthians 4:4) because of his sway on so many. If misguided youth could see the true deformed nature of sin and the certain self-destruction to which it leads, they might think more seriously, but the tempters are *devious in their ways* (Proverbs 2:15), deceiving even themselves. The *crooked* path these young people choose doesn't allow them to see around the corner to where it leads. Satan presents the bait, makes sin taste sweet, hides its huge offensiveness to God, puts people to sleep, and blinds them from seeing where it is taking them—ultimately to Hell (Psalm 125:5; Romans 6:21; 2 Corinthians 4:3,4). Their habits and attitudes are so much a part of them that they can't turn back to wise ways. They *walk in the ways of darkness...rejoice in doing evil...delight in the perverseness of evil...are devious in their ways.* A fatal epitaph!

To Help You Meditate:

1. Tell of a time when you or someone you know was not careful to check with a more experienced person than you about a purchase you were going to make. Who would you have chosen to talk to and why?

2. Why do young adults and others rush ahead with a decision to believe something without carefully evaluating what is being persuasively urged as a true or wise choice?

3. How important is pleasure to people? How do Satan and his agents use pleasure or the promise of pleasure to deceive people? What is the antidote that God provides so we can escape this deception?

3:1,2   How to Live A Long Life—Usually

ESV

1 My son, do not forget my teaching, but let your heart keep my commandments,
2 for length of days and years of life and peace they will add to you.

NIV

1 My son, do not forget my teaching, but keep my commands in your heart,
2 for they will prolong your life many years and bring you prosperity.

Wisdom Lived Out Today:

It's not always true in our broken world, but usually the way we live affects how *long* we live and the *peacefulness* we can enjoy along the way. These two verses link both *length* and *peace* of life to God's teaching and his commandments.

I learned from some missionaries that in one Native American tribal region of Arizona the average length of life is between 35 and 36 years of age—a lifespan less than half the national average. The chief reason: alcohol addiction—even for children as young as eight. The addiction rate among this one large tribe of about 22,000 is five times greater than the overall U.S. average. The suicide rate is also way beyond the national average. Unemployment, drug abuse, poor educational options, street crime, and unhealthy living conditions contribute to the very low life expectancy. Imagine this pattern going back for three or four generations. The result: hopelessness and very little motivation to achieve in school or to plan for the future.
"After all, nothing is going to change or get better." They have no hope.

This tragedy and hopelessness is real life for these people. It exists in many city neighborhoods, too, because as Solomon implies in these verses, they don't *remember* God's good *teaching or* his *commandments.* Maybe they've never been given his *teaching* or his *commandments* in the first place! That's why missionaries go to remote, needy places like these Native American areas. Life without God's law and gospel usually results in loss of *length of days and years of life and peace.* Not always, of course. But there is usually that kind of connection. That's the way God has designed life to work—and it still does, even in this broken world.

My father, and his brother, my uncle, and my youngest brother Bob, all died right around age 60—10 years younger than I am now as I write this. They were wonderful men in lots of ways, but all three lived their lives disregarding God's wise counsel about life. All three faced the life-ending effects of their addictions. In my dad's case, he disciplined me firmly throughout my childhood and taught me how to submit to authority and to value hard work when we moved to our farm. These are lessons that have been invaluable. But sadly, alcohol, tobacco, and unfaithfulness to his wife (my mother) controlled his life. Because God saved me in my early high school years, he spared me from life-style patterns that my dad had. This was not true of my youngest brother. His life ended early, too, for the same reasons. I'm certainly not a perfect person, but Jesus has made a difference in my values and my habits. Christ's church was a major guide for me for *teaching* me biblical values in my teen years after I became a believer. My church leaders taught me to *remember* God's *teaching* and *commandments*. With the 10 extra years (to the time of this writing God has given me), I've been able to enjoy my wife (your grandma) and all of you and serve him full-time in my mission work. In my case, because of his grace (certainly not my goodness), *length of days...and peace* have flowed from *remembering* his *teaching* and his *commandments*. These have made the difference. It's all God's grace!

Likewise, if you *don't forget my teaching and let your heart keep my commandments* you can enjoy God's blessings of years of life and peacefulness. No one knows how long he or she has to live. The end of life is an appointment God has set and for which no one will be late. Hebrews 9:27 says "...it is appointed for man to die once, and after that comes judgment..." The length and quality of your life, however, do not need to be either cut short or be full of fear, anxiety, worry, or doubt. *Length of days and years of life and peace* are what he has in store for those who are his *remembering* and trusting family members. Make it your goal not to *forget his teaching* or neglect his *commandments*.

> **Prayer:**
> Father, give me the humility to trust you and not wander from your teaching or commandments. Help me to keep them carefully, from the inside of me to the outside of me because of my relationship to Jesus, my Savior. Allow me to live every year of life you give me for your glory with the peacefulness that shows the world that you are a good and accepting God and Savior. In Jesus' name, Amen.

Bridges' Comments:

No one is a fool who re*member*s God's commands! *Remember*ing is the opposite of forgetting or *dismember*ing. *Remember*ing is putting things together that ought to be together—God's wise Word and my heart belong together. *Forgetting* is separating them, keeping them apart, or neglecting or ignoring those wise truths.

Keeping God's wise counsel, his *commands*, is a *heart* matter. The *heart* is the place of intimacy and personhood. The heart is the place where we connect with someone at a level below the surface to enter a close relationship. When this connection is with God and his wise counsel, it yields *long life* and *peace*. "Shalom" is the Hebrew word for *peace* in this verse. It means wholeness, prosperity, and completeness. This quality of life usually follows such *"remembering"* in this life, but it always does in eternity. Sometimes, though, pain, suffering, and even martyrdom may follow people who seriously *remember* God's law. Think about Joseph, Naomi, Job, Jeremiah, and the Apostles Paul, James, and his brother John. All of them suffered.

Because of his grace, most people who follow the LORD, the living Word (the Lord Jesus, John 1:1,14), enjoy him and the shalom he grants. In this life "the path of the righteous is like the light of dawn, which shines brighter and brighter until full day" (Proverbs 4:18). Consider again all the same people listed above who suffered severely in their lives. Their lives did not end with a whimper or sigh, but with great joy. Even Paul, who suffered tremendously (beatings, attacks, scorn, imprisonments, etc.), said, "For to me to live is Christ, and to die is gain" (Philippians 1:21).

The world can't understand this. How can suffering people be at *peace*? But this is what God's counsel, his *teaching and commandments,* produces. It's the way he's made the world to work when his law and his wise counsel are followed. Even in a fallen, broken world, his shalom operates for the blessing of his people.

Are you *remembering* or *dismembering* God's wise counsel in your young years? This question in Proverbs does not come from a stern, unfeeling king. It's a father's voice who is lovingly speaking to persuade his child, his *son,* to do what will result in life and peace. In the last chapter, he urged his son to "seek" and to "search" for wisdom (Proverbs 2:4). Now he counsels his son to *not forget my teaching.* Solomon is warning his son about pushing God's wisdom, his *teaching* and wise *commands,* out of his mind by trying to *forget* them or by giving his attention to other distractions (see Proverbs 2:17; Psalms 9:17 and 10:4 and compare them to Proverbs 4:5, Deuteronomy 4:23 and Psalm 119:93,176). He's not worried about his son's intelligence. He knows his son **can** remember, but he must **want** to remember, so his father urges him to *not forget* these things. The help of the Spirit is truly needed here so we don't neglect or *forget* the wisdom of God (John 14:26).

All obedience that God accepts and blesses begins from the heart.

Solomon says...*let your heart*...be the keeping place of *my commandments*. Make it like the ark of the covenant that held the tablets of the law (see Deuteronomy 9:18; Isaiah 51:7; Ezekiel 11:20; Hebrews 9:4). This is the child of God's desire. "O that my ways may be steadfast in keeping your statutes" (see Psalm 119:5,69,129). This is especially true when he is conscious that, on his own, he is helpless to apply God's wise counsel and the Father's covenant promises to his life. God, YHWH, the Redeemer said, "I will put my law within them, and I will write it on their hearts" (Jeremiah 31:33). Ultimately, only God can bind or tie these laws to our hearts. All obedience that God accepts and blesses begins from the heart, and yet this is the first part of us that wanders from God and the first part that he activates or makes alive by true faith. The heart is the source of life (Proverbs 4:23; Romans 6:17). All our religious activity, thinking, and intentions to do good come from our heart. If our heart is not the source, we are like a shell of a person without any internal organs. The outside may look good, but the real person just isn't there.

Anything that an empty professing believer does to please God, even if he does thousands of good things, will fall short and not be accepted by God. Such behavior cannot make him or her right with God. "...their root will be as rottenness, and their blossom will go up like dust" (Isaiah 5:24). If every moment of their lives was filled with good deeds for the benefit of others or with religious activity, without a renewed *heart,* made alive to God to *keep my commandments*, they will still hear God's rebuke. Isaiah told disloyal Israel that even while they performed their religious sacrifices, God rejected them. Isaiah wrote:

> What to me is the multitude of your sacrifices? says the LORD; I have had enough
> of burnt offerings of rams and the fat of well-fed beasts; I do not delight in the blood

of bulls, or of lambs, or of goats. When you come to appear before me, who has required of you this trampling of my courts? (Isaiah 1:11,12)

The "delight" of our "inner being" (Romans 7:22) is what stamps all that we do as acceptable service. Our pleasure and our stick-to-it-iveness with works of faith flow from the gracious change that God produces in our hearts (Ezekiel 11:19; 36:26,27). It is obedience from the heart that brings a great reward: a long and happy life—the highest earthly good (Psalm 34:12,16; Proverbs 4:10; 9:11; 10:27; Job 10:12). The wicked may die in outward comfort, the righteous may die in outward trouble (Ecclesiastes 9:2), but *length of days and years of life* is the promise to the righteous to take place either on earth or in heaven or in both as the Father determines.

God's promises to the believers in this life do not appeal to unbelievers. To the ungodly, they are more like a curse (Genesis 4:11-15). On the other hand, the promises to the people of God are often linked to the trial of their faith and exercise of patience when they must wait for God's plan for them to unfold fully in eternity (Genesis 27:46; 47:9; 1 Kings 19:4; Job 7:16; Philippians 1:23,24; Revelation 22:20). To everyone, though, days on earth are a source of weariness (Proverbs 15:15; Psalm 90:10; Ecclesiastes 12:1).

But weariness is not the last word for God's people. *Peace* adds sunshine along this toilsome way for the believer (Psalm 119:165; Isaiah 32:17; 48:17,18). This peace is "...peace with God through our Lord Jesus Christ...by the blood of Christ...by the blood of his cross" (Romans 5:1; Ephesians 2:13,14; Colossians 1:20). This is eternal peace in our Lord's home and in his arms (Psalm 37:37; Isaiah 57:2). This is where all the fightings of our rebellious fleshly sinful nature, all our fallen patterns of thinking, desiring, and acting that still cling to us, and all our willful disobedience shall end forever. "Blessed are those who wash their robes, so that they may have the right to the tree of life and that they may enter the city by the gates" (Revelation 22:14).

To Help You Meditate:

1. Do you know of people whose length of life and peacefulness have been cut short or were absent because of ignorance of God's wise law or their refusal to heed it? What could motivate people to ignore God's wise counsel about life?

2. Considering the number of needy people in the world who have never heard the life-giving, life-extending, peace-producing gospel, how can you be involved in helping them?

3. What strategies can you use to "remember" God's wise commands and laws? What is there about this kind of self-discipline that keeps many from making the effort?

4:1-2   Are You Listening to Me?

ESV

1 Hear, O sons, a father's instruction, and be attentive, that you may gain insight,
2 for I give you good precepts; do not forsake my teaching.

NIV

1 Listen, my sons, to a father's instruction; pay attention and gain understanding.
2 I give you sound learning, so do not forsake my teaching.

Wisdom Lived Out Today:

Imagine Marcus as a young teen. "Marcus, have you cleaned your room the way I told you?" Aunt Deb might call up the stairs to check on him, but there is no answer. She calls again a few minutes later and a little louder this time: "Marcus, did you clean your room?" A little more time passes and she calls even more loudly, "Marcus, are you listening to me? How many times do I have to call you? Did you clean your room?"

Do your parents have to call you over and over for some things? Listening doesn't seem to come naturally, does it? Sometimes this is because we are focused on some of our own things, like listening to our music. Sometimes we are hard of hearing because we think we're in trouble and just don't want to hear it. Solomon knew being "hard of hearing" was true about himself and his teens, so he begins this section of his practical counsel in Proverbs by calling for his sons' attention. Listen, he is saying. *Hear...be attentive...*

Solomon knows that our hearts can be in totally foreign worlds, away from the focus on the wise *instruction, good precepts,* and *teaching* we need for *insight* or "understanding." He isn't only interested in having his teens parrot back wise sayings. He wants them to gain *insight* or "understanding," as the other versions translate the Hebrew word. He's not simply looking for them to *do* the right stuff, but to *think* the right stuff. Both are important—doing *and* thinking. He knows that doing comes from the way we think—the way we mentally process things; how we understand what things mean. This is the *insight* about things he wants his son to gain.

Insight gets a teen thinking about why something is wise. It gets a teen comparing what is wise with what is foolish about friendships, doing homework, spending money, being honest with parents and teachers, and hundreds of other experiences he has each day. Young adults can compare outcomes of choices their parents and friends have made. This *Proverbs'* dad wants his teens to consider the cost of their decisions to their reputation, wealth, health, safety, and God's approval.

Every choice has outcomes. Some outcomes are obvious. Some only appear later. Some are positive and some are negative. But the starting place for making wise decisions, beneficial ones, safe ones, and God-blessed ones is with *hear*ing *instruction* and being *attentive* to God's thoughts. This starting place is Solomon's focus in this chapter and the rest of the book of Proverbs.

"There is a lot at stake, so listen!" is really what he's saying. Gaining *insight* or "understanding" is the biggest value this *father* has in mind. He says, *Hear!* It's a loving, life-preserving command to his *sons*. Solomon is not just giving casual advice. He's saying, "To gain the *insight* that will pay off in this life and the next, you are going to have to give some serious attention, some concentrated thought, some intentional focus to what I'm saying."

> **Prayer:**
> Father, don't allow me to tune out the people you place in my life to help me grow and mature. Especially don't allow me to tune you out when things my friends want to do may differ from what you want for me. Make me wise. Help me to focus on gaining *insight* by carefully listening and thinking about what others are saying and evaluating all my options with your wise counsel. In Jesus' name, Amen.

If Lesley and Becca don't pay attention to their gymnastics coaches about mounting and dismounting the balance beam, or if Nate or Katie or Nicole don't follow the lead of their band conductors or play director, there will be a price to pay. One that costs them something, but also one that costs the team, their bands, or the success of the school drama program.

Even more seriously, we need to listen when God speaks about trust in Christ as the only way to have an eternal relationship with him. Trust in him is the only way to conquer the fear of what others think of us, or the way to conquer anger, discouragement, or any other temptation. The cost for not listening to God's wise counsel is enormous—eternal judgment in the future and loss and troubles in this life. "If you are wise, you are wise for yourself; if you scoff (one who doesn't listen to God's wisdom), you alone will bear it" (Proverbs 9:12). Others certainly are affected by our unwillingness to *hear*, but the biggest gainer or loser is me, depending on whether I tune in to God's wise instruction or not.

Bridges' Comments:

The reminders in these first chapters urge young adults, over and over, to "listen to me." They are intended to startle Solomon's sons like the angel's words when he came to the prophet Zechariah. The angel spoke to him, waking him out of a sound sleep to get him focused on the vision he wanted him to see (Zechariah 4:1). Solomon's knowledge was huge. It was as extensive as "…the sand on the seashore" (1 Kings 4:29). But remarkable, intriguing knowledge is not the most important thing for young people to have. More important, given our naturally lazy and forgetful hearts, are the *good precepts…* [and] *teaching* that will give…*understanding…and…sound learning*.

Sadly, many children do not have parents with this concern. Solomon, though, seriously takes up their need by urging them to…*hear a father's instruction…*and to…*be attentive…*This is similar to Paul's later challenge to the Thessalonians: "For you know how, like a father with his children, we exhorted each one of you and encouraged you and charged you to walk in a manner worthy of God, who calls you…" (1 Thessalonians 2:11,12).

Solomon speaks God's Word to his son. He declares his law as *sound learning* (compare Ecclesiastes 12:9-11). To many people, exciting, mysterious, speculative, compromising, self-righteous, and self-exalting teachings are more attractive (Ezekiel 33:31,32; 2 Timothy 4:3,4; Isaiah 30:10; Jeremiah 5:31; Galatians 1:6,7), but young adults need to remember that which gives them a humble, accurate sense of themselves before God. They need to *hear* the gospel. It's that which shows us the free, transforming grace of God, which melts down the stubbornness of our will, which draws the dedication of our heart to himself, and which fills us with the humble, sacrificial spirit of the cross. This is the *...good...teaching* we need to *hear* regardless of how uncomfortable our own human nature finds it.

Therefore *...do not forsake my teaching.* Don't be influenced by the opinions of the group or the popular people in the culture because they say "everybody's doing it" or "nobody believes that anymore." What is the worth of all the opinions of mankind when it comes to determining how to find God's favor? Their way is folly (Psalm 14:1). "There is a way *that seems* right to a man, but its end *is* the way to death" (Proverbs 14:12). This is God's stamp on all the beliefs and sayings people have throughout all generations regardless of how popular they have been.

This is the path of those who have foolish confidence; yet after them people approve of their boasts. *Selah* (A word in Psalms that means something like, "think about this."). Like sheep they are appointed for Sheol (the grave); death shall be their shepherd, and the upright shall rule over them in the morning. Their form shall be consumed in Sheol, with no place to dwell (Psalm 49:13,14).

To Help You Meditate:

1. Describe a time when someone was trying to get your attention but, because you were concentrating on something else or for some other reason, you just did not hear him or her calling or talking to you. What are times that you are tempted to "not hear" when someone is trying to get your attention?

2. Why can being alert to others talking to you be important? Can you think of a situation when actually hearing what someone was saying had a serious outcome?

3. How is listening to understand different from listening to know something? Why is listening for understanding stressed by Solomon in this passage?

4:3-9   Chasing Wisdom

ESV

3 When I was a son with my father, tender, the only one in the sight of my mother,

4 he taught me and said to me, "Let your heart hold fast my words; keep my commandments, and live.

5 Get wisdom; get insight; do not forget, and do not turn away from the words of my mouth.

6 Do not forsake her, and she will keep you; love her, and she will guard you.

7 The beginning of wisdom is this: Get wisdom, and whatever you get, get insight.

8 Prize her highly, and she will exalt you; she will honor you if you embrace her.

9 She will place on your head a graceful garland; she will bestow on you a beautiful crown."

NIV

3 When I was a boy in my father's house, still tender, and an only child of my mother,

4 he taught me and said, "Lay hold of my words with all your heart; keep my commands and you will live.

5 Get wisdom, get understanding; do not forget my words or swerve from them.

6 Do not forsake wisdom, and she will protect you; love her, and she will watch over you.

7 Wisdom is supreme; therefore get wisdom. Though it cost all you have, get understanding.

8 Esteem heart, and she will exalt you; embrace her, and she will honor you.

9 She will set a garland of grace on your head and present you with a crown of splendor."

Wisdom Lived Out Today:

Decisions, decisions, decisions. You make thousands of them daily, don't you? Some are very common and inconsequential and others more critical. Luke may ask, "Is it wise to hang out with Steve and his friends?" "Why not share my answers with other kids in English class? Everyone else does it." "Does it matter if I'm at someone's house when mom thinks I am still at school?"

All decisions are not the same. Some are helpful and some are harmful. The counsel in these verses tells young people how to *get wisdom* and how to *get insight* or understanding so their decisions can be beneficial ones.

Making good decisions is called *wisdom*. It is making choices that fit with the way God wants us to think about life. *Insight* is a little different from *wisdom*. It is the understanding that makes something a *wise* choice. God does not just want us to do the right things (*wisdom*). He wants us to understand why they are the right things to do (*insight*).

So how does a young adult *get wisdom* and *insight?* There is no magic method, but there is a way to think that God says produces them. *Get wisdom, get insight; do not forget, and do not turn away from the words of my mouth...The beginning of wisdom is this: Get wisdom, and whatever you get, get insight* (Proverbs 4:5,7).

Solomon is pushing young people to pursue *wisdom and insight*, like someone hunting and chasing an animal. That's the force of the word *get*. Solomon wants you to chase *wisdom and insight* mentally, emotionally, and spiritually. Be relentless. Don't let them get out of your sight and get away. In Proverbs 3:21-22 Solomon says "My son, do not lose sight of these—keep sound wisdom and discretion (another name for *insight*), and they will be life for your soul and adornment for your neck."

In other words, if you want the BENEFITS of *wisdom* and *insight,* you must WANT *wisdom* and *insight.*

Socrates was a wise Greek philosopher who lived more than 400 years before Christ. He was deeply respected for his wisdom and understanding about life. One day, the story is told, a young man approached him and asked him, "How can I become wise like you?" Socrates told the young man to follow him and led him to the ocean beach. He continued walking out into the ocean water and told the young man to follow him. When the water was up to the young man's chin, Socrates told him to turn around and look at the shoreline. Socrates was reputed to be a tall, strong man, and this arrangement put Socrates behind the young man. Without warning, Socrates folded his arms and put them over the young man's head and pushed him under water. He held him there until the young man struggled violently for breath. Finally, Socrates let him go. The young man shot out of the water, gasping and choking. He sputtered the question, "Why did you do that?"

> **Prayer:**
>
> Father, I know I can be foolish. My heart often wants to focus on things that really are not important or things others want me to pay attention to, but I need your wisdom. I need understanding that you give so that I stick with your wisdom. Otherwise, I will be led away to foolishness the way my heart naturally wants to go. Help me to chase wisdom and insight passionately. Help me to see them and imitate them as they are lived out by godly people and especially the Lord Jesus. In Jesus' name I pray, Amen.

"Young man," Socrates said, "when you hunger for wisdom like you craved that breath of air, you will find it."

This is what Solomon was telling the young people to whom he was writing 500 years before Socrates lived. Don't be enamored or infatuated with the sparkle and noise of the advice of this world. Crave wisdom. Hunger consciously for godly decisions in every situation. Then, just as desperately, crave *insight* to determine what makes these decisions *wise* and not foolish. Look at their outcomes. Look at the consequences that come upon people who choose to go other ways (see Proverbs 9:12).

This kind of driving motivation about living, decision-making, and choosing among the hundreds of options you have every day will pay incalculable dividends. You will find honor to be the reputation you wear like a *graceful garland.* You will earn authority, gravitas, or weightiness, in your influence on others like a *beautiful crown. Wisdom* and *insight* are great rewards. You must seriously want them, though, to get them. Chase wisdom!

Bridges' Comments:

Solomon's father, David, was his model when David taught him as a young boy and then as a young man (1 Chronicles 22:5; 29:1). His dad loved him in special ways, and the more he loved him the more he showed it by carefully teaching him the wisdom of God's ways. This is God's pattern for us all: to be brought up by a "man after God's heart"

(1 Samuel 13:14; Acts 13:22) who instructs us in the fear and service of the Lord (compare 1 Kings 2:2-4; 1 Chronicles 22:6-16 and 28:9,10,20; Genesis 18:19; Deuteronomy 6:7).

It is a special sign of God's mercy to us if we have had an Abraham or a David, or moms or grandmothers like Lois or Eunice (2 Timothy 3:14,15) to bring us up with godly training. Parents: remember that a child untaught will be a living shame (Proverbs 29:15). Training young people in discipline, and not just indulging them, is the truest evidence of love to our young ones (see also Proverbs 13:24 and 1 Kings 1:6).

Notice what Solomon says about this training here in Proverbs 4:4. First, he urges his son to *let your heart hold fast my words and keep my commandments*. While exact words may often escape our memory, the sense of the truths we've heard may be kept in our hearts. Even this heart-keeping effort is the path of life (see also Proverbs 4:13; 6:23; 8:34,35; Isaiah 55:3; Zechariah 3:7). If our hearts are not affected, all the rest of our lives are dead or dying.

Solomon expresses, to the extreme, his father's counsel: *Get wisdom...get insight!* Then he repeats himself, using the same words but with even more emphasis: *get wisdom*

At any cost, and with whatever pains necessary, get wisdom!

...and whatever you get, get insight! At any cost and with whatever pains necessary, *get wisdom* (see Proverbs 23:23 and compare 1 Kings 10:1; Matthew 12:42). The *beginning* or starting place to acquire *wisdom* as the supreme or principal thing of value is your determination to *get wisdom*. Don't forsake it but remind yourself of its great importance (John 8:30,31; Colossians 1:22,23; Hebrews 3:6,14 contrasted with Matthew 13:20,21). Do not *forsake her. Love her. She* will *keep you* and *guard you.*

She, wisdom, is a *keeper* of your soul and a treasure for your happiness. She will promote and honor you, even in this life! She is an ornament of grace in the church. She is a crown of glory in heaven. This father's appeal does not come from a cold, detached advice-giver. It comes from one who passionately pleads to his child who he thinks will self-destruct unless he is led in wisdom's ways. Parents! Do you know this stirring concern, anxiously watching for the first dawn of light in your child's soul (Proverbs 4:18)? Are you earnestly pointing out to him or her that the *beginning of* getting *wisdom* is to desire it, to want it, to pursue it—by paying any price necessary to get it (Matthew 6:33)? Are you modeling that desire as your first choice - above all that the world makes glitter (1 Kings 3:5-12; Philippians 3:7,8)? Is it not just important to you, but seriously important? *Wisdom* and *insight* and your desire for them can have no place if they do not have first place. If these mean anything at all to you, they will be everything to you. That's their nature. Earthly wisdom may be a nice pearl, but this *wisdom* from above is the "pearl of great value" (Matthew 13:46). It can only be gotten by selling all that we have to buy it (Matthew 13:46).

To Help You Meditate:

1. Describe someone you've known who doesn't seem to be satisfied with just surface, bare-facts knowledge, someone who wants to know things more deeply than most people.

2. What can be the spiritual outcome for someone who acts wisely, does good things but doesn't really understand why such things are wise to do?

3, What are three ways you could increase your efforts to get wisdom and insight about God's counsel for your life?

Sex In-Bounds and Out-Of-Bounds
An introduction to Proverbs 5 and 6

These are two of the most extensive sections in Proverbs in which Solomon and other writers counsel us about sex. Most of Proverbs chapter seven is a third section about sex, but that's not included in this book.

Earlier, in the introductory pages of this book, I urged you to read from Proverbs every day and every month by following the number of the day of the month. If you do this, each month this reading cycle will remind you of the urgency of *keeping* or guarding your heart (Proverbs 4:23) in this important area of life.

Solomon knew that this reminder was necessary. He had experienced the tragedy in his own family life of seeing sex running wild. Don't get tired of the subject Solomon is bringing to your attention in these chapters. The repetition is because the wisest man, next to Jesus himself, says you and I need to keep these thoughts in front of us.

These sections in Proverbs are in three parts, as presented by Charles Bridges in his commentary. Each of the three parts is a segment of the total extended lesson he wants us to think about. Read and meditate on each part, one after the other, in your devotional times. Don't skip around. That way you will get the full impact of the wise counsel Solomon is offering in this important area of your young adult life.

Part I of Proverbs 5

5:1-14   I'm Free to Jump!

ESV

1 My son, be attentive to my wisdom; incline your ear to my understanding,
2 that you may keep discretion, and your lips may guard knowledge.
3 For the lips of a forbidden woman drip honey, and her speech is smoother than oil,
4 but in the end she is bitter as wormwood, sharp as a two-edged sword.
5 Her feet go down to death; her steps follow the path to Sheol;
6 she does not ponder the path of life; her ways wander, and she does not know it.
7 And now, O sons, listen to me, and do not depart from the words of my mouth.
8 Keep your way far from her, and do not go near the door of her house,
9 lest you give your honor to others and your years to the merciless,
10 lest strangers take their fill of your strength, and your labors go to the house of a foreigner,
11 and at the end of your life you groan, when your flesh and body are consumed,
12 and you say, "How I hated discipline, and my heart despised reproof!
13 I did not listen to the voice of my teachers or incline my ear to my instructors.
14 I am at the brink of utter ruin in the assembled congregation."

NIV

1 My son, pay attention to my wisdom, listen well to my words of insight,
2 that you may maintain discretion and your lips may preserve knowledge.
3 For the lips of an adulteress drip honey, and her speech is smoother than oil;
4 but in the end she is bitter as gall, sharp as a double-edged sword.
5 Her feet go down to death; her steps lead straight to the grave.
6 She gives no thought to the way of life; her paths are crooked, but she knows it not.
7 Now then, my sons, listen to me; do not turn aside from what I say.
8 Keep to a path far from her, do not go near the door of her house,
9 lest you give your best strength to others and your years to one who is cruel,
10 lest strangers feast on your wealth and your toil enrich another man's house.
11 At the end of your life you will groan, when your flesh and body are spent.
12 You will say, "How I hated discipline! How my heart spurned correction!
13 I would not obey my teachers or listen to my instructors.
14 I have come to the brink of utter ruin in the midst of the whole assembly."

Wisdom Lived Out Today:

Tom came into the guidance office. He was angry.

He talked for a while and told me about how unfair his English teacher was, and that he was going to do what he could to make life miserable for her because she was making life miserable for him.

"Tom, you have the freedom to be as mean and nasty as you want to be. I can't stop you from that. God has created you with the ability to make decisions as a young adult and there are very few people who can *make* you do anything."

"I wish Smith (his English teacher's name) would understand that. She's always trying to control me and make me do things her way."

"Tom," I said, "do you see my office windows here? You are a big guy. If you wanted to push past me and jump out my second-floor window, you probably could. I'd try to stop you because to jump would be crazy and dangerous, but you are taller and stronger than I am and could probably catch me off guard. You could shove me out of the way, if you wanted to, and jump out of the window. God has given you the ability to make that kind of choice—even if it is a crazy one.

"But once you are out the window, another law takes over and your choices don't matter too much at that point. You can't say, 'Uh, well, maybe this wasn't too smart. Maybe I'll go back into Dr. Horne's office.' It's too late for that. Another law now takes over and you are going down, whether you like it or not."

Sex is not the same thing as Tom's choice to be mean to his teacher or to jump out of a second-story window, but it is just as much a decision—with consequences.

Sex is something young people think about a lot, and Solomon, the writer, doesn't avoid it. He's saying to his young adult son, "This is something you must think about if you are going to live wisely—and safely. In addition, this area of your life will have a serious impact on your relationship with God."

Solomon thinks this topic is so important for young adults that he mentions it in a few verses in chapter two, all of this chapter, part of chapter six, and all of chapter seven. That's almost a third of the first nine chapters, which make up this first section[8] of Proverbs.

Like Tom, God has created you with the freedom of choice. You can use your body and sex as God intended them to be used or try to make your own rules, but once you are out of the window, another law takes over. You are free to make choices. You are not free to choose the consequences that go with them.

A key word in this chapter is "ponder." It's used twice (Proverbs 5:6 and 21). First, the woman who is seducing a young man *does not ponder the path of life* (Proverbs 5:6). Neither she nor the young man mentioned later are thinking about where their behavior leads. There is a *bitter end* that she isn't considering, Proverbs 5:4 says. This could be just as true of a young man trying to seduce a girl or a young couple giving in to their passion for each other. Solomon is not picking on girls.

Especially in this chapter and the next two, Solomon tries to give his sons a picture of the dangers of using the gift of sex in ways God *does not* intend, but he balances that warning with the richness of sex in marriage, the way God *does* intend it to be enjoyed.

---

[8] Chapters 1-9 of Proverbs are extended passages of wisdom on several different topics. Pertaining to sexual temptation, some of the passages have just a few verses and some take up whole chapters. Chapters 10-29 are mostly one or two-verse sayings of short, pithy, pointed wise counsel. These first chapters are like an athlete's stretching exercises to get him or her ready for the needed quick bursts of energy and sharp movements in an event. Chapters 10-29 are where those bursts of energy and sharp choices about living happen. Meditating on the truths in these first nine chapters will prevent you from pulling a spiritual hamstring or crippling yourself in the many event choices you must make throughout your young adulthood.

Ponder! Think. You are free to jump out the window, but you are not free to choose the consequences of doing so. Other laws God has created into life, like gravity, take over and have their impact. Sometimes the outcomes last a lifetime.

Proverbs 5 ends with someone else *pondering* - God. God has created a world in which such a *lack of discipline* (Proverbs 5:23) *ensnares* people and *holds* them *fast* (Proverbs 5:22). Sin always produces death in some kind and degree, though not necessarily in the literal sense. Some feature of your future will be affected—emotionally, psychologically, relationally, physically, and spiritually. In other words, the patterns and effects of using sex contrary to God's wise design result in some degree of bondage. Who doesn't know some couple whose relationship has been damaged or ended because of sexual foolishness? It doesn't look or feel that way at the moment you are enjoying it, but as the chapter begins, there is an *end* (Proverbs 5:4,11). That *end* is out of sight at the moment, but it will surely follow.

Sexual sin can be forgiven. God will forgive any person who genuinely repents or turns from sin to God and asks forgiveness (1 John 1:9). "The blood of Jesus his Son cleanses us from all sin" (1 John 1:7), but that doesn't mean there won't be lasting effects.

Imagine someone doing this stupid experiment: A guy puts his hand on a stove burner to see how long he can keep it there with the stove turned on high heat. Suppose he has the willpower to keep his hand there until his hand turns black with a burn. Will God forgive that foolishness if he genuinely asks for forgiveness for abusing his body? Of course he will. Forgiveness, though, won't erase the scars and restore the full usefulness of his hand. Full usefulness may have been lost for the rest of his life. God has created us with the ability to make choices, but we cannot choose the consequences.

God has a better idea! *Blessed...rejoice...delight...be intoxicated always in her love* (Proverbs 5:18,19) are his words to describe sex as God intends it within his marriage boundary. *Drink* up (Proverbs 5:15), God's way! That's wonderful, beautiful, and without regret!

Prayer:
Father, help me ponder my ways. Help me to not just go with the flow of my feelings and passions in my relationships with guys or girls. Help me to keep myself pure for the partner and the sexual enjoyment you want for me in marriage so that you will be glorified in that part of my life as well as all others. In Jesus' name I pray, Amen.

Bridges' Comments:

Ponder this chapter. None of us knows the extent to which sin has poisoned and twisted our physical desires. Perhaps Solomon's painful experiences (1 Kings 11:1-8; Ecclesiastes 7:26) had given him wisdom and understanding about this, so listen to his counsel with caution and carefulness.

Our own strength, education, and self-discipline are as powerless against our sexual passions as the green vines Delilah used to tie Samson while she was trying to trick him (Judges 16:8). Only God's wisdom, deeply etched on our hearts, is a safeguard. His wisdom teaches us to exercise discretion or good judgment so that we can guard our own souls and warn our friends of the dangers of giving in to these desires before God's time (see Proverbs 2:10,11,16; 6:20,24; 7:1-5; Psalm 17:4; 119:9,11).

The serious reality of sexual temptation, which comes at all of us, demands our attention. The deluded or self-deceived victim thinks or hopes he will only taste the *honeycomb* sweetness of sex and its pleasure, even when he goes outside of God's boundaries for it. He only hears the seductive smoothness of the girl's or maybe his own heart's desires that are tempting him (Proverbs 2:16; 6:24; 7:21), but the beginning is never as sweet as the end is bitter. Here, God shows consequences that include bitterness and regret like *wormwood* (a bitter tasting plant), a double-edged painfully slashing sword like seductive words (see Psalm 55:21), and even a pathway leading to death. Every step she takes is *taking hold of hell.* It's as if she is invading hell defiantly, grasping it cheerfully, but is ignorant of its horror.

One feature of the tempter's deceptiveness is remarkable: she shifts herself in a thousand moveable ways according to whatever she thinks is seductive at the moment (see Proverbs 7:21). She

Ponder!

uses every weakness she senses in her target and every one of his unguarded moments. Her one hidden goal is keeping her victim from thinking or *pondering the path of life.* She wants his conscience to be distracted. She doesn't want him to reflect on the possible outcomes of this encounter. If he gives one serious thought, it might break the spell she has him under and open a way for him to escape (see Psalm 119:59; Ezekiel 18:28; Luke 15:17).

Would we be surprised by a mom or dad forcing their children to play back away from the edge of a cliff? *Hear me now, kids! Move away from the edge!* So Solomon warns his sons as godly parents would do: "We are not trying to keep you from enjoying the pleasure of sex that God has designed for you. We want you to enjoy it God's way! Every other way is an illusion."

When we put ourselves in the way of temptation, we also put ourselves out of the way of God's protection.

When we put ourselves in the way of temptation, we also put ourselves out of the way of God's protection. The closer the snare or trap comes to us, the more it becomes deceptively attractive and appealing. The voice of wisdom, therefore, is *flee youthful passions* (2 Timothy 2:22). Avoid the tempter's touch, her words, even the looks she gives you. *Keep your way far from her.* Not only don't give in to her, don't *go near her door* (compare Proverbs 4:14,15; 6:27,28).

Think of the bad fruit of ignoring this warning: losing your honor and trust (Proverbs 6:32,33; Genesis 38:23-26; 2 Samuel 12:11; 15:30; Nehemiah 13:26), opening yourself up to years of mockery, a bad reputation, and misery (Proverbs 6:26; 31:3; Judges 16:18-21); wasting future opportunities and family wealth (Proverbs 6:26,35; 29:3; Job 31:12; Hosea 7:9; Luke 15:13,30), living with remorse, regret, and guilt and the ways they can contaminate future relationships with a spouse and children (Luke 15:15,16), or slowly seeing your body deteriorate and even slide toward an early death (1 Corinthians 6:18).

Add to these thoughts the voice of your conscience throughout life. It reminds you of privileges you've wasted from your upbringing, the beliefs and desires about truth and character you've betrayed, the warnings that you've suppressed, and the knowledge you've received but which you've simply ignored. This will be the sting many feel who have been taught in school and by godly parents but now ignore the warnings by God and the voices of their teachers. Some boldly live in openly shameful ways among their families. In some cases, they bring this outright violation of God's laws right into Christ's church (Numbers 25:6,7; Ezekiel 8:5-16).

This is the picture of sin. It offers "pleasure for a season" (Hebrews 11:25), but its "wages" are death (Romans 6:23). Every sin not repented of in this life will bring perpetual torment in eternity. Talking myself into believing that this is "no big deal" does not put away the sorrowful fruit that crossing God's boundary lines will bear. It only delays the consequences, until the judgment when mercy shall have fled away forever (Proverbs 1:24-31). Then, nothing will remain except the piercing cry of the accusing conscience: "Son, remember..." (Luke 16:25). There are no people who doubt God's existence or the Gospel's truthfulness in eternity and few on their death-beds. Sinner, *the path of life* is now open to you. *Ponder* it thoughtfully and prayerfully. May the light of the Word and the teaching of the Spirit guide you to that *path of life*.

To Help You Meditate:

1. Have you ever made a stupid choice? What could be some of the outcomes of making a choice about sex that is out of the boundaries God has set?

2. What are some of the most powerful reasons people give for crossing boundaries God has set for sex?

3. What are some of the greatest influences that Satan and the world use to attract us to giving in to sexual desires outside of God's plan for it in marriage?

Part 2 of Proverbs 5

5:15-19   A Beautiful Romance

ESV

15 Drink water from your own cistern, flowing water from your own well.

16 Should your springs be scattered abroad, streams of water in the streets?

17 Let them be for yourself alone, and not for strangers with you.

18 Let your fountain be blessed, and rejoice in the wife of your youth,

19 a lovely deer, a graceful doe. Let her breasts fill you at all times with delight; be intoxicated, always in her love.

NIV

15 Drink water from your own cistern, running water from your own well.

16 Should your springs overflow in the streets, your streams of water in the public squares?

17 Let them be yours alone, never to be shared with strangers.

18 May your fountain be blessed, and may you rejoice in the wife of your youth.

19 A loving doe, a graceful deer— may her breasts satisfy you always, may you ever be captivated by her love.

Wisdom Lived Out Today:

Not too long ago I had the privilege of visiting believers in Addis Ababa, the capital city of Ethiopia. One brother took me to the national museum there. On the second floor we paused in front of a famous painting of a beautiful queen with her husband. "That is King Solomon," he said. "Solomon wrote a whole book about his romance with the queen of Sheba of Ethiopia, about 1000 BC, according to many scholars." He went on, "The book, Song of Solomon, is a beautiful love poem in your Bible and celebrates the beauty of sex and intimacy in the marriage relationship. Solomon's relationship with the queen introduced her and Ethiopia to Judaism and prepared us for the gospel when Philip led the Ethiopian eunuch to faith in Christ a thousand years later, as we're told in Acts 8." Some scholars would not agree with all the details of my guide's summary of history, but the point is still true, The Bible has much to say about sexual intimacy.

Sex is God's idea! It is beautiful and rewarding in a marriage relationship that aims for God's glory and has Jesus at its center. The book, Song of Solomon, does celebrate sex God's way, but even more, it points, like all marriage intimacy, to the beauty of the relationship between Christ and his people. The most intense human intimacy points to the deep and rich spiritual relationship God intends his people to have for eternity with the Savior. "And this is eternal life," Jesus said, "that they know you the only true God, and Jesus Christ whom you have sent" (John 17:3).

Examples abound in the Bible and in the news of today of the hurtfulness of sex outside of God's design. No one has to look very far to see the damage such intimacy does. But this section of Solomon's counsel to us in Proverbs 5 paints a candid picture of the beautiful marital intimacy that God intends to give us as a taste of the delight and enjoyment that he has planned for his people forever (see Ephesians 5:31,32).

Prayer:

Father, allow all the desires I feel to point me to the wonder you have for me for eternity with the Lord Jesus. Help me to save myself so that the sexual intimacy I am able to have with my husband/wife may be a beautiful, strengthening part of our relationship. Help me keep the commitment to keep myself pure for my spouse so that our marriage intimacy may truly point to the relationship of pleasure that you want us to have with you. In Jesus' name, Amen.

Bridges' Comments:

Our desires for pleasures that God says are out of bounds spring naturally from our dissatisfaction with what he has already provided for us. If we are not content with what we have at home, drinking *from your own cistern,*[9] we will look for it elsewhere. Sexual pleasure in marriage is one of the extraordinary good things God has mercifully given to his fallen and rebellious people, so thankfully enjoy your own and not your neighbor's *well* (Exodus 20:17; 2 Samuel 11:2,3). God wants to bless your sexual intimacy (Psalm 128) so that it will be as flowing water (compare Numbers 24:7; Deuteronomy 33:28; Psalm 68:26; Isaiah 48:1) that results in a godly influence through your children to many others (compare Zechariah 8:5).

Rejoice in the wife of your youth (Deuteronomy 24:5; Ecclesiastes 9:9). Consider her a special gift from your Father's hand (Proverbs 19:14). Cherish her with gentleness and purity (Genesis 24:67) *as a lovely deer, a graceful doe.*

Whoever neglects this beautiful intimate relationship with his wife or her husband opens the door to immediate temptation. Tender, regular, private lovemaking is the best defense against roaming desires and sinful passions. The Word of God honors this lovemaking by making it an image of the greatest relationship "mystery" of which Paul speaks. He compares the one flesh intimacy of the husband and wife to the relationship of Christ and his church (Ephesians 5:25,29).

To Help You Meditate:

1. When you think of a close friendship with someone, what are some of the ways it can be created and strengthened?

2. What boundaries make such a friendship lasting and deeper?

3. Why do you think the world often thinks that the Bible is against people enjoying pleasurable experiences—like sex? In what sense can it be said that such people are "nearsighted" (only see things right in front of them, here and now, and miss the big picture of life)?

---

[9] The beauty of the figure is illustrated from the cultural situation in which the houses of the East appear each to have had their own cistern or water source (2 Kings 18:31).

Part 3 of Proverbs 5

5:20-23   Taken Captive

ESV
20 Why should you be intoxicated, my son, with a forbidden woman and embrace the bosom of an adulteress?
21 For a man's ways are before the eyes of the LORD, and he ponders all his paths.
22 The iniquities of the wicked ensnare him, and he is held fast in the cords of his sin.
23 He dies for lack of discipline, and because of his great folly he is led astray.

NIV
20 Why be captivated, my son, by an adulteress? Why embrace the bosom of another man's wife?
21 For a man's ways are in full view of the LORD, and he examines all his paths.
22 The evil deeds of a wicked man ensnare him; the cords of his sin hold him fast.
23 He will die for lack of discipline, led astray by his own great folly.

Wisdom Lived Out Today:

Sex is intoxicating! That's a good thing—when it's enjoyed as God planned it to be.

Solomon knew about the power of sex to dominate him. He had seen it in his family with the failures of his dad, and he experienced it himself with his wealth and the influence having many wives had upon him.

Here he warns his own sons to be on guard against sex's destructive, controlling, *ensnaring,* binding power. It can trap or addict one. It can make one captive to his lusts and desires. Ultimately, because of its dominion, it destroys self-control and leads to death. Not a pretty picture. Not the ecstatic fantasy that the world pictures sex as providing. Sex has effects. It changes people. It can distort the way they think about sex itself, about the opposite sex, about trust, about people as people or objects, about the way intimacy is related to real love, and about its place in the marriage relationship.

Discipline, Solomon warns, is critical for security and trust in a relationship. Sex outside of God's boundaries erodes *discipline.* To refer to another proverb, "A man without self-control is like a city broken into and left without walls" (Proverbs 25:28). He's defenseless. Vulnerable. Easily taken over, influenced, and controlled by others' wishes and wills. He is unable to protect himself and move himself in positive, creative, free directions.

So, Solomon concludes this chapter with the question, *Why be intoxicated* or "captivated..." (NIV)? Why be *led astray by* [your own] *great folly?* Such entrapment is not necessary for any who keep their relationship with the *LORD* (God's loving, redeeming, personal name used in Proverbs 5:21) in view and want to live with his gracious, thoughtful, loving eye upon them.

Bridges' Comments:

Solomon contrasts the deadly seducing temptation of sexual sin in Proverbs 5:20-23 to the beautiful happiness that God provides for a married couple in Proverbs 5:15-19. It's clear that only an infatuated, seduced person would want to leave the healthy fountain for the poisoned spring. One would have to be under a spell to insult the "honorable" state of marriage (Hebrews 13:4) by *embracing the bosom of an adulteress* to have sex that would be loveless, joyless, and impersonal.

> **Prayer:**
>
> Father, I don't want my life to be controlled by anyone or anything except you! But the feelings and desire for sex can be strong and I need you to help me turn away from them and remind myself of your love, acceptance, power, purpose, and plan for me. I need to be on guard against the world's fantasies that lead to broken-down walls of discipline. I want the freedom that you produce, the freedom to be who you made me to be and not be taken captive by any of the world's fantasies. In Jesus' name, Amen.

One would think just knowing that sex outside of God's boundaries is open before the *eyes of the LORD* would slow down such self-destructive and ungodly behavior, but sadly it often does not! Our human, lost, sinful, broken condition (our depravity), at its root, is a form of practical atheism. We are willing to live like God does not exist (Psalm 14:1-3). Being conscious that someone might see us commit a wrong might slow down our poor behavior (Job 24:1,15; Isaiah 29:15), but the thought that the invisible though all-seeing God may see us (Psalm 10:4) often seems to raise no alarm, conviction, or restraint. Oh, that we would simply read and believe our Bibles! How this solemn truth, that *he* (God) *ponders all his* (man's) *paths,* would flash through our minds and consciences.

Not only would such reflection point people to the God who knows all (Job 31:4; Psalm 119:1-4), but it would also point them to the One who *ponders all his paths* and justly judges all (Proverbs 16:2; 1 Samuel 2:3; Daniel 5:27). No one is hidden from his piercing eye (Hebrews 4:13). "God will bring every deed into judgment, with every secret thing..." (Ecclesiastes 12:14). "Everyone who is sexually immoral or impure...has no inheritance in the kingdom of Christ and God" (Ephesians 5:5).

But if one is not restrained from crossing these boundaries by thinking about God's all-seeing eye, maybe considering the troubles he can bring upon himself will do it. God does not need chains or any physical condition, like a prison, to control someone who flaunts or dismisses his law. He has made life work in such a way that wherever one goes, his sins and its effects usually go with him. The *cords of his sin ensnare* or trap him for judgment (see Proverbs 11:3,5,6; 29:6; 1 Samuel 28:5-10). Is it possible for someone who lives with a pattern of sin simply to give it up whenever he pleases? Most addicts believe that about themselves, but repetition forms the habit. It cultivates a pattern. Sin becomes a ruling, dominating power in his life. Every such desire pressures and seduces him as Delilah pressured and seduced Samson. He just closed his eyes against the light and was captured. He finally died as a consequence of ignoring God's life-giving instruction (see

Proverbs 1:29; 5:12; 10:21; Job 4:21; Job 36:12; Hosea 4:14,17). *...because of his great folly he is led astray* (2 Peter 2:14,15).

Is there no remedy for this deadly curse? Thanks be to God! Yes! Cleansing is provided for the impure (1 Corinthians 6:11); deliverance is proclaimed for the captive (Isaiah 56:1). Blessed Savior! Cleanse the leper in your precious fountain. Fulfill your mighty commission: set the captive free.

To Help You Meditate:

1. What are some of the evidences of the power of sex to control people in our culture?

2. What can you envision as effective ways to guard yourself from allowing sexual desire to control you?

3. How important is it to keep God's all-seeing eye and his abundant forgiveness in view for ourselves and others regarding sex that is outside of God's boundaries?

Part 1 of Proverbs 6

6:20-24   Fire to Heat Your Home or Burn It Down

ESV

20 My son, keep your father's commandment, and forsake not your mother's teaching.
21 Bind them on your heart always; tie them around your neck.
22 When you walk, they will lead you; when you lie down, they will watch over you; and when you awake, they will talk with you.
23 For the commandment is a lamp and the teaching a light, and the reproofs of discipline are the way of life,
24 to preserve you from the evil woman, from the smooth tongue of the adulteress.

NIV

20 My son, keep your father's commands and do not forsake your mother's teaching.
21 Bind them upon your heart forever; fasten them around your neck.
22 When you walk, they will guide you; when you sleep, they will watch over you; when you awake, they will speak to you.
23 For these commands are a lamp, this teaching is a light, and the corrections of discipline are the way to life,
24 keeping you from the immoral woman, from the smooth tongue of the wayward wife.

Wisdom Lived Out Today:

Sex is God's good idea! It's his gift to married people. It's for them to enjoy, to bring them happiness in their relationship, and to have children, but sex is like fire. It's only safe, healthy, and valuable when it's in its right place. That place is marriage. Outside of marriage, after the immediate thrill, sex often brings anger, danger, harm, hurt, regret, guilt, heartache, distrust, alienation, and disappointment.

Fire that is out of control, instead of providing heat for your home in the winter, will burn your house down. Sex, when not under God's control in your life, can also bring your life down.

God does forgive sin of all kinds—even sexual sin—but that doesn't mean there aren't bad consequences that one may have to battle with all his or her life. This section of Proverbs sketches some of the lifelong effects of immorality. Some effects are immediate. Others linger for a lifetime.

Often guys and girls who become sexually involved before marriage struggle with guilt and the fear of getting a disease (an STD—a sexually transmitted disease) that could affect their health and even how long they live. Unwanted pregnancy is often a result too. Pregnancy will send its effects into all of one's future choices. And the world's option to end a pregnancy by abortion will send shock waves that often seriously distort one's personal spiritual, emotional, and psychological adjustment and his or her relationships for the rest of life. In addition, the seeds of guilt, regret, distrust, and fear may have been planted in your mind and conscience. These affect relationships and can show up in unpredictable ways.

Of course, God does forgive sin—even sexual sin. But even his forgiveness often does not end all of the effects that sex outside of God's boundaries may have. Often, years of doubt, anxiety, and fear may linger, and then be stirred up again when one's own children begin to have friendships with the opposite sex. One pastor has said, "Sin takes you where you don't want to go, costs you more than you want to pay, and keeps you longer than you want to stay."

Prayer:

Father, I can be tempted in this area easily. I need regularly to keep your wise counsel in front of my eyes and, even more deeply, in my heart. Help me to use your Word in that wise way—every day. Help me to save sex to be the beautiful act you want it to be in my future marriage, without any contaminating memories, regrets, or hurt. Help me to be on guard in my modern culture against the many ways the world wants to make the thrill of sex common, easy, and self-centered. Rather help me keep the wonderful marriage act you intend as a way to build an intimate marital relationship and family. In Jesus' name, Amen.

Today, caution is even more important than in past generations. Guys may use "date rape" drugs. Girls may use seductive dress and touching. Both may use alcohol and other drugs to deceive and seduce an unsuspecting partner. Adults may even make it easy to cross the boundaries God has established for our health, safety, and good. For example, a university near our home gives out condoms to young men and women before every holiday or extended weekend. Most colleges provide contraceptive information and medications to young women. The message is clear: "Sex is OK, pretty much any way you want to have it. Enjoy yourself, just do it safely. And if you get pregnant, abortion services are nearby."

But here, Solomon is warning young adults about the real dangers that the world hides or denies. There is an "end" that is "bitter," he says in Proverbs 5:4. It includes groaning, dishonor, regret, addiction, and, finally, death. In this chapter, verse 33, *Wounds...dishonor...*and *disgrace...*are the likely outcomes—maybe sooner, maybe later.

How can you guard yourself in our sex-conscious and sex-crazed culture? Solomon answers this in the first couple of verses of this section: keep God's wisdom in front of you and inside of you at all times (Proverbs 5:20-23)—especially if you are in the company of flirting, sexy, beautiful young women (Proverbs 5:24,25). Later in chapter seven, Solomon urges his sons to *keep your way far from her* and not go *near the door of her house* (7:8).

Allow this fire to heat your home, not burn it down or damage it in ways that can last a lifetime.

Bridges' Comments:

Here again, God reinforces the importance of parental guidance (see also Proverbs 1:8,9 and 4:1). God never intended young people to be independent of their parents. Other sources of instruction are important, but God's plan is for godly parents to provide it. They will bring God's wise words of counsel, not their own, to you. So, *bind them on your heart always* (see also Proverbs 3:3; 4:21; 7:3) and *tie them around your neck (*see also Proverbs

3:3 and compare Job 31:36). Let these truths be the wardrobe you wear most. Let God's law be your friend for all times and all situations, by day (see Proverbs 3:22, 23; 4:12) and by night (see Proverbs 3:24; Psalm 63:5)—a friend for every waking moment (see Psalm 119:17,18).

Don't allow anything to hinder your interaction with this faithful counselor in your heart. This is the best means of keeping the world's influence out of your life before it is able to gain a toehold in your mind and heart. One wise man said, "Happy is the mind in which the Word is an unchallenged companion." *A lamp*, like such a focused mind, full of *light* (Proverbs 6:23) in this dark world, is a gift of incalculable value. Its *reproofs of discipline are the way of life* (see also Psalm 19:11; 2 Timothy 3:16,17; compare Matthew 7:13,14).

This *lamp* and *light* are especially valuable when facing sexual temptations (see Proverbs 2:10,11; 16-19; 5:1-8; 7:1-5). Those who choose their own *light* fall into a seductive trap (see Proverbs 2:16; 7:21). If a young person ignores this kind of parental warning, he will come to an end with bitterness and consequences that repentance cannot wipe away (see Proverbs 5:11-13). Oh, young people, hear the Father's often repeated instruction: "How can a young man keep his way pure? By guarding it according to your word" and "I have stored your word in my heart that I might not sin against you" (Psalm 119:9,11; see also Psalm 17:4).

To Help You Meditate:

1. Relate a story you've seen or heard from a song or movie where sex is presented to be a normal part of a relationship and where the consequences of practicing it outside of marriage are totally ignored or minimized.

2. How does Solomon urge his son to guard or preserve himself from immorality in these verses?

3. Would a plan to memorize some of the Proverbs for guidance in this area be wise for you to practice? Select several from chapters 5, 6, and 7 that you think will be helpful. Write them out and begin to memorize them, one per week.

Part 2 of Proverbs 6

6:25-29   Eyes in the Sky

ESV

25 Do not desire her beauty in your heart, and do not let her capture you with her eyelashes;
26 for the price of a prostitute is only a loaf of bread, but a married woman hunts down a precious life.
27 Can a man carry fire next to his chest and his clothes not be burned?
28 Or can one walk on hot coals and his feet not be scorched?
29 So is he who goes in to his neighbor's wife; none who touches her will go unpunished.

NIV

25 Do not lust in your heart after her beauty or let her captivate you with her eyes,
26 for the prostitute reduces you to a loaf of bread, and the adulteress preys upon your very life.
27 Can a man scoop fire into his lap without his clothes being burned?
28 Can a man walk on hot coals without his feet being scorched?
29 So is he who sleeps with another man's wife; no one who touches her will go unpunished.

Wisdom Lived Out Today:

Not everything that is dangerous is obvious.

It was night time, Christmas Day, 2007. Uncle Jed was a HumVee driver in the U.S. Army, in Iraq in a war zone. He had a crew of soldiers he was transporting through a dangerous location. A drone operator radioed Uncle Jed about what looked like suspicious activity on the road ahead of his truck. He immediately turned off his truck lights. Within a minute, an insurgent remotely exploded an IED (Improvised Explosive Device) as the truck passed over it, but the enemy had miscalculated. It exploded at the rear end of the truck because Uncle Jed had turned the truck lights off and the Iraqi soldier couldn't see the truck clearly enough to judge when to send the signal to detonate the bomb. The IED created a hole the size of a house, but only caught the back of the truck. A few of the men were injured, but none seriously. Because Uncle Jed had "eyes in the sky" he was able to prepare for the danger.

In this passage in Proverbs, Solomon is warning his sons about what they *can* see, too. In fact, his warning is about an *explosive* that is often in plain sight. It's just as dangerous as the enemy's hidden IED and can blow up your life just as violently if you don't take protective action to guard against it. The threat he is warning about is the sexually attractive man or woman who crosses your path at school, on the beach, on the basketball court, on the TV beer, cosmetic, or Victoria's Secret commercials, on the movie or TV screen, in the lyrics of your music, in a magazine advertisement, or on a website.

Sex appeal brings fantasies and desires to the front burner of our hearts and imaginations quickly, doesn't it? That's what Solomon is cautioning us about in these verses. This sounds a lot like Jesus' teaching in Matthew 5:28, "…everyone who looks at a woman with lustful intent has already committed adultery with her in his heart."

Sexual immorality, the general term for sexual sin of any kind, begins with our physical eyes or our "mental eyes," the thoughts in our heart. This is where Jesus and Solomon direct our attention if we are to keep ourselves safe from temptations that can seduce, disarm, and damage us in our dangerous, life-threatening world.

Proverbs 4:23 warns, "Above all else, guard your heart, for it is the wellspring of life" (NIV). Our hearts are where our vulnerability lies first of all. Our eyes are often the first portal through which sexual temptation enters. Solomon warns young adults not to be *captured* by tempting sights or *carry fire* close to you—it will *burn* you. You will likely be *scorched*, he says.

Prayer:

Father, I have experienced this kind of temptation. My eyes and my heart have been attracted to sexual interests. Please forgive me, and please help me to turn away from such views when they occur. Help me to spot the tempting situation before it settles in my mind and heart and even draws me into a relationship with the wrong kind of person. Help me to live with my mind being transformed and renewed by the Lord Jesus so that my relationships with the opposite sex are wholesome, godly, and blessed by you. Give me your eyes, please, Father. In Jesus' name, Amen.

Bridges' Comments:

Solomon gives Jesus' own rule of thumb about looking at and desiring a sexually appealing woman (see Matthew 5:28; compare James 1:14,15; Job 31:1; Psalm 119:37). *Do not desire her beauty in your heart* (see Proverbs 31:30; Genesis 6:2; 39:6; 2 Samuel 11:2). Resist sexual desire when you first sense it. Delay can be fatal. Many victims have become deluded by seductive *beauty* and captivating *eyes* (see also Genesis 39:7; 2 Samuel 11:2; Isaiah 3:16; 2 Peter 2:14). Like the hunter who keeps his prey in his sights until he shoots it, some young women will keep up the pressure until they have *hunted down a precious life* (see Genesis 39:14; Judges 16:18-21; compare Ezekiel 13:18,20,21).

But some who have followed their desires and gone down this forbidden path have done so even though they've been warned of the dangers in this life as well as those in eternity. "Self-confidence sees and fears no danger." "I can handle it. I know when to stop. I'm different. Nothing bad is going to happen to me."

This temptation is like throwing gasoline instead of water on a fire. One may escape the outcomes of following his sexual desires as surely as he can *carry fire next to his chest and his clothes not be burned* or *walk on hot coals and his feet not be scorched* (see Exodus 20:14,17; Leviticus 20:10; 2 Samuel 12:9; Malachi 3:5). Even a sin of ignorance was liable to be judged in biblical times. In other words, not intending to sin in the first place doesn't cancel sin's effects (see Genesis 12:15; 20:1-6; 26:10). The Lord put strict boundaries around the holy ordinance of marriage! Even unintentional sexual offenses could carry heavy penalties. Sin and consequences are linked together by an unbreakable chain. "The fire of sexual desire kindles the fire of hell" (compare Job 31:12 James 1:14,15).

Excuses like "the temptation was too strong" won't work before God. Solomon counsels the young to avoid the temptation. One who is carrying a can of gasoline probably will not light a match with the gasoline in his hands. To run into a tempting setting is just like that. It invites personal moral failure—sin. Temptations do not always look crazy. They can seem harmless, but the young man who wants to resist them must get away at the first sensations of the temptation in order to resist it successfully. Be careful of walking too close to the edge of where temptations lie (see Genesis 39:10; Romans 13:13; 1 Thessalonians 5:22). Crossing these borders can even bring legal consequences...*none who touches her will go unpunished* (Proverbs 6:29; see also Genesis 20:6; 39:9; 1 Corinthians 7:1).

To Help You Meditate:

1. What avenues of sexual attraction and temptation would you be wisest to keep alert to and turn from?

2. Can you think of ways to keep alert to the temptations presented by the world, the Devil, and your own human nature's vulnerability or weakness for sexual thinking and fantasizing?

3. Why does Solomon put so much emphasis on the mind, the thinking that his sons do in this area of spiritual challenge?

Part 3 of Proverbs 6

6:30-35   The Same and Not the Same at the Same Time

ESV

30 People do not despise a thief if he steals to satisfy his appetite when he is hungry,
31 but if he is caught, he will pay sevenfold; he will give all the goods of his house.
32 He who commits adultery lacks sense; he who does it destroys himself.
33 He will get wounds and dishonor, and his disgrace will not be wiped away.
34 For jealousy makes a man furious, and he will not spare when he takes revenge.
35 He will accept no compensation; he will refuse though you multiply gifts.

NIV

30 Men do not despise a thief if he steals to satisfy his hunger when he is starving.
31 Yet if he is caught, he must pay sevenfold, though it costs him all the wealth of his house.
32 But a man who commits adultery lacks judgment; whoever does so destroys himself.
33 Blows and disgrace are his lot, and his shame will never be wiped away;
34 for jealousy arouses a husband's fury, and he will show no mercy when he takes revenge.
35 He will not accept any compensation; he will refuse the bribe, however great it is.

Wisdom Lived Out Today:

Jerome was caught! The police saw him on his bike only two blocks from the 7-11 store where he stole a pair of sunglasses. The store manager called the police when he ran out with the glasses. He ended up with a $200 fine and 20 hours of community service as his punishment. His parents also made him return to the store and ask the manager's forgiveness.

Four years later, Jerome was in his dorm room. He had developed an addiction to dope, but had been clean for the last six months. He was now in his second year of college. His roommate was out and he was in the dorm alone. He had just failed an English exam and that afternoon his girlfriend had broken up with him. He was discouraged, angry, and felt like a failure all around. He wanted to feel good. He craved the high just one more time. A friend sold him a single bag with the same amount he used months earlier. He shot up, but his body was not used to this amount now. There was immediate euphoria, and then his body reacted—he went into cardiac arrest. His roommate found him barely breathing just a short time later. By the time the paramedics got there, Jerome had stopped breathing altogether.

Solomon describes how breaking some commandments earns more serious shame and has more lasting effects than others. All sin is sin. All of it is condemned by God and has the wages of death if one does not seek God's forgiveness because of Jesus' death, but not all sin gets the same reaction from others.

Jerome's shoplifting was bad. His reputation took a hit from it among family and friends. But his use of drugs in the dorm room was fatal. Both were wrong. One, though, had a long-lasting effect. It ended his life.

All immorality is sin. Much of it has lasting, though often hidden, effects. Sexual immorality is that way too. Especially after one is married, as these verses in Proverbs 6 conclude. Solomon's caution here is that the effects of sex outside of God's boundaries cannot be tamed or controlled. In addition to physical outcomes like STDs (sexually transmitted diseases), shame and a reputation for untrustworthiness, a lack of self-control, and unfaithfulness may follow one for many years to come—maybe a lifetime.

None of these results needs to be the last word about one's life if one turns to Christ from his sin. Effects may still linger, godly counsel may be needed to help with the healing process, some medical conditions may be life-long, and testimony and reputation matters may not be restored quickly or maybe ever with some people, but none of that means life is over for a repentant, trusting child of God. God used David after his tragic sin and failure with Bathsheba (read about this in 2 Samuel 11). He was even used to write Scripture that has been used for the eternal benefit of millions over the centuries. God used Rahab, a prostitute, and even included her in the line of Christ's ancestors (see the genealogy in Matthew 1:5). The gospel does bring healing. Tragic spin-off effects often do follow such failures, even for believers, as David's family life reveals, but God is in the business of redeeming brokenness. That is the good news of the gospel.

> **Prayer:**
> Father, the outcomes of foolishness are often hidden. The Liar, Satan, doesn't want me to see them. Help me to do the thinking and praying that will keep me from making excuses for what the world may call little sins as well as the ones that can have enduring effects throughout this life. Help me not to minimize any sin, especially in this sexual area, but to seek your help to live wisely and righteously. Help me to be a testimony of the beauty of living according to your good and wise law in this area of sex. In Jesus' name, Amen.

Don't make the mistake of deceiving yourself into thinking that crossing sexual boundaries is not that serious because "everybody is doing it." Everybody isn't! And you can move on to the important relationships of life in which sex will be a richer experience because you have saved sex for God's appointed season of marriage. You can enter these relationships without any baggage to weigh down your intimacy.

Bridges' Comments:

These verses do not give any excuse for a thief to steal. He will have to pay everything back that he stole and *seven* times more. "Sevenfold" is not to be taken literally. Four or fivefold was what the Law required (see Luke 19:8). It really means this thief will have to pay someone back fully or satisfactorily. It is an indefinite number (compare Genesis 4:15,24). Making full restitution, perhaps sweeping away *all the goods of his house*, shows that even poverty doesn't excuse breaking God's law by stealing (compare 1 Corinthians 6:10 with 1 John 3:4). Even the poor must earn his living by honest work. If his work doesn't help him earn enough, let him, trusting in God, seek the help of others. If one has the faith to trust in God's provision, he will never be forced to steal (see Matthew 6:25-33). Yet, even in this extreme situation and temptation, if he does give in to it, people will not tend to heap scorn on him. Rather, seeing his desperate situation, people will look on him with sympathy. *People do not despise a thief* in such a setting.

But the sin of an adulterer is something else. No sympathy is offered. He can't use the plea of survival. It's his lust. Not need, but out-of-control passion. Not a lack of bread, but of understanding (compare Ecclesiastes 7:25,26; Jeremiah 5:8,21). He willfully gives himself to his sinful desires. He *destroys himself* (see Leviticus 20:10; Proverbs 2:18,19; 5:22,23; 7:22,23; Ephesians 5:5). He gets *wounds*—not like a soldier or martyr for Christ, full of honor—but he gets conviction in his conscience (Psalm 32:3,4) and *dishonor* and *disgrace* to his name (see also Proverbs 5:9; Genesis 38:23; 49:4; 2 Samuel 3:13; 13:13; 1 Kings 15:5; compare with Deuteronomy 23:2, Nehemiah 13:26, and Matthew 1:6). The tremendous passions of *jealousy* and *revenge* shut out all human forgiveness (see Genesis 34:7; 49:5-7; Numbers 5:14; Esther 7:7-10; Ezekiel 16:38). One so offended *will accept no compensation* (Genesis 39:19,20; Judges 19:29,30) regardless of how much is offered.

...wounds...convictions in his conscience and dishonor and disgrace to his name.

Such are the outcomes of many sins (2 Samuel 11:6-24). Terrible miseries flow from this breach of God's holy commandment. St. Augustine declared,

> Oh! How great iniquity is this adultery! How great a perverseness! The soul, redeemed by the precious blood of Christ, is thus for the pleasures of an hour given to the devil; a thing much to be lamented and bewailed; when that which delights is soon gone, that which torments remains without end.[10]

This scary picture of sin and its consequences, of which Solomon was all too well aware, teaches us to avoid everything that may present temptation to us, to be sensitive to the first attractions to immorality, to shut off every avenue of our senses that could allow seductive poison to enter, and to cut off conversations with others that may be off-color or carry any suggestion of impurity to which a godly person would recoil with disgust. Let us learn to seek God's strength to "watch and pray" continually and while we "think we stand to take heed lest we fall" (1 Corinthians 10:12).

To Help You Meditate:

1. While all sin is sin, some may have more serious outcomes in this life than others. What makes sexual sin the kind that often has serious effects on someone who engages in it?

---

[10] Augustine cited by Bridges.

2. David committed sexual sin. What were some of its effects in his and his family's lives?

3. Why do you think sexual sin seems to be treated so much more seriously than other sin such as stealing?

7:1-5   Keep Your Guard Up for Any Temptation

ESV
1 My son, keep my words and treasure up my commandments with you;
2 keep my commandments and live; keep my teaching as the apple of your eye;
3 bind them on your fingers; write them on the tablet of your heart.
4 Say to wisdom, "You are my sister," and call insight your intimate friend,
5 to keep you from the forbidden woman, from the adulteress with her smooth words.

NIV
1 My son, keep my words and store up my commands within you.
2 Keep my commands and you will live; guard my teachings as the apple of your eye.
3 Bind them on your fingers; write them on the tablet of your heart.
4 Say to wisdom, "You are my sister," and call understanding your kinsman;
5 they will keep you from the adulteress, from the wayward wife with her seductive words.

Wisdom Lived Out Today:

How will Julissa become a high school basketball standout? How can she develop the moves under the basket that will make her a strong scoring player for her team? If she has to stop and think about every move she makes, she'll lose time, miss opportunities to pass or score, have the ball stolen, or be tied up for jump balls.

By practicing her moves underneath the basket over and over and over and over again, they will become second nature to her. She won't have to stop and think in game pressure situations. Her reactions will be more spontaneous. Aunt Jen was considering going out for women's basketball in college. In the interview, her prospective coach said, "Players are made in the off-season; teams are made during the season." Players are made by repeating over and over the shots and ball-handling moves that they will need to be second nature in game situations. If an athlete has to stop and think about basic moves, he or she will lose opportunities every time.

That's what Solomon is saying in Proverbs 7:1-5. You need to have a plan to *keep my words and treasure up commandments* so that they will *keep* or guard you from *the forbidden woman*. This *forbidden* or immoral *woman* can be a literal person or can represent the temptations with which the world, our sinful nature, and Satan himself will try to attract us.

God has not left you without protection! Be in the Word day by day so that you can *write* God's truths *on the tablet of your heart.* Make your time with the Lord your most important relationship. Call *wisdom* and godly *understanding* by the most *intimate* names. In biblical poetry *my sister* was an expression of intimacy for one's wife.[11] The closest possible human relationship is godly marriage. Your marriage to *wisdom* and *insight* is the kind of relationship that Solomon said will guard you against self-destructive temptations and alluring come-ons.

---

[11] Bruce Waltke, 2004, pages 369-370.

Do you have a plan to read and think about the Word of God daily? There are many plans that can help. Talk to some godly adults whom you respect and ask how they practice their private devotional times. Make memorization a part of your plan, writing God's truths *on the tablet of your heart*. This is a big but not impossible task. Approach your private time with the Lord like the answer to the question, "How do you eat an elephant?" Answer: "One forkful at a time." You have a lifetime to feast with your intimate friend—the Word and the Lord of the Word. *Keep my teaching as the apple of your eye.* Everything you or I substitute for God's *wisdom* and *insight* from his Word will disappoint, frustrate, and betray us. *Keep my commandments and live.*

Prayer:

Father, I need to be in your Word every day. So many things come up to crowd out that time, though. Please help me to discipline myself for this godly exercise so that the *wisdom* of your Word becomes second nature to me at all times. Help me to "hide your word in my heart that I might not sin against you" (Psalm 119:11 NIV). Give me the strength to keep my guard up. Help me to be prepared for the lures to evil that will certainly come my way in this life by having your Word as my intimate friend on the *tablet* of my *heart*. In Jesus' name, Amen.

Bridges' Comments:

Solomon earnestly and artfully urges us to study wisdom in this chapter. Meditate on these valuable guides for practical living.

First, let your whole mind and heart be taken up with this counsel. *...keep my words...and live* (Proverbs 3:21,22; 4:4,13; Isaiah 55:2,3; Jeremiah 22:15). Sir Matthew Hale told his children,

> If I skip my Bible reading in the morning, it never goes well with me throughout the day. "*...lay up,* or *...treasure up*" (Proverbs 10:14; Deuteronomy 11:18; Luke 2:19,51) God's word carefully, not on our shelves, but on our hearts. Let the **whole** Word of God be our precious treasure. Receive his gracious promises with simple affection and his holy *commandments* with ready obedience. Stand with your eye in the land of promise but your feet in the land of uprightness on level ground (Psalm 143:10).

Second, be jealous and passionate about living out God's law. Consider how carefully we are to protect *the apple* (the pupil) *of* our *eye*—the most tender part of the most delicate member of our body (Deuteronomy 32:10; Psalm 17:8; Zechariah 2:8)! Keep the *commandments* with that same care. Let every one of them have their full weight in your life. If you make excuses for why one command does not apply or lower a commandment's requirements, you reduce its protection and make yourself vulnerable to common temptations. One who lives by doing what makes him feel good and not by keeping God's will in mind may be deceiving himself. He may not be a believer at all.

Keep God's laws right at hand by using them and reminding yourself of them constantly. ...*bind them on your fingers* (see Proverbs 3:3; Deuteronomy 6:8; 11:18). By keeping them always in sight, you will be ready to remind yourself of his wise counsel and will every moment. For their practical day-by-day influence, *write them on the tablet of your heart.* Make this your prayer:

> O, Lord God! This is your Almighty work (Isaiah 26:12; 2 Corinthians 3:3). I must have your help and Spirit to write these things on my heart. You have said that you would do this for your people. "I will put my law within them, and I will write it on their hearts" (Jeremiah 31:33). At the same time, by your power, I know I must make the faithful effort to make your words part of me. Lord, seal this promise to my heart by your grace.

...make God's wisdom your intimate friend...

My young son and daughter, make God's *wisdom your intimate friend*, your wife. Call her your sister—a name used in biblical times for one's wife—to show family closeness. By wrapping your heart around God's *wisdom,* and treating it like a very dear relative about whom you think often and care about lovingly, you will make the attractions and temptations of immorality of all kinds less inviting. People are motivated by what they think will give them pleasure. If they do not consciously seek to love wisdom for the pleasure God promises, they will follow their own natural desires for the pleasures that will be self-destructive. The Bible, therefore, not merely read, but truly cherished, loved, and respected as an *intimate friend,* will show itself as a powerful, godly force to cancel the power of evil temptations (see Proverbs 2:10,16, 6:23,24; 23:26,27).

To Help You Meditate:

1. How is a regular devotional time like an athlete practicing her moves over and over and over again?

2. What kind of a regular plan of daily Bible reading and prayer would work for you? (Don't be afraid to be creative. What is most important is the daily consistency of your meditation on the Word of God, not necessarily how much Scripture or how much time you spend reading it. Your time in the Word will naturally increase as this becomes a habit.)

3. What feelings should you be alert to that will hinder you from a regular time of meditation in the Word?

10:1   How to Make Your Mom and Dad Smile or Frown

ESV

1 The proverbs of Solomon. A wise son makes a glad father, but a foolish son is a sorrow to his mother.

NIV

1 The Proverbs of Solomon: A wise son brings joy to his father, but a foolish son grief to his mother.

Wisdom Lived Out Today:

How hard is it for a *son* to bring *sorrow* to his *mother*? It seems dads can more easily or more quickly become frustrated, disappointed, and sad with their *sons* than moms. Of course, this same kind of thing can be said about daughters, too, but this proverb was especially written to give boys a wake-up call about how their wisdom or foolishness can affect their parents.

When Jed, Jr.'s parents got a report about his good grades and the teacher's encouraging words about the way he shows sensitivity to his classmates, his mom and dad were very proud of him. Likewise, when Tyler got the "Christlikeness" award in basketball because of his attitude on the court, his mom and dad were really happy and proud of him. That kind of mature behavior *makes a glad father...and...mother*. Their happiness isn't because it makes them look good, but because they know this kind of *wise* behavior will be good for their child's life if it becomes a settled pattern. It will be for their good. It fits with the way God has designed life to work best for people throughout life.

On the other hand, it's usually harder for kids to disappoint their *mothers*. Moms tend to be optimistic and hopeful about their children—even when they mess up. They believe in their son's potential. They often see that there is more to this young one than what he's done or is doing at the moment. For sure, *mothers* can be brought to the point of *sorrow*, but it takes a lot. That is the point of this verse. A foolish *son* is one who lives in his own way as a pattern of life. He is focused on himself, his own feelings, thoughts, values, and goals. He's one who doesn't give serious thought to God's mind and will about life decisions. He is the center of his universe. Such a *son* or daughter, over time, can bring deep *sorrow* to his or her *mother*. Parents know that such self-centered living is self-destructive. They've lived long enough to see the results of such patterns in other young people and grieve over the possibility that such pain and loss could land on their children too.

A wise *son* or daughter, though, one who respects God's thoughts, will, and counsel, brings *joy* to his *father* and *mother*. He or she is living in a way that brings his parents contentment and real happiness, especially if he's living this way with the heart desire to "fear the LORD" (Proverbs 9:10). They are proud of him. If this motive underlies all that he does, he will still face the same challenges any other young people face, but he lives to please his Savior. Not perfectly, of course. No one does. But this is the pattern of his life! It brings incalculable *joy* to his dad and mom.

Prayer:
Father, help me to live such a life of wisdom that I make my father and mother glad. Jesus clearly lived that way (Luke 2:51,52), so help me to imitate him. Enable me to spot foolishness and avoid it. Wisdom is lived out from the heart, not just in my outer actions, so help me to live to please you by my trust and faithfulness in you and bring honor and pleasure to my mom and dad. In Jesus' name, Amen.

Bridges' Comments:

The first nine chapters of Proverbs have shown over and over the nature and value of God's wisdom. That wisdom contrasts with the sinful foolishness that can be so attractive to young adults. In this section of Proverbs, from chapters 10 to 31, Solomon and other wise sages will observe and then display God's wisdom, over and over, in word pictures, metaphors, and similes. Then they will show, with clear contrasts, the wisdom that is needed and foolishness that can be so appealing to young people.

Many of the proverbs appear to be simple, unconnected sentences, but they are remarkable for their profound thoughts, sharp observations, and widespread personal, family, and social applications for all people. Chapters 1 to 9 lay a strong foundation for the rest of the book. The counselor introduced in chapter one, and more fully described in chapter eight, offers his gracious instruction to us as the principles of true happiness and practical godliness.

This first sentence in chapter 10 may be here to point us to the value of a godly education for personal, social and even national influence—in this life and the next. Parents hope for rest and comfort in their children as a wonderful gift from God (Genesis 5:28,29; 33:5; Psalm 127:3). A young person's faith may be severely tried as he moves through his years (Ecclesiastes 12:1), but the child watched over, prayed over, instructed, and disciplined, shall most often, in the Lord's best time, choose wisdom's paths (Proverbs 22:6) and *make his father glad* (Proverbs 15:20; 23:15,16,24,25; 27:11; 29:3; Genesis 45:28; 46:30).

On the other hand, many a *mother* is burdened with the *sorrows* caused by a *foolish son* (Genesis 26:25,34). In such cases, the training of their children has often been marked by giving in to the desires of their teen. Parents may invite *sorrow* by not saying "no" when they should, by overdosing on pleasure instead of godliness, and by being distracted by the world instead of the Word. Often, parents who neglect early life discipline and do not hold their young children and teens accountable for their faults, disrespectful words, attitudes, and actions, will see their pattern of parenting lead to foolishness. It commonly results in *sorrow* in their young adults and in themselves (1 Samuel 2:24; 3:13; 1 Kings 1:5,6; 2:25).

God has laid down plain rules, duties for young people, and consequences that flow from keeping or neglecting them (Proverbs 22:6; 23:13,14; 29:15). If a young person forgets to look at God's wise counsel every day and instead chooses to live with his own brand of wisdom Proverbs 22:15), we will not be surprised at the inevitable *sorrow* for his *father* and *mother*.

To Help You Meditate:

1. What are some of the most common ways you've seen young people bring sadness to their parents?

2. What are some of the ways you've seen young people bring gladness to their parents?

3. What is there about wise living that makes one's father and mother glad?

10:20, 21   **Your Tongue or Your Heart**

ESV

20 The tongue of the righteous is choice silver; the heart of the wicked is of little worth.
21 The lips of the righteous feed many, but fools die for lack of sense.

NIV

20 The tongue of the righteous is choice silver, but the heart of the wicked is of little value.
21 The lips of the righteous nourish many, but fools die for lack of judgement.

Wisdom Lived Out Today:

Your *tongue* or your *heart*! Which is more important for life?

It is difficult, but mute people can communicate in ways that let you know that life is still possible even though they cannot talk. On the other hand, no one lives without a functioning heart.

In the hands of the Lord this lesser important muscle, our *tongue*, becomes a healthy, caring, helping organ. Under God's control, our *tongue*, meaning our speech, what we say, is refined to become purified and nurturing. It encourages others. Nicole's speech was this way to her neighbor girlfriend who was not from a Christian family. She showed care to her friend and invited her to church where she heard the Word of God.

Aunt Deb's speech was like this to a young Chinese girl living with us and a young Dominican woman in the Dominican Republic. Both of them made professions of faith in Christ through Aunt Deb's compassion and witness. Her speech was literally life-giving.

It was March, and March Madness was in full swing. I was looking forward to seeing the semifinals that evening in New York when visiting Aunt Michelle and Uncle Eric and the kids. Grandma had a different idea for that evening—playing a game of Speed Scrabble. I grumbled and eventually came to the table with the family. To make matters worse for me, as the game progressed, I was losing. I usually win or do well in this game. Aunt Michelle saw my moodiness and heard it in my voice. I was casting a heavy cloud of unpleasantness over both families as we played.

"Dad, you don't look very happy,"
"I'm not doing well in this game," I said.
"It's just a game, Dad," she said,
"But I like to win."
Grandma said, "He wants to be in watching the basketball game."
"So, maybe it's good for you not to be winning, Dad," Aunt Michelle said.

Her words were *choice silver*! They were the gentle rebuke I needed to hear. I knew that she was referring to God's use of frustrating experiences to grow us. I knew she was right. The Lord does bring situations into our lives to challenge our priorities and our heart-loves. At that moment, I was able to confess my sin to the group, know the Lord was pleased, thank Aunt Michelle, and go on to lose the game and miss the basketball game on the TV. Her words were beautiful and valuable—*choice silver.*

Unlike these examples, we don't have to look too far to see examples of how *foolish* speech is of *little worth.* Even the most sincere speech of a fool fits into this category. A *fool,* in the Bible's meaning, is not a dumb person. Instead, these are people with little or no regard for God's values and law. Their hearts, as well as their speech, are of *little worth,* meaning they have just a trifle of value. Instead of *feeding many,* their speech brings loss and *death* to people, including themselves. Their talk is discouraging. They kill people's spirits, their joy, their willingness to live constructively, and because of their negativity, they even drain the life out of themselves. Like a noose that gets tighter and tighter around their own necks, the effects of their speech slowly strangle them. They *die for lack of sense.*

We can speak with *choice,* or purified *silver words* that *feed many* or with *worthless* drivel that not only doesn't *feed* others healthfully, but also saps life out of them and our-

> **Prayer:**
> Father, make my heart like Jesus' so that my words are like his to my family, friends, and even enemies: *choice silver* that *feeds many.* Make my words life-giving, not life-taking words. In Jesus' name, Amen.

selves. Jesus, of course, is the best example of the first kind of speech. "The words that I have spoken unto you are spirit and life" (John 6:63). Satan and his followers are the clearest examples of the second. "...he is a liar and the father of lies" (John 8:44) and he comes to "steal and to kill and to destroy" (John 10:10). Even the name "Devil" means "slanderer" or "accuser."

Bridges' Comments:

It is wise to give thought and effort to how we may skillfully use our words.

As our tongues are our source of foolishness and sin (Proverbs 10:18,19), they also may be the source of praise and glory (Psalm 57:7-10; 108:1). When we use them to extol or praise the King (Psalm 45:1; Song of Solomon 5:10-16), our words are *choice silver* purified or refined of this world's contaminating elements and shining all the more brightly with spiritual brilliance. Who would not eagerly gather up such *silver* scattered in the streets? Aren't we all the wiser if we enrich ourselves with the *choice silver* from *the tongue of the righteous* when we have the opportunity to be instructed by it? Even the poor of this world, if they belong to the Lord, though they may say "I have no silver and gold..." (Acts 3:6), may scatter *choice silver* to many. They may be "...as poor, yet making many rich..." (2 Corinthians 6:10).

Think about the ways the Lord may use your tongue. If you are living with God, it will be like salt, like a heavenly yeast. It can be a valuable source of holy encouragement to many of your friends. *The lips of the righteous feed many* when they speak from your heart. When the "word of Christ" is spoken (Colossians 3:16) it *feeds* "those who hear..." (Ephesians 4:29; Job 4:3,4; 29:22,23). This is the soul's true and needed nourishment! It is "...food to others, as well as life to them."[12] As our great Master broke the bread and gave it to his disciples to distribute (John 6:11), so, now, as well, he breaks the bread of his word

---

[12] John Flavel, cited by Bridges.

to his servants to spread it further to meet the needs of those to whom they talk. Every Lord's Day we witness this gracious and miraculous gift. Pastors and teachers multiply the imperishable bread of the Word as they break it and distribute it. The Word refreshes and strengthens hungry mourners, the weary, and those who are weak and feel their need.

On the other hand, *the wicked* may have a bank account with more money than they know how to use, but their hearts, since they are empty of *choice silver,* are *of little worth* (Jeremiah 22:28). Far from *feeding* others, the fool dies *for lack of sense,* or without the *heart* to seek it. He despises the *lips* that would *feed* him and *dies* of famine in the midst of the rich pastures of Gospel wisdom. We are often reminded that our sin is the cause of our own self-destruction (Hosea 13:9)!

To Help You Meditate:

1. Tell of a time when your words were negative and when they affected the spirit of others.

2. Tell when your words or those of a friend were "choice silver," adding value and positiveness to another person.

3. Who are people you can depend upon to have the "lips of the righteous" and to use their tongues as "choice silver"? What makes their words this way?

11:1   You're Cheating!

ESV
1 A false balance is an abomination to the LORD, but a just weight is his delight.

NIV
1 The Lord abhors dishonest scales but accurate weights are his delight.

Wisdom Lived Out Today:

Have you ever been cheated? It doesn't feel good, does it? It takes the fun out of a game if the other team cheats, doesn't it? It's frustrating when you work hard for a test and someone else cheats and does well on it without studying, but it's even more serious than just making us feel bad. God's take is that cheating is an *abomination*—something he hates!

Imagine Joey and Eon playing basketball on an unusual basketball court. The boundary lines can shift on this court. So one moment Joey can bring the ball down toward their basket along the sideline and make a good pass to Eon who scores. The next time, though, when Joey brings the ball down and passes, the referee blows his whistle and calls him out of bounds—at the same spot. "That's not fair," Joey declares. "This was in bounds a minute ago."

The ref says, "This court is different. The lines change and you were outside the lines this time when you passed the ball." It's a ridiculous example, of course, but you can see how discouraging and frustrating it would be if the lines change.

This is the point in Solomon's example. The *weights* Solomon refers to are what merchants would use with their *balance* scales to weigh food or spices or other products that they sold in the marketplace. Dishonest merchants might have two bags of *weights*: one with *weights* that were marked with a heavier *weight* than they actually were and one that was accurate. If the merchant wanted to cheat someone, he'd use the falsely-marked *weights,* ones that were marked heavier than they actually were. The customer would have to put more of his goods on the scale to make it balance than if the merchant used accurate or *just weights.*   Proverbs 20:10 and 23 use some of the same images to echo these truths.

You can probably recognize unfair treatment by a teacher in class, an unfair test or grade, unfair discipline by mom or dad, unfair criticism by friends, or a coach's unfair treatment of his players. We want fairness or justice for ourselves and our friends. God has wired that desire into us. The Apostle Paul explains that God has written this sense of right and wrong on our hearts (Romans 2:15). Theologians call this heart-writing God's moral law. That just means that we all have an awareness of basic right and wrong because God has built it into our human nature. That's where our consciences come from.

But there are ways we use *false balances* or unfairness in our treatment of others. For example, cheating in school as mentioned in the first paragraph is a way *false balances* often show up. Cheating is unfair to others who don't cheat for a grade. It's unfair to the teacher who is trying to teach effectively and help students learn. It's misleading for any who need to evaluate the student for advanced classes or maybe admission to a special program or school. It's also unfair to the cheater himself because it doesn't allow him to truly grow. It doesn't allow him to gain confidence in his true achievements or abilities. Cheating gives the impression of being honest but is really deceptive. It is done by students who share homework and test answers in school, by workers who lie about being sick to get out of going to work, by salespeople who lie about their products, and by parents who tell their kids to say to a caller that they're not home. Sadly, it's very common.

In a visit I had to the country of Azerbaijan in Eastern Europe, one missionary told me that if they needed medical attention or a hospital, they would go to the extra expense of traveling to a hospital in Western Europe. She said, "Most of the surgeons and doctors in the hospitals in this country are dangerous. They have purchased their degrees by bribing university professors. Cheating results in seriously unsafe health conditions here. The nurses in the States probably have more medical expertise than our surgeons. They often buy their medical degrees."

Such *false balances* are an *abomination to the LORD*. *Abomination* is a very strong word. God is more than a little dissatisfied or a little bit bothered by falseness. His whole character is against it. He hates it. The word *abomination* is reserved for conditions God hated most. Idols are called *abominations* in the Old Testament. Sacrificing children to idols was called an abomination. Rape, homosexuality, and incest are all called detestable or an *abomination* by God, too.

Do you want the LORD to *delight* in you? *Just weights* are the LORD's *delight*. Integrity, honesty, and truthfulness fit with his holy character. He loves truthfulness and fairness. They are his *delight*. Jesus, himself, is called the "truth" (John 14:6). Having a relationship with Jesus makes you hate what he hates: *false balances* or deception and cheating are some of what he hates. Being in him makes it natural for you to love what he *delights* in: the *just weights* of truthfulness and fairness.

Bridges' Comments:

How valuable is the Book of God for every detail of life! *Balances,* or weights as they were used in old times, were used to keep business dealings fair and honest, but when the balance is rigged or the weights are wrongly marked, *a false balance,* even man's laws convict the deceiver (compare Proverbs 20:14). The Old Testament Law and the gospel forbade this kind of dishonesty (Leviticus 19:36; Matthew 7:12; Philippians 4:8).

Some people may think "getting it over" on someone is wise (Luke 16:8), but God forbids and, more than that, hates it (it is *an abomination* or detestable). See Proverbs 20:10; Deuteronomy 25:13-16; Amos 8:5.

A just weight, however, typically goes unnoticed because it is as it should be. It is a *just* or perfect stone for weighing things that is precious in the sight of God. It is his *delight* (Proverbs 16:11; 12:22), and this is the highest seal of approval, above all human praise. We must not minimize the seriousness of this proverb. It is needed badly. Taking advantage of an unsuspecting brother or sister earned Paul's warning to the Thessalonian church (1 Thessalonians 4:6). Such wrongness toward others also earned a shameful reputation for believers within the Corinthian church (1 Corinthians 6:7,8).

Isn't it a sobering thought that the eye of God marks all our common work and business dealings as either *abomination* or *delight?* Have you found your conscience troubling you when thinking about God, prayer, or time with others in his church because of some unfairness, dishonesty, or deception (Psalm 66:18)? Examine your heart now to see that you "have a clear conscience toward both God and man" (Acts. 24:16). "For the LORD is righteous; he loves righteous deeds; the upright shall behold his face" (Psalm 11:7). He only "…shall sojourn in your tent…" and will "dwell on your holy hill…" who lives "…blamelessly and does what is right and speaks truth in his heart" (Psalm 15:1,2; 24:3-5; 140:13).

To Help You Meditate:

1. Think of a time when you were cheated out of something. Why did it bother you?

2. Why do you think God hates cheating? What is there about it that makes it an abomination (something he hates)?

3. Satan is a liar and Jesus is the truth. How can my allegiance to one or the other affect my friendships?

11:24 She's Not Collecting Sea Shells

ESV

24 One gives freely, yet grows all the richer; another withholds what he should give, and only suffers want.

25 Whoever brings blessing will be enriched, and one who waters will himself be watered.

NIV

24 One man gives freely, yet gains even more; another withholds unduly, but comes to poverty.

25 A generous man will prosper; he who refreshes others will himself be refreshed.

Wisdom Lived Out Today:

She's a single woman[13] in her early 60s. Many of her friends are retired. She is still working full-time and is very successful at her job and deeply appreciated by her employer and those she serves as an administrative assistant. But she was lonely.

She has no husband and no children. Her mother passed away several years ago and a brother to whom she was close had died just a year before. Distraught, she called me to talk, and this was our conversation:

"I come home from work and I'm alone. I clean, make some dinner, and sit alone to watch a TV program and go to bed. The next day, I do it all over again. Many of my friends are out enjoying movies together, playing cards, visiting with each other, and going out to eat together several times a week—they are retired. I can't be with them because of work, and I'm lonely. The only men in my life the past few years have not been serious about any kind of relationship, and I wouldn't trust them anyhow because of their past ways of treating women. I'm alone and depressed. I feel hopeless about future relationships, friendships, and work. I don't know what the point of living is about. I'm not worth much to anyone! I don't know what I'm supposed to do."

Linda felt like her life was pointless. Meaningless. That it was going nowhere. When she read my summary of our conversation, above, she added, "If I were not a Christian, I might have taken my life at this point. There comes a point in most people's lives when they need to suck it up, humble themselves, and ask for help. If I didn't have you to turn to, who knows where I'd be right now."

I had to remind her of investments she was making in the lives of many people. She had lost sight of how the Lord was using her and the way others valued her.

"Linda, Jesus said if you lose your life you will find it. You have lost perspective about your life. You give of yourself at holiday times by inviting people who have no place to go to come to your home. You serve your church youth in the summer at Vacation Bible School. You are a regular worshiper and helper at your church. You get a group of the older folks together on Sundays after the service for lunch. You are faithful at work, consistently

---

[13] Aunt Linda gave permission for this true story to be written and gives glory to God. He has used her to *water* many and has showered her with riches from himself, friends, and family.

showing a Christian example to the men among whom you work. That's a way of 'preaching' the gospel. You serve in the singles' community by organizing events for gatherings. And you are Aunt Linda to our 17 grandkids and our six adult married kids. They love you and adore you and you serve them selflessly. You are losing your life for others." She began to be hopeful about her life—seeing how generously she was investing in others and the way that investment was coming back to her.

During a storm they drove their car over a cliff and were killed. Piper asked, "Was that a tragedy?"

After we prayed and ended our call, I scanned two stories[14] told by Pastor John Piper and sent them to her.

One story was of two single women serving in their retirement years, in their 80s, as missionaries in Cameroon, West Africa. During a storm they drove their car over a cliff and were killed. Piper asked, "Was that a tragedy?" "No," he answered. They did not "throw away their lives on trifles. Their lives were not wasted."

A second story was about a couple he read about in a *Readers Digest* article. They were from the Northeast U.S., and when they retired they moved to Florida. They spent their time sailing on their boat, playing softball, and collecting shells on the beach. "Imagine that you come to the end of your life, and the last great work of your life before you give an account to your Creator is playing softball and collecting shells. Picture them before Christ at the great day of judgment: 'Look, Lord. See my shells.' *That* is a tragedy!"

When Aunt Linda read the two stories, she contacted her pastor and began to plan a Christmas toy give-away ministry to poor single moms who could not afford gifts for their kids for Christmas. She collected hundreds of toys and was able to give several moms the opportunity to "shop" for their kids. They got to hear the gospel Sunday morning and then "shop" for Christmas gifts for their children while their kids got to eat lunch provided by the church. The whole church is now mobilized to give major attention to this ministry of mercy and outreach for the next year.

Aunt Linda called me and described the toy ministry she organized and the church provided. I said, "No shell collection here!" We both laughed.

She's shared those two stories with several others and has been encouraged to serve Christ with more energy and purpose. Losing her life has resulted in finding her life. She *gives freely, brings blessing, waters* others, and *grows all the richer,* is *enriched* and *watered.* There still may be times of loneliness, but she knows now that there is much more to the story of her life than those times.

In this proverb, Solomon isn't talking only about financial *riches.* He's talking about the *riches* that have to do with eternity. *Riches* that last. The treasures stored up in

---

14 John Piper, *Don't Waste Your Life,* Crossway Books, 2003, 45-46.

heaven (Matthew 6:33). Aunt Linda has been making investments for years. She temporarily lost sight of them. She continues to be enriched and to add to her spiritual portfolio by her sacrificial service to others. She has come to see that she is a very wealthy child of God!

Prayer:

Father, I can be selfish so often, but you are generous. You've loved me and given your blood for my rich salvation. You became poor so I could become rich, so help me to be a giving person to the poor around me too—to the poor spiritually as well as the physically needy. Give me a *watering* spirit for people around me and around the world who do not have the full lives like the one with which you have *enriched* me. In Jesus' name, Amen.

Bridges' Comments:

God has set a mark of special favor upon those who imitate his character by the way they practice mercy toward others. He scatters his blessings generously to others (Psalms 33:5; 36:5-7). Those born of his Spirit do the same. One may give lavishly or squander what he has thoughtlessly or sinfully only to get poverty in return (Proverbs 21:17), but there is also *one who gives freely yet grows all the richer*.

The farmer who scatters his seed liberally or *freely* over his field expects a bountiful crop. Likewise, the man of God who *gives* his seed of godliness *freely* (Psalm 112:9) is enriched. As he dedicates his material possessions and personal influence to the Lord, as he has "…opportunity…" to "…do good to everyone" (Galatians 6:10), he is likely to grow *all the richer* (2 Corinthians 9:6-11).

People of the world often risk all their wealth in unsure and often disastrous investments, but in the giving that Solomon cites, there is no uncertainty or groundless speculation. Generosity is the pathway to plenty. To trust God and to lay out all we have for him will make us *grow all the richer* (Proverbs 3:9,10; 19:17). This outcome will become clearly visible in either the material prosperity that God grants or in the rich satisfaction that he gives with less (Deuteronomy 15:10). The reward that comes because of God's grace is that he is pleased with us (Hebrews 13:17) and is willing to receive us "into the eternal dwellings" (Luke 16:9; 1 Timothy 6:18,19).

But is the selfish and covetous man or woman of the world happier or richer when he *withholds what he should give* to others in need? Read Haggai 1:3-10 as an example of the loss that comes their way. Seldom does such a person prosper in this world, for God gives to men in a measure that corresponds to the way they give: bad crops, bad debts, expensive sickness, and a variety of similar troubles that soon add up to far more than generous giving would have totaled.

The Lord's blessing, however, is more clearly revealed in the spiritual realm. The one who *brings blessing will be enriched* as he practices healthy and energy-producing godliness (Proverbs 11:17; Isaiah 32:8). While he *waters...* he *...will himself be watered* with showers from above (Isaiah 53:10,11). The minister is refreshed by his own message of salvation to his people. The Sunday School teacher learns many valuable lessons in the very lessons she teaches. The brother or sister who visits others in need in the name of Jesus is enlivened. Every holy disposition, every spiritual gift, and every active gracious feature of character is increased by faithful use. Similarly, all of these wither with neglect (Matthew 25:29).

To Help You Meditate:

1. Describe a situation in which you served others without any material reward but were rewarded with a great sense of satisfaction.

2. What produces the satisfaction from service for the Christian? How does that differ from satisfaction a non-Christian may receive when he serves others?

3. Why do you think someone who "withholds what he should give" suffers with a sense of neediness?

12:12   Spreading a Net

ESV

12 Whoever is wicked covets the spoil of evildoers, but the root of the righteous bears fruit.

NIV

12 The wicked desire the plunder of evil men, but the root of the righteous flourishes.

Wisdom Lived Out Today:

It's easy to admire and imitate the methods people use to prosper, even if those methods are shady or outright evil!

When I was in college and seminary, I sold books during the summer months to earn enough money to pay for my education and have enough money to live on through the year of school. I sold lots of books and made lots of money and was able to pay for college and seminary over the next three years. Selling was hard work, but I did well with it.

But my methods...I did what people who sold lots of books did—I closed sales hard. That means I was very persistent—high pressure. It worked, but was it honest? I think I crossed the line into unethical treatment of some people in a way that made the sale but took advantage of them wrongly. My methods grew out of my desire, my *coveting* of the end results, *the spoil* that I wanted. I wanted a sale, even if it meant pushing people where they didn't want to go. I was cutting corners, or short-circuiting the love that the Father wanted me to be living out. I was *coveting the spoil of evildoers.* The word translated "coveting" here can also mean *spreading a net* to set a trap. I sadly confess that I did that sometimes. My desire for the sale was greater than my desire for *righteous* living.

Righteous living plants a *root* that *bears fruit* that God grows in our lives that can benefit others. The net of *covetousness* might get some immediate results, but God's description here is that those who spread it are *wicked.* This is not a good label to earn from God, and such methods of getting stuff usually don't produce the same stability or *fruitfulness* in the long run that come from a good *root.*

When I went to deliver the books to many of the people I pressured, they often backed out of the deal. I don't blame them. Those who had put down a deposit were angry with me because they felt forced into something they had to buy that they really didn't want to buy. I pushed them beyond what they truly wanted and they realized it after I left. The *fruit* wasn't pleasant for them or for me. On the other hand, those books that folks really did want, they were eager to get and the *fruit* was much more enjoyable—for them and for me. Many invited me for meals, to their churches, and even referred me to other friends of theirs for more sales. But not the ones for whom I spread the net or pressured.

Don't let your heart envy the shady things kids do in school or at work to get ahead or to get cool stuff like they have. Cheating, sneaking, stealing, gossiping, threatening, or pressuring others to get them to do what you want can get you what you want sometimes, but such net-spreading usually has bad side-effects too. Distrust and anger are two of the big ones. Even more serious, though, is God's displeasure. In the long run, none of those ways of relating to others will plant a *fruitful root* in you or for you. These strategies earn God's label for you as *wicked* and rob you of his smile, his being pleased with your life.

Prayer:

Father, help me to be a person of integrity, of honesty, of compassion. Deliver me from imitating the methods of the unbeliever to get what looks or feels good. Help me to plant a root of fruitfulness by helping me to live in godly ways—even if I'm not getting what others seem to be getting by the nets they are spreading. Thank you, Lord Jesus, for not cutting any corners or spreading any nets to take advantage of others when you lived and died on planet earth. Thank you for the fruit that root bears today. Help me to plant the same kind of root by my trust in you and by avoiding a coveting heart. In Jesus' name, Amen.

Bridges' Comments:

People are always restless to push themselves toward something they have not yet enjoyed. This is true of the believer, *the righteous* in this verse, and the unbeliever, called the *wicked* here.

The Christian reaches for higher privileges *of service and enjoyment of the Lord* and increasing holiness. The Apostle Paul illustrates this when he reveals his heart:

Not that I have already obtained this or am already perfect, but I press on to make it my own, because Christ Jesus has made me his own. Brothers, I do not consider that I have made it my own. But one thing I do: forgetting what lies behind and straining forward to what lies ahead, I press on toward the goal for the prize of the upward call of God in Christ Jesus (Philippians 3:12-14).

On the other hand, unbelievers imitate and envy each other in wickedness. If they see evil men more successful than themselves and *"desire their net,"* they may imitate their evil methods.

He sits in ambush in the villages; in hiding places he murders the innocent. His eyes stealthily watch for the helpless; he lurks in ambush like a lion in his thicket; he lurks that he may seize the poor; he seizes the poor when he draws him into his net. The helpless are crushed, sink down, and fall by his might (Psalm 10:8-10; see also Jeremiah 5:26-28).

These deceivers want to discover the plans of those who have been more cunning and more successful than they have been and want to learn from them and imitate them. They are not satisfied with the honest "gain of godliness" ("…godliness is of value in every way…," 1 Timothy 4:8). Rather, they *"desire a net"* in which they may grasp richer treasures of this world. These, in the end, will prove to be empty and vain (1 Timothy 6:10).

Sadly, the church throughout history has often vividly illustrated this envious pattern. Immorality, lavish lifestyles, and power struggles of church leaders—one net spread after another—have produced deception after deception for personal gain, power, and fame. Such is a root *or core of evil,* and it is full of destruction.

Sadly, the church throughout history has often vividly illustrated this envious pattern.

But the root of the righteous bears fruit that is true, healthy, and abundant. It is not always visible to others but it is always acceptable to God.

Through him then let us continually offer up a sacrifice of praise to God, that is, the fruit of lips that acknowledge his name. Do not neglect to do good and to share what you have, for such sacrifices are pleasing to God (Hebrews 13:15,16).

Dependence on Christ is the source of this blessing. It is this relationship of dependence that makes fruitfulness inevitable. "I am the vine; you are the branches. Whoever abides in me and I in him, he it is that bears much fruit, for apart from me you can do nothing" (John 15:5).

As surely as the vine-branch can have no powers independent of the root, so surely the Christian cannot think, act, or live, apart from Christ; he can only do these as he derives his abilities from the tree into which he is grafted (see John 15:4; Romans 7:4).[15]

The spiritual branches "are nourished and increased by the living root of God's grace and blessing.[16]

To Help You Meditate:

1. Describe a situation you've seen in which someone "spread a net" for another because of what he or she wanted that another had.

2. Sometimes suffering comes because of righteous living, but sometimes fruitfulness is the outcome. When have you enjoyed or flourished because of living in a righteous way?

3. How have some religious leaders coveted or "spread a net" and been like the "wicked"? How would they be different if their "root" was different?

---

[15] Paraphrased by Bridges from quotations by Rev. William Jones' *Enquiry Upon The Spring,* p.36.
[16] Diodati, cited by Bridges.

13:16   Think Backwards!

ESV
16 In everything the prudent acts with knowledge, but a fool flaunts his folly.

NIV
16 Every prudent man acts out of knowledge, but a fool exposes his folly.

Wisdom Lived Out Today:

Our Father wants his people to be shrewd, to be thoughtful and *knowledge*able people about life. It's called being "street smart" in the 'hood. *Prudence* in this sense means being aware of the threats that can derail me or knock me off balance in any decision-making that I need to do. *Prudent* young adults think about outcomes of their possible decisions before they commit themselves to an act. One youth speaker used to say we need to "think backwards" - start with the possible outcomes of our choices, then consider what likely decisions will lead to those results, and then choose which decision to make. This sounds like the way Proverbs wants us to think.

Before Lesley begins a gymnastics routine she thinks about how each move or skill will lead to the next one and how she'll end it. She thinks about the ending and thinks backwards about what will lead to it. She doesn't just do one move and then at the end of that one pick another from her possible skills, and then another, and another until she gets to the end of her time. Thoughtfulness ahead of time is *prudence*. It's thinking how things go together and work toward an end.

Solomon says that is what is true about wise young men and women. They act out of knowledge about what is happening and where things might lead them. Some friendships, for example, can take someone down a pathway of mostly thinking about himself or herself. He might be willing to imitate his friend's harmful decisions about "having fun," or she might be influenced to focus on how she looks, how she dresses, what brand names of nail polish she uses, how to act around guys, and much more. All imitating doesn't have to be unwise or imprudent. The thing that tilts a decision one way or another is *acting with knowledge* or *folly*—that is, *foolishness.* But if my friends nudge me or pressure me into being demanding or disrespectful to my parents, or encourage me to make fun of some other kids who aren't part of the "in" crowd, or to say or do hurtful or mean things to another, then these acts are really those of "a fool" who "flaunts" or makes a show of his folly or foolishness.

Instead of being one who is thoughtful, *acting with knowledge, prudent,* about the end of those hurtful things, the guy or girl who causes pain or hurt to himself and others is *exposing his folly.* It's like not thinking about a gymnastics routine ahead of time and not smoothly moving from one element of it to another and then running out of time before the gymnast is able to finish her routine precisely.

Jesus was *prudent*. In John 2:24-25, the Bible says he didn't just let people control him by going along with them even when they were saying good things about him. They wanted to make him an earthly king right then and there, before God's timing. It says that "he knew all people...he knew what was in man." In other words, knowing human nature as he did, he was *prudent*, thoughtful, shrewd. He knew that some of these same people would be hollering "crucify him" in a short time.

We don't have the luxury of the thorough kind of knowledge about others that Jesus had, but we do have the wisdom of Scripture and the example of Jesus to guide us into being thoughtful about decisions about life. Give thought to the Word's wisdom. When you don't know what principles the Word of God may have for you in any given situation, ask someone who is more mature in the Lord. That, too, is a form of *prudence* or thoughtfulness. It's a way of thinking about the end result of a choice before making it.

> **Prayer:**
> Father, it's easy for me just to live from one thoughtless moment to another without thinking about where my decisions will lead me. Deliver me from that kind of foolishness. Make me a prudent young adult, one who acts with knowledge and wisdom, Jesus' way. Help me make choices because of the ends he wills for me. Not just spontaneous, thoughtless, or pointless words and actions—folly. In Jesus' name, Amen.

Bridges' Comments:

It is so easy to fritter or dribble away valuable knowledge because of a lack of careful forethought—*prudence*. To get the full benefit of opportunities, we need to think about our immediate situation, the seriousness of matters at hand, the helpfulness or hurtfulness of what is getting our attention, and the ways to take good advantage of what's happening.

For example, someone can think carefully and speak *prudently* about something that is happening to her or something that someone is saying to her, or she can just blurt out the first thing that comes to her mind. "The tongue of the wise commends *knowledge* (makes it acceptable), but the mouths of fools pour out *folly*" (Proverbs 15:2).

This kind of carefulness should be applied in every area of life. It can guard us against dangers we can see coming or think are likely to happen. "The *prudent* sees danger and hides himself, but the simple go on and suffer for it" (Proverbs 22:3). It can also help us to escape if we are caught in the middle of some troubles (Acts 16:7,38; 22:25; 23:7). The same *prudence* can help in raising children (Judges 13:8-12), in making life-relationship decisions (Judges 14:1; 2 Corinthians 6:14 and following verses) and especially, in church and spiritual growth matters (Galatians 2:2; Titus 1:9).

If we want to be truly helpful to others, this kind of thoughtfulness is important (Acts 15:22-29; Romans 15:14). What we want to do to help can turn out to be more harmful and hurtful without loving carefulness. "Whoever blesses his neighbor with a loud voice, rising early in the morning, will be counted as cursing" (Proverbs 27:14). Here a person who thought he was being helpful by blessing someone, was really annoying. He did it loudly—in the morning. The ministry of the Spirit and the compassionate right use of God's Word are critical (1 Corinthians 12:7) to be truly helpful.

Our *prudence* will affect our relationships with unbelievers. It will help us avoid falling into temptations and enable us to speak a word of wisdom and think accurately about what we see happening around us, including what others are thinking about us (1 Peter 3:15,16).

Even in political, economic, and social matters God calls us to *prudence*—not just "shooting from the hip" or saying the first thing that comes to our minds. This wide range of *prudent* responses is the responsibility of every believer (see Proverbs 14:8,15).

How does this *prudent* kind of living contrast to that of the fool? Look at the different translations of the words that describe his actions in the second half of the verse: he "*flaunts*," "*lays open*," "*exposes*," "*displays*" his *foolishness* (see Proverbs 12:16; Numbers 22:29,30). He shows openly his shallowness (1 Samuel 17:44). He *exposes* his thoughtlessness (Matthew 14:7). He uses no good sense and brings shame back upon himself (Proverbs 18:13). Want to see how *prudence* is lived out? Look at Jesus' well-lived life. Isaiah prophesied that the coming Messiah would "act wisely" or *prudently* (Isaiah 52:13). This marked his character and his work. His *prudence* frustrated and silenced his enemies when they tried to trick him (Matthew 21:24; 22:42-46), and it could be seen in his tender sympathy with the needy people he encountered (Isaiah 11:4). How good it is to have him as our *prudent* example to caution us and guide us in our living and serving.

To Help You Meditate:

1. Describe a time when you thought about steps to take to accomplish a task successfully. What were the benefits of thinking ahead of time about how to move forward with the project?

2. Can you think of a time you did not think things through beforehand and it did not go well? Describe it.

3. When was a time you thought carefully ahead of time about something you wanted to say or ask someone—maybe a parent, boss, friend, or teacher?

13:25 If I Get One of These, I Won't Ever Ask for Anything Else!

ESV
25 The righteous has enough to satisfy his appetite, but the belly of the wicked suffers want.

NIV
25 The righteous eat to their hearts' content, but the stomach of the wicked goes hungry.

Wisdom Lived Out Today:

Your grandmother is an amazing shopper. No one can squeeze more out of a dollar than she. I'm sure that some of that skill comes from being raised by parents who owned a general store and the hours she worked in it.

When we were first married, I thought I'd do something romantic with Betty—go food shopping with her. I really don't like shopping at all, but I wanted to serve my new bride. In the supermarket, I pushed the shopping cart, following her lead. We came to a huge barrel of large dill pickles. I said, "I'd really like to have one of those."

She said, "That is really big. You won't be able to eat it all."

"But I'm really hungry for one. I'm sure I'll be able to eat it."

So we bought one large dill pickle.

When we got home, I wasn't in the mood for a dill pickle, so we put it in the refrigerator. The next day, next week, and next month, I never got in the mood for the pickle. When we tell this story, your grandma asks, "Do you know how long it takes for a dill pickle to get moldy?"

I was driven by my appetite—at the moment, but soon I lost interest and the appetite for what I thought would satisfy me.

What's it take for you to be content? Jesus meets all the needs of his adopted family members (John 15:15; Philippians 4:18). Jesus will not leave any of us who are *righteous* as orphans (John 14:18). He *satisfies* us for eternity with what matters—himself.

The spillover effects of that relationship are amazing for this life and the next. He doesn't just give us stuff. Stuff can rot, be stolen, wear out, break, or run down. He said, "I am with you always, to the end of the age" (Matthew 28:20). That's why Paul said, "For to me to live is Christ, and to die is gain" (Philippians 1:21).

This proverb warns that we can be like a child who wants an especially popular toy and says, "If you get me that, I won't want anything else." Then, parents often notice that soon after getting it, the child is tired of it. It no longer has the fascination it had at first—often in just a few days. Now he *wants* more to keep him happy, but no created thing has that kind of lasting, satisfying power. Only a relationship with Jesus offers that kind of contentment. God the Father provides everything his family needs. He satisfies "our needs, not our greeds," one pastor said. The Psalmist said, "In your presence there is fullness of joy; at your right hand are pleasures forevermore" (Psalm 16:11).

When your parents went to the Dominican Republic with some of our mission teams and worked in the desperately poor villages of Juan Tomas and Caballona, they were often impressed with the joy the believers had—in their poverty.

Satisfaction comes because of contentment with God and his grace in Christ, not with stuff. Things were never intended to have much of a satisfaction shelf-life. Only Christ is the treasure worth selling everything for. "Seek first the Kingdom of God and his righteousness, and all these things will be added to you" (Matthew 6:33). "...the path of the righteous is like the light of dawn, which shines brighter and brighter until full day" (Proverbs 4:18).

Prayer:

Father, don't allow me to mistake what I want for what I need. Don't allow me to be driven by the feelings of the moment. Help me to be content with what you provide for me. That's what I truly need. Especially help me to be satisfied with Jesus and with what you give me for this life and the next. "He must increase, but I must decrease" (John 3:30). "For me to live" must mean being satisfied with Christ, just as "to die" means having more of that satisfaction (Philippians 1:21). Help me not to be distracted in this world with the wrappings and toys it offers and miss the richness you want me to find in Christ. In Jesus' name, Amen.

Bridges' Comments:

This is one of the many ways in which *the righteous* is "...a guide to his neighbor" (Proverbs 12:26). God assures his people that they will enjoy his goodness in this life—insofar as it is truly beneficial for them. He will provide little or much—enough to satisfy his child's need, not necessarily to fulfill his "craving" (Proverbs 10:3; Psalm 34:10; 37:3,18-19). In fact, the *righteous'* needs are never more than his Father provides. He wants what is within his Father's wise boundaries for him and he wants to use God's blessings with carefulness. He *has enough to satisfy his appetite* while the *wicked suffers want.*

Joseph was fed with the best of Egypt while his own countrymen were destitute (Genesis 47:11-13). A widow fed Elijah. Later ravens fed him. All the while, the wicked nation of Israel was experiencing famine (1 Kings 17:1-17; 18:5). Sometimes, of course, the conditions of the *righteous* may appear to be scantier than those of *the wicked.* This was the case of Daniel and his friends, but they were

more *satisfied* and more nourished with their meals than their fellow captives who had more royal provisions (Daniel 1:12-16).

As to higher food and heavenly *satisfaction*, Christ is the substitute for everything. Nothing is the substitute for him! Luther said, "If we live here by begging our bread, isn't this well rewarded by the nourishment we receive from the food of angels, eternal life, and Christ himself?" (Author's paraphrase of Bridges' quotation.)

The believers' *satisfaction* contrasts with the chaos of desires in the soul of the *wicked.* There is no abundance that can satisfy his *want.* Ahab's crown could give him no rest without Naboth's vineyard (1 Kings 21:1-4; Job 20:20,22). The ungodly heart is an insatiable, bottomless pit of cravings (Psalm 17:14; Isaiah 65:13,14; Hosea 4:10; Micah

6:14), but how intolerable will this conscious craving be throughout eternity! He will be denied even a drop of water to cool his tormented tongue (Luke 16:24).

To Help You Meditate:

1. When have you craved or seriously wanted something that you eventually got, but soon thereafter got tired of it or lost interest in it?

2. Can you think of people who have little materially but seem to be content?

3. Why will the righteous be satisfied and the unbeliever go hungry when both of them have strong desires?

14:18   What Crown Will You Wear?

ESV

18 The simple inherit folly, but the prudent are crowned with knowledge.

NIV

18 The simple inherit folly, but the prudent are crowned with knowledge.

Wisdom Lived Out Today:

Shaun's temptation was to grab his rod and rush ahead of everyone else to get to the best fishing spot around the pond. That was his temptation, but he knew he was the leader of the seven other cousins and his two sisters who were in the group. Instead, he helped the younger family members select rods, bait their hooks, and even escorted some to pond locations to get them started. His *prudence*, good sense and good judgment earned him respect and authority that Solomon describes as a *crown*. Shaun *knew* that more was expected of him than the younger kids in the group who weren't as sure of themselves as he was. He knew his example was important. His good sense gave him a big-picture awareness of what was really important, even though he was eager to do his own fishing.

In this verse Solomon was describing the kind of *prudence* that Shaun was practicing. The *simple* are people who don't think things through very well. They often run their lives by their emotions. They only do what they feel like doing at the moment. They *inherit folly*, Solomon says. In other words, they act foolishly and they get foolish outcomes from their actions.

The Bible gives many examples of such *simple* people. Evil king Ahab was one. He wanted Naboth's vineyard. He tried to negotiate a purchase price with Naboth, but Naboth didn't want to sell. Ahab became depressed, moody, and sulking in bed—until his wife, Jezebel, told him she'd take care of the problem. She hired false witnesses to bring phony evidence against Naboth and then had him executed because of the charges. Then Ahab took the vineyard. He and his wife earned God's wrath for their evil, covetous, manipulative injustice. You can read more about this in 1 Kings 21. But the bottom line was that he and Jezebel inherited folly and the self-destructive consequences that followed because of it. He and his wife were smart and devious, but they were not *prudent*.

You can be like Shaun, rather than Ahab, by acting *prudently*. You can act with understanding and good judgment, with godly character and servant-mindedness. If you do, you are recognizing that there is more to any event than the event itself. There was more to the fishing activity than fishing. God is involved! He is over all and in all and through all that is going on. He wants us to recognize his presence, goodness, and rule in every decision we make. He wants us to imitate him. That is true *prudence*.

This kind of decision-making results in being *crowned with knowledge*. This means God blesses someone who practices *prudence* and thoughtfulness by giving him or her deeper levels of *knowledge* of himself and his workings in this life. In addition, one who is *prudent,* especially in thoughts about how to live for Christ and how to honor God in his life, will be *crowned* with greater levels of respect, authority, and honor (what *crowns* represent). These cannot be bought, manipulated or wrenched out of others. True, some people will hate the *prudent* person. Think of what was done to the most *prudent* person who ever lived, Jesus. But even then, in the big picture of things, which the *prudent* person seeks to keep in mind, Jesus was not defeated. He would be raised and would receive a name that is above every name and is one that every knee will bow before and every tongue confess that he is Lord, to the glory of God (Philippians 2:9-11).

The same is largely true for you, too. You won't be declared Lord of all, as Jesus is and will be declared to be by everyone, but if you are *prudent,* you will be *crowned* with levels of *knowledge* that will produce honor, authority and blessing, which the *simple* will never *inherit.* They only *inherit folly.* Imitate Jesus' *prudence.* Wear the *crown* he grants!

> **Prayer:**
> Father, teach me always to be looking at the big picture, past my immediate feelings, in all my decisions. Especially help me to be thoughtful about the big, eternal purposes you have for me in every choice I make. Make knowledge of you and your will to be my crown. Make it set me apart for your glory in this world like it did the Lord Jesus. In Jesus' name, Amen.

Bridges' Comments:

Solomon contrasts the *simple* and the *prudent* once again. The descendants of Adam are born to naturally live lives of *folly* or foolishness (Job 11:12). We all inherit that trend. We have "inherited...futile ways from our forefathers" (1 Peter 1:18), especially from our first father, Adam (Genesis 5:3; Psalm 51:5). As long as we remain in this original, natural condition, we confirm our title as *simple* people by the decisions we make and the loves we embrace.

Unlike an earthly *inheritance,* we cannot relinquish or detach ourselves from this title on our own. We are marked by our *simpleness* in life, and when we "return...naked" to the grave, if we are without Christ, the way we were born, in *foolishness,* this will be the way we die and enter eternity.

But God generously offers wisdom to you just for the asking (James 1:5). There is no injustice in God's wise plan for our lives. There is no reason to complain about the *knowledge* he gives us as a *crown.* If you do not commit yourself to Christ, you will continue to live as a *simple* one by willfully going with the flow of your emotions or impressions about life and eternal matters. If knowledge of eternal matters is at hand for you and you choose to be satisfied with ignorance, you will be throwing away a treasure: *knowledge* of him and how to live, a *crown* of incalculable value.

The *prudent,* however, whom God instructs in heavenly knowledge, think about and understand God's wisdom about life. They see such wisdom as the true light in a dark world. *Knowledge* is truly their *crown.* This *crown* contrasts with the fading and wilting leaf wreaths warriors wore in ancient Rome and Greece. It contrasts, also, with the gold crowns of Roman emperors. These only lasted for the few years of their rule. This godly *crown* enhances the splendor and beauty of a young man or woman with the light, holiness, hope, joy and glory of eternal life. Acquiring this *knowledge* is not just a once-and-done magical or mystical experience. It does not come by focusing on the opinions of popular celebrities.

Modern sayings and wisdom often dim God's glory. The blemishes of the *simple* person's life and his self-centered pattern of living show the *folly* of his choices. In stark contrast, however, the Spirit stamps his steady consistency on his people's character. This usually draws honor and respect even from those who are not sympathetic to godly

---

We cannot detach ourselves from the title of "simple" on our own.

---

principles (1 Peter 2:12). Thus, in this life, "The wise will inherit honor, but fools get disgrace" (Proverbs 3:35). But not always. Think of how Jesus, the wisest One who ever lived, was treated. Yet, what shall be the glory of his followers in eternity? They will sit around the throne of God and be crowned by the hand of God himself!

To Help You Meditate:

1. When have you acted prudently as you served others and learned some things about people or yourself as you thought about your time with them?

2. Have you known anyone who was with a group of people in need of some help and seen him or her begin to help out without being asked? What is the difference between what they "inherit" and what the person "inherits" who doesn't even see the need?

3. What is the main spiritual difference between the simple and the prudent? What makes the difference?

15:1   Nobody Does That to Me!

ESV
1 A soft answer turns away wrath, but a harsh word stirs up anger.

NIV
1 A gentle answer turns away wrath, but a harsh word stirs up anger.

Wisdom Lived Out Today:

He was so mad!

He got his friends together and they were going to teach this idiot a lesson. They were going to give him a piece of their mind and maybe more!

Dave had helped Bull with a number of his homework assignments and even substituted for him at the market where they both worked so Bull could get his work done. But then Dave learned that Bull had told some of his friends that Dave was gay. The word spread like wildfire through the junior class. Some classmates even put insulting signs on his locker.

Dave's reputation as a Christian was well known. Now he thought all that was ruined because of Bull's lies and jealousy. As Dave and his friends waited outside the market for Bull's shift to end, Bul's former girlfriend, Abby, came up to him and asked to talk to him for a minute. They walked to the side of the parking lot.

"I know why you are here," Abby said. "Look, Dave, you have a strong reputation as a Christian. Bull is jealous and nasty, and everyone knows it. No one really believes anything he says. If you guys beat him up the way you look like you are planning to do, you'll just show that you're not any different than he is. But you are different. You are known to be kind and helpful. Most of us know you have even helped Bull with his homework so he wouldn't flunk Chemistry. You've even covered for him at work sometimes to give him more time to study.

Dave, Abby and Bull—A modern version of 1 Samuel 25

"The Lord has given you a good reputation at school and in our youth group. People respect you. Kids will quickly see this gossip to be just Bull's jealous slander. Let him alone. Take your friends back home. Turn the other cheek as Jesus said to do. The Lord will continue to bless you and favor you with even more opportunities to represent him the way you really want to. Your loving reaction, even to Bull, because of your trust in Jesus to take care of your reputation, will say so much more about who you truly are than any attempt to get even with him. He's not worth it."

It's easy to want to speak or react harshly and angrily to mistreatment. Solomon shows, though, that it's *soft*, comforting, healing words and actions that *turn away anger*. Abby used that kind talk with Dave. She reminded him of who he really was and what he was about to sacrifice by being "*harsh*" or nasty in return for Bull's lies about him. "*A harsh word stirs up anger.*"

Abby's wise counsel was to trust Christ's instruction about vengeance—don't take it into your own hands! Trust him to take care of your reputation. Show your trust in Christ by your love, even to an enemy. Show it by your *soft answer*. It will usually turn away someone's *wrath* (intense anger).

But that is not always the response to a *soft answer*. Jesus is an example of that. He often used soft answers or no answer at all with folks, but the religious leaders didn't like it and ended up crucifying him. Pilate said it was because they were jealous of him.

> **Prayer:**
> Father, it's so easy for me to want to defend myself. So easy to fire back with words that are calculated to hurt the way I've been hurt. But you have accepted me. You have brought me into your kingdom and given me a future that you guarantee—in this world and the one to come. Help me to live like a child of that kingdom; to love my enemies and not try to get even with them when they show up in my life. Let your love radiate through me so that you are glorified by my life. In Jesus' name I pray, Amen.

Jesus' response was to "entrust himself to him who judges justly..." and then "bore our sins ...on the tree..." (1 Peter 2:23,24). In other words, Jesus committed himself to the Father and trusted his control and then died for his accusers. That's the pattern Jesus wants for us: trust the Father and then serve the very people who are offending or hurting us. Peter says that God's will for us, in suffering situations, is to "follow in his steps" (1 Peter 2:21).

This kind of *soft answer* makes a difference, and God takes note of it—big time (see Matthew 5:10-12).

Bridges' Comments:
God's Word is so practical! What wisdom is here! The principle here is valuable for family peace, church unity, and especially the personal benefits that come with self-discipline with my tongue.

Scripture illustrates many different effects of the "soft" answer. *It is like water that quenches fire.* Consider Jacob with Esau (Genesis 32-33), Aaron with Moses (Leviticus 10:16-20), the Reubenites with their brothers (Joshua 22:15-34), Gideon with the men of Ephraim (Judges 8:1-3), David with Saul (2 Samuel 24:9-21), and Abigail with David (1 Samuel 25:23-32). On the other hand, harsh words are *like oil. They stir up the fire.* Think about Jephthah (Judges 12:1-6), Saul (1 Samuel 20:30-34), Nabal (1 Samuel 25:10-12), and Rehoboam (1 Kings 12:12-15).

It is this last tendency that controls most of us. We are more likely to *stir up* the fire than *quench* the angry flame. We are easily irritated, have a sarcastic or cutting answer to someone's comment, quickly justify ourselves, insist on having the last word, say far more than we should say, and think it's our right to be angry (as Jonah thought in Jonah 4:9).

Often, in times of verbal sparring, neither person gives in to the other—even to the smallest degree. Pride and strong feelings drive both people and make the sparks fly. And, "...how great a forest is set ablaze by such a small fire" (James 3:5)! We are commonly motivated by self-gratifying sarcasm. Having the last word may mean more to us, in order to win with a cutting word, than keeping and building a healthy friendship. People often excuse such hurtful responses by saying they are "just being honest," or "just being my-self," or "simply saying what is on my mind."

Having the last word may mean more to us than keeping and building a healthy friendship.

But the gospel shows us something different. Jesus inspires us with his spirit of humility (Philippians 2:3-5); he shows us his love is not "irritable or resentful" (1 Corinthians 13:5). As a result, he is careful not to rouse anger in one who is hurt or frustrated. If another person begins to act with rough or testy words, let us hold ourselves back from reacting the same way. Proverbs 17:14 says, "The beginning of strife is like letting out water, so quit before the quarrel breaks out." Patience is the true peacemaker. Soft and healing words gain a double victory—over ourselves and our brother (James 3:17,18; see also Proverbs 16:32; Romans 12:19-21).

To Help You Meditate:

1. What made Abby's advice appealing to Dave?

2. How did Jesus' response to injustice compare to Dave's first approach to his enemy?

3. Has anyone ever responded with a soft gentle word to something hurtful you angrily said or did? What was there about what they said that seemed to settle you down?

15:22   "Myself Do It!"

ESV
22 Without counsel plans fail, but with many advisors they succeed.

NIV
22 Plans fail for lack of counsel, but with many advisers they succeed.

Wisdom Lived Out Today:

Aunt Deb was about three years old.

She wanted to swing on our new swing set in the back yard. She wanted to do it without any help or advice about how to hold on to the chains. "Myself do it!" she exclaimed.

I tried to hold her hands on the chains, but she was insistent, "Myself do it!"

The swing was only a few inches off the ground and the grass was soft, so I thought this is going to be one of those teachable moments for Deb to learn something about taking advice and accepting help.

I said, "Debby, don't let go of the chains or you'll fall."

"Myself do it," she firmly stated.

I let her hands go when she had hold of the chains, but very soon she opened her hands and immediately fell backwards off the swing and onto the soft grassy ground.

The fall surprised her. She took a deep breath and then let out a loud screaming cry. She was not injured, but she was startled and the fall onto the ground scared her. She tightly grasped me as I picked her up and held her close and hugged her.

Without counsel plans fail, Solomon said. Think that you have all the answers and don't listen to others who have had experiences in life that you haven't had, and, he says, you won't *succeed.* Life's bumps and bruises will become more serious as you get older because your decisions will become more serious. They often have longer and longer-lasting effects.

Solomon's counsel to us is to seek the advice of trusted others before we make important decisions. "Myself do it!" is a temptation that our pride invites us to assert, but God's wisdom is that such a spirit is foolish. Failure will often be the result of going my own way and using my own solitary judgment in decision-making situations. Success is much more likely if I seek the advice of other brothers and sisters in the church, moms and dads who know me and love me, and others I respect and trust because of their maturity and desire to follow Christ. "...in an abundance of counselors there is safety" (Proverbs 11:14).

Bridges' Comments:

The value of this proverb as a political truth is obvious. A nation *without counsel* can never *succeed* or be established. "Where there is no guidance, a people falls, but in an abundance of counselors there is safety" (Proverbs 11:14). An *"abundance of counselors"* is an indispensable advantage for the government leader who wants to advance his plans and purpose. "Plans are established by counsel; by wise guidance wage war" (Proverbs 20:18). "...by wise guidance you can wage your war, and in abundance of counselors there is victory" (Proverbs 24:6). Similarly, by the neglect of counselors, *plans fail.* Consider Rehoboam (1 Kings 12:13-19), Ahab (1 Kings 22:18-29), and even King David (2 Samuel 14:1-4,15).

Prayer:

Father, please don't allow me to live as though I have all the answers. Teach me the humility of Jesus who, though he was God in human form, submitted to and was open to teaching by his parents as a young person (Luke 2:51). Please give me the sense to seek out godly advice and thoughts from people with more experience in life matters than I have. I want to succeed in the things you have for me to accomplish. Help me to rightly take advantage of the people you've placed in my life to learn from them and move ahead to make wise choices. In Jesus' name, Amen.

In the Church also good counsel advances the Christian mission. "The apostles and the elders were gathered together to consider this matter..." (Acts 15:6-31). They were addressing an important difference of opinion among the churches. The wisdom of godly and able people, *many advisors,* helped to move the group's purposes forward.

In many of our personal matters, too, we are urged to value greatly the advantage of good counsel. On our own, we are weak and ignorant! If our judgment were perfect, our first impressions would always be right. But weak, unstable and inconsistent as they often are, because of the fall, every decision we make needs careful thought. How much evil and hurt has been done by acting out of impulse, in a hasty moment, or by a few words or written lines without reflection or serious forethought. "Desire without knowledge is not good, and whoever makes haste with his feet misses his way" (Proverbs 19:2). Our wisdom lies in self-distrust. It is advanced by a suspicion that we may be wrong.

At the same time, we must avoid the overreaction of thinking that we must hear everyone's opinion about what we should do when we need to make a decision. The benefit of seeking experienced *counsel* for important decisions is clear, but even our wisest advisers can make mistakes in judgment. As we take advantage of the help God gives us from others, let us look mainly to the great "Counselor" (Isaiah 9:6) of the church for guidance. Take his "testimonies..." for your "counselors" (Psalm 119:24) with reverent thankfulness. Blessed be God for this special privilege of his *counsel* always at hand in his word by his Spirit! In humility and confidence we shall not err seriously (Proverbs 3:5,6).

To Help You Meditate:

1. Describe a time when you thought you had "all the answers" and ended up failing at something.

2. What is there about asking others for advice that makes such requests helpful? What makes "going it alone" more risky?

3. What does Bridges mean when he says "Our wisdom lies in self-distrust"?

16:1,9   Plans Are Really Prayer Requests

ESV

1 The plans of the heart belong to man, but the answer of the tongue is from the LORD.
9 The heart of man plans his way, but the LORD establishes his steps.

NIV

1 To man belong the plans of the heart, but from the LORD comes the reply of the tongue.
9 In his heart a man plans his course, but the LORD determines his steps.

Wisdom Lived Out Today:

Did you know that all your *plans* are like prayer requests? That's one way of reading these proverbs. You can carefully *plan* with all your *heart* what you are going to do on the weekend, in the summer, after school, after college, what car you'll buy, where you'll drive tomorrow afternoon, what sport you'll play, or any of hundreds of other things, but at best, all your *plans* are desires that you want to have happen. They are like prayer requests. These interests are like asking God or, more thoughtlessly, some "force" to "please let this happen."

Some time ago, I was scheduled to fly to Liberia to teach a course to some church leaders. I was to fly by Air Canada to Brussels and from there to Monrovia, Liberia. At the airport, though, I was told my flight to Brussels was canceled due to a worker strike in Brussels. I would need to be rerouted to Casablanca, Morocco. I was told this would involve more than a 12-hour layover in Casablanca, and that I'd need to retrieve my luggage and report back later in the day to check in and check my baggage again for the trip to Liberia.

In the Casablanca airport, I got my baggage and was standing in the baggage claim area wondering what I'd be doing for the next 12 hours. A woman approached me. "Your name is Rick," she said. "I can't remember your last name but it begins with an H.

I was stunned. I was almost 3,700 miles from home. "Yes, Rick Horne," I said.

"Yes, now I remember," she said. "You taught my kids at Delaware County Christian School. I'm Leigh, and my husband is one of the few Christian pastors allowed here in Morocco. What are you doing in Casablanca?"

I explained my trip rerouting and my layover in Casablanca.

"Well, my husband is coming to pick me up and we are going to be driving around in Casablanca to look for a camera shop to repair my camera. Why don't you spend the day with us? We'll show you around the city and get you back here for your flight later tonight."

What a remarkable turn of events! 3,700 miles from Philadelphia, someone knows me and offers to be my host for the day.

It turned out that the very pastoral counseling course I was going to Liberia to teach was what she was teaching the leaders of her church—but without a comprehensive set of notes. I was able to give her a copy of the workbook we'd developed with the notes from the same approach to biblical counseling that she used. She was so appreciative. So was I.

The Lord readjusted my plans so we could meet and I could provide her with a resource for her ongoing ministry.

In your heart, you know that you don't have the power to control whether or not your *plans* will work out. God is in control. *...the answer of the tongue is from the LORD.* Or, as verse nine states, *The LORD establishes his steps.* He makes his plan our reality.

Have you ever missed a deadline, been late for a meeting, or had a special event or trip canceled that you were looking forward to? Maybe you got sick. Maybe the leader of the meeting didn't show up. Maybe the electricity went out last night and you couldn't get an assignment done. *Plans,* even carefully thought out ones, which is what this word *plans* means in both verses, are still in the LORD's control.

Life is a gamble for unbelievers.

People who are living by looking to the LORD for his will to be done in their lives can take great comfort in this. God has their back. Nothing that their short-sightedness might miss can happen to truly hurt them or put at risk what is good for them. Luke can surprise an opponent by jumping in front of another player and intercepting a basketball pass, but God is never surprised by anything that seems to jump in front of us. The Father of believers has everything under control even when it might look like things are spinning out of control in our personal world.

This doesn't mean there are no surprises for us—even painful ones. This is a broken and sinful world and sometimes it breaks on us. But because of his love for his children, young people or older ones who have the Lord Jesus as their Savior and Ruler have someone in charge who guarantees that they can never make a fatal mistake—a mistake that can injure what really matters about our lives. That's because the *answer of the tongue is from the LORD.*

When *LORD* is in all capital letters in the Bible, it is referring to God as the Savior, the Redeemer, the one who sent his Son to die for sinners. And if he is going to come and die for his people to save them for true living in this life and for eternity, is he going to be skimpy on other less important things he will provide? Paul the Apostle made a statement like that. He said, "He who did not spare his own Son but gave him up for us all, how will he not also with him graciously give us all things?" (Romans 8:32). If he gave the greatest gift, his Son, everything else good for us is a lock—regardless of how it looks or feels at the moment. No matter what choices a believer makes, God is there to care for him or her. He will not let our plans go through to the end if they are not really in our best interest and for his glory (Romans 8:28).

The person without a relationship to Jesus, though, has no such protection or assurance about the wisdom or foolishness of his or her decisions and their outcomes. Life is a gamble for unbelievers. Their *plans* are still basically prayer requests since they can't guarantee they will happen. They are more like wishful thinking. The *answer of the tongue* is still *from the LORD,* but someone who is not a believer in Christ is "alienated" or estranged and separated from him (Colossians 1:21). He or she is living on borrowed time, in a foreign world, with an imaginary god or gods. Such a one is just waiting for God's anger to fall on him in judgment (John 3:36). The wisest thing for anyone in that condition to do is to submit himself to the Lord Jesus and be made right with God.

Prayer:

Father, it's easy for me to think life is under my control. I know that is not the case. You are in control. Thank you for your loving management of everything that comes into my life. Help me to rest in the confidence that there are no fatal mistakes going to come into my life. Thank you that even "accidents" are not surprises to you. Help me to make all my plans with a sense that I only want your will to be fulfilled in my life. In Jesus' name, Amen.

So, plan humbly, carefully, always recognizing that "if the Lord wills it" (James 4:13-15) your plans will come to pass. And if they don't happen, allow the change of plans to bring your heart into full submission to his wise will with thankfulness. In Christ, his *plans* for you are good! Never a mistake.

Bridges' Comments:

This is a wonderful description of God's sovereign rule in the world! It is a mystery how his complete control works to fulfill his purpose along with the freedom that he gives us to think and make decisions. Humankind without freedom to choose is a machine. God without his unchangeable purpose ceases to be God (Malachi 3:6). Freedom and Sovereignty are both realities.

As rational creatures, we think, talk to others, gather information, make decisions, and act freely, but as dependent beings, the LORD exercises his own power in our lives—permitting, overruling, or furthering our acts (see Proverbs 19:21; 21:30; Psalm 33:11; Isaiah 46:10; Lamentations 3:37). Someone has said, "Man proposes; God disposes." *Man plans; the LORD establishes.* He orders our wills without canceling or invalidating our freedom and without interfering with our responsibility, for while we act as we please, we are still accountable to him. There is mystery here!

We confess his supremacy in directing, not only the important ends toward which our lives inevitably move, but every step we take toward that end. This includes the big events and what appear to be insignificant twists and turns in life.

For example, consider the international and eternal effects of Ahasuerus' sleeplessness (Esther 6:1; see also Psalm 37:23; Proverbs 20:24; Jeremiah 10:23). Joseph's brothers had no idea how their plot against him would be overruled by God's plan of goodness (compare Genesis 37:26-28 and 45:5). When Saul of Tarsus (eventually called Paul) was planning the murder and imprisonment of Christians (Acts 9:1-6), and when the runaway slave, Onesimus, was looking for freedom by his escape (Philemon verses 10-16), they had no idea that their steps would lead to their gracious salvation.

When David simply followed his father's orders to take food to his brothers, little did he know how that would affect all of Israel's history (1 Samuel 17:17,18,23,58). The LORD had *established his steps.* A captive girl could not begin to calculate the weighty results from her being taken into a foreign country away from her home (2 Kings 5:2,8).

Often, through Israel's history and the church's history, their enemies were frustrated just when they were ready to snatch their prey (1 Samuel 23:27; Isaiah 37:7,8). Bridges quotes Bishop Hall, a pastor from Bridges' day, who said, "Every creature walks blindfolded. Only he that dwells in light, sees where they go" (2 Kings 5:2,3).

This doctrine of Providence is not like the doctrine of the Trinity—a mystery that cannot be reasoned out and must be accepted by faith. Rather, God gives us evidence in the apparently small experiences of his people that have become major parts in his plan of redemption over the span of thousands of years. A matter of missing donkeys (1 Samuel 9:3,15,16), a small man's curiosity (Luke 19:4,6,9), a thirsty woman (John 4:7), a woman by a riverside running her business (Acts 16:14), all are connected to infinitely important and traceable results by One who *established* their *steps.*

It often happens that other doors of opportunity open taking us another way, which we later testify was the wise right way.

Often, when our purpose seems clearly fixed, and sure to happen, our *plans* have been blocked by unexpected difficulties. At the same time, it often happens that other doors of opportunity open taking us another way, which we later testify was the wise right way (Psalm 107:7; Isaiah 42:16). God's control of Paul's movements, landing him in prison, turned out "to advance the gospel" (Philippians 1:12,13). Philip was led to leave a ministry to thousands in Samaria and go to the desert where he met the solitary Ethiopian eunuch who was probably a major channel of the gospel to tens of thousands in Africa (Acts 8:37-39). Paul was turned aside from a wide field of labor to a narrower ministry, but saw the conversion of a few women and a family and the beginnings of a church (Acts 16:6-15). Yet these small beginnings resulted in his planting of flourishing churches (Philippians 1:1; 1 Thessalonians 1:1).

We need much discipline to turn us away from depending upon our own planning and beginning any plan by seeking his direction first and foremost. If we develop the habit of seeking his will first, the fruit of our own private planning will be something we come to dread (Psalm 143:10). We truly find happiness and security in submitting to our Heavenly Guide. He knows the whole way; every step of the way. He knows "the end from the beginning," and we shall never miss the right path or the end of the way if we commit ourselves with total trust and confidence in his *established plan* for our *steps.*

To Help You Meditate:

1. What is one incident in your life or your family's experience that didn't work out as you planned but later turned out for good in God's providence?

2. Why do the Lord's "answer" and his "establishment of our steps" allow a Christian to live with confidence—even in uncertain situations?

3. What are some of the things non-Christians tell themselves to still feel okay when their plans don't work out?

16:2   There Are Wants Behind What I Do

ESV
2 All the ways of a man are pure in his own eyes, but the LORD weighs the spirit.

NIV
2 All a man's ways seem innocent to him, but motives are weighed by the LORD.

Wisdom Lived Out Today:

The Bible teaches that we are more than what we do. Doing is important, but doing is only a part of us. We also *think* about what we do and have *heart reasons* for our thinking and doing. Sometimes we are aware of some of our reasons and sometimes we're not.

When Grandma and I were in college, before we really knew each other well, I began to hang out with her—in order *to get to know her best friend.* Terrible! I agree. I thought I would date this girl named Betty a few times so that I could get to know Suzie. My interest in Betty wasn't as I made it look. My heart intentions were different from my actions. The Lord thankfully interrupted my plans. He knew what was best for me and overruled my foolish heart motives. I began to see the woman who became your Grandma as the treasure she is. I was soon smitten by her, and eventually married her. That was 50 years ago from the time I'm writing this.

Or consider your reasons for studying and doing homework. This is part of your *ways* or actions that the verse mentions. But why do you do it, really?

Maybe Jaydn wants to avoid the punishment he might get if his parents think he is wasting time. Maybe Silas doesn't want to miss the reward his parents have promised him for getting his work done. Maybe Cami wants to keep getting the attention and acceptance of the academic in-crowd at school. Maybe Ty just wants to stay eligible for the next athletic season.

These can all be heart "motives" or the *spirit* that this verse is talking about. This doesn't mean these reasons for studying and getting good grades are necessarily bad reasons for doing something, but studying hard, or doing anything else out of fear or for any other reason, as your main reason, is a clue to what the center and controlling force of your life is. Eventually, these motives or reasons for doing what you are doing will run out of gas—they will become weak forces for driving you to action. (Parents won't always be there to punish me if I'm lazy or to reward me if I do my work. The in-crowd and meeting minimum athletic grade standards won't always mean future success.)

Only one motive can offer a changeless reason for doing anything well—doing everything I do for the glory of God (1 Corinthians 10:31). This will drive me past failures, disappointments, changing life situations, the uncomfortable disapproval of others, and other challenges that come at me to hinder me from doing what is wise with my life.

Our motives, reasons for doing what we do, get lots of attention in the Bible. It's not just the outside doings that are important. It's the heart as well. "Keep your heart with all vigilance, for from it flow the springs of life" (Proverbs 4:23). If one is a Christian, these motives, if they are the main ones that drive a person, may miss the point of doing all you do for the glory of God (1 Corinthians 10:31).

God made us different from the animals. God made us in his image so that we could make choices (our *ways)*, guided by our thinking (which can *seem pure* or "innocent" to us), but these are driven by what we want deeply in our heart (our *spirit or* motives).

I may go to my friend's house (my choice) to do homework with him or her (the reason I give my mom), but my decision could be because I don't want to face her. The teacher said she was going to give her a call about my poor work in class. Going to my friend's place sounded good to me to avoid my mom—my real motive.

Sin has affected our actions, our thinking about our actions, and our motives for why we act the way we do.

Sin has affected all three of these parts of us: our actions, our thinking about our actions, and our motives for why we act the way we do. Sometimes our *ways* or actions look *pure* or innocent to us in our thinking, but our *spirit* or deeper motives, our heart desires, fears, loves, or ambitions, actually drive us. The Bible is totally realistic about who we are and how we are wired. This is Biblical Psychology 101. There are no accidental choices. We do things for reasons in our heart.

This verse in Proverbs isn't specifically about studying for tests, dating with false motives, or doing homework with a friend. It's about reasons we do things that God clearly sees, even if our heart motives are not so plain to us. People can think they are doing the right things but not be thinking too seriously about why they are doing them. Some parents refuse to discipline their kids if their kids put up a fuss. They tell themselves that giving the kids what they want will make them happy and pleasant to be with. But what the parents really want is peace and quiet—kids who don't annoy them—so they give in to their foolish demands. *The Lord weighs the spirit.* He knows what drives us.

Some young people dress in ways, talk in ways, act in ways that look good, but down deep inside, they are afraid of what other kids will think if they don't. That fear is called the "fear of man" in Proverbs 29:25. "Fear of man" is like bowing down to the idol called "I-want-you-to-like-me." This is doing what others want me to do, even okay things, but for the wrong reasons. This is what God sees and *weighs* or judges. *The Lord weighs the spirit* or motives of our hearts.

Jesus had confrontations all the time with the Pharisees because their motives were out of sync with what God wanted them to want. They were out for themselves. Their hearts were far from him, Jesus said (Mark 7:6).

Prayer:

Father, I want what you want. Help me to live that way in every kind of situation, at home, in school, with my friends, and with those who aren't my friends. Help me to think about why I do what I do and to guard my heart so that I'm making my choices to glorify you first and foremost, and then truly to care for others. Make me a careful watcher of my heart's desires. In Jesus' name, Amen.

How important is having right heart intentions or motives? Living wisely means having "no other gods before me," the first of the Ten Commandments (Exodus 20:3). It's wanting God's approval more than anybody else's—no matter what the cost. God created us to care more about what he wants than what anyone else wants, but while we all fall short of this requirement, Jesus died for our foolish heart motives. When he is our Savior, he saves us even from ourselves, our own natural, self-centered desires. Then he begins to change our heart's loves so that, more and more, as we grow in him, we want to do what he wants us to do for his good reasons. He forgives our mixed heart desires and strengthens our love for his desires by his Spirit more and more throughout our walk with him. That is called growth in Christ.

Living wisely means that I want Jesus' approval for what I do and what I think. It means that I want, at the heart level, his will more than anyone else's will or approval. *The LORD weighs the spirit.* He searches our heart motives. Pray for a heart that wants what the Lord Jesus wants more and more.

Bridges' Comments:

If any of us were our own judges, few of us would ever judge ourselves to be guilty of anything. People judge by what they can see. God judges by principles, his law, the truth. His eye, therefore, sees the amazing mass of pollution in people's hearts. But what we see is often different. This verse says, *all the ways of a man are pure in his own eyes* (see also Genesis 6:5; Psalm 14:3).

People will never believe what they are really like on the inside until the mirror of God's Word is held up to their faces with a clear image of their hearts reflecting back to them (Romans 7:9). We also get a dose of reality about our sin-contaminated hearts when some temptation surprisingly erupts and shakes us up. Maybe it is angry words, a violent reaction, a selfish sexual act, or a self-protecting lie. "How could I have done that, said that, thought that, or believed that?"

People may see that they are sinners of some sort, but they will often add, "...but I'm not really that bad, and my good points outweigh any bad points." Jesus has a different view—a realistic one. He said, "…you are those who justify yourselves before men, but God knows your hearts. For what is exalted among men is an abomination [cursed, hateful] in the sight of God" (Luke 16:15).

Sometimes our self-deception is not too clear. Pilate washed his hands and was *pure in his own eyes* from the blood of Christ whom he handed over to be crucified (Matthew 27:24). The murderers of Christ were clean in their *own eyes* from moral uncleanness. They stayed out of Pilate's Gentile judgment hall to accuse Jesus (John 18:28). That place would have made them "unclean" according to their Jewish traditions. Those who persecuted the early Christians thought they were doing the right things, even God's work, by imprisoning or killing believers in Jesus (Acts 26:9). The Scriptures show people who are self-deceived and pass into eternity as lost men or women even though they seemed to have the right words to say while in this life.

It's not looking or sounding right in my *own eyes* that matters. It is my condition before God, the way he sees me, that matters most—not what I or anyone else thinks about me. Someone can look like a Christian and have the reputation of being a Christian, but not be one. Jesus said it is possible to "...have the reputation of being alive, but you are dead" (Revelation 3:1).

Sometimes our self-deception is not too clear.

Doing Christian-like things without true trust in Christ alone for salvation can give someone an empty, false hope. The Lord weighs the *spirit,* not just the actions (1 Samuel 2:3; 16:7). He discerns clearly and accurately such self-centered hollow and wrongly-placed faith (1 Samuel 15:11; Daniel 5:27). Saul was "weighed in the balances and found wanting." The Psalmist prayed, "If you, O LORD, should mark iniquities, O LORD, who could stand?" (Psalm 130:3; Psalm 143:2).

We must run from the guilt that our omniscient (all-knowing) God sees. Jesus' blood alone cleanses us from our guilt. We must run to the only refuge where God's justice has been completely satisfied and where forgiveness is freely given—to Jesus (Galatians 3:10,13; Psalm 130:4). On one side of an imaginary judgment scale, God's perfect law rests. On the other side Jesus' perfect obedience is placed. We must say, "Here, O my God, is my peace and my security. You alone smooth my way before your presence. 'The path of the righteous is level; you make level the way of the righteous'" (Isaiah 26:7).

But, oh, how critical is the saving blood of the beloved Son of God! (1 Peter 1:18,19). The scale of God's justice demanded it (1 John 2:1) and it is only satisfied by his blood (1 John 2:2). What a privilege we will have to give him glory forever for this wonderful work because of his grace (Revelation 5:9).

To Help You Meditate:

1. What is one thing you've done or said to a friend or family member that was good or looked good, but you did it or said it because you wanted him or her to like you or approve of you? How could you have done or said the same thing with the reason behind it to serve Christ with your life?

2. In a recent TV or movie episode, can you identify any evil motives that drive an actor's good-looking choices?

3. The deeper we look into our motives, the more we see they are self-centered to some degree. They violate the very first of the Ten Commandments. How, then, can anyone be accepted by a holy God?

17:17   He Helped Her While She Was on Her Crutches

ESV
17   A friend loves at all times, and a brother is born for adversity.

NIV
17   A friend loves at all times, and a brother is born for adversity.

Wisdom Lived Out Today:

Aunt Julie went to the first-grade teacher-parent meeting. She wasn't sure what she would hear from the teacher about Ty's progress. She walked into the classroom while the students were getting ready to be dismissed. The teacher waved to Aunt Jul. She went over to her. The teacher nodded toward Ty and said to Aunt Jul, "keep watching."

Tyler had gotten up from his desk and moved across the room to Maria's desk. He handed her crutches to her and she got up on her feet.

Maria had broken her leg. She had a hard time getting around and maneuvering on her new crutches, but she had a friend who was looking out for her—Tyler. No one asked him to do it, and first grade puppy love was not the reason. Tyler was just being a kind *brother* for someone who was in need of some support in *adversity*. He helped her gather her books, pack her book bag, get her lunch box, and he pulled out and pushed in her chair—all without being asked to do it. Aunt Julie got tears in her eyes, so grateful to see this kind of thoughtfulness.

Friends are around all the time, but *a brother*—well, that's a special relationship that shows up especially in times when things are tough, like in Maria's broken leg situation. Proverbs speaks of friends who are around when things are going well and even when they may think they may get something of value from a friend. Proverbs 19:6 describes someone like this: "Many seek the favor of a generous man, and everyone is a friend to a man who gives gifts." But Tyler was not out to get something. He was out to give something— true friendship, true brotherhood.

This is the pattern God wants us to imitate. Of course, Jesus is the best overall example of such friendship and brotherhood. He said, there is no greater love than this, "…that someone lays down his life for his friends"— exactly what Jesus did for all his people (John 15:13). He didn't do this because we were good people or because he needed something. He did it because of his love. God wants us to be that kind of friend at all times, especially in times of trouble.

Prayer:

Father, make me this kind of friend to people in need so that they will see you through me.

Help me not to be a fair-weather friend—only there when things are going well. Instead help me to sacrifice my comforts and inconvenience myself for others, to be like the Lord Jesus and to draw the attention of others to you as the best friend and brother. In Jesus' name, Amen.

Bridges' Comments:

This beautiful picture of friendship has been drawn by people who teach others to be and do good just because that's good to do (moralists), by people who tell others that doing good will make them feel good and will look good to others (sentimentalists), and by poets. But in reality, the only place this kind of friendship can be found is where God's grace has melted away people's natural selfishness into true loving concern for others.

If godly virtue, good character, is the best foundation for friendship, then this is the most solid kind of friendship of all. One contemporary of Bridges, Bishop Hall, describes the common kind of friendship he's seen as "brittle stuff." In other words, it can break easily. It can't hold much weight. It cools by distance or by the coldness of our friend. Hard times in the world transform this friendship into indifference or even hatred (see Job 6:14,15 and Proverbs 19:7). Such a "friend" forsakes his "friend" if he drifts from the right life path and faithful living instead of following up on him, watching over him, and making efforts to help him back onto a righteous pathway.

…the only place this kind of friendship can be found is where God's grace has melted away people's natural selfishness…

But the true friend loves at all times, through the good and the bad. He does not change when circumstances of his life change. He's the same whether his buddy is prospering and succeeding or collapsing and failing. He proves himself in troubling times by stretching himself to offer help. He is not ashamed of any extremes in his friend's life such as poverty or prison! Nothing will keep him from loving his friend (see Philippians 2:25 and 2 Timothy 1:16-18 for two great examples of friendship). In any great times of trial, the pains of troubles cement the love of true friendship and brotherhood. The *loving friend* now becomes *a brother born for adversity* (contrast this with Job 2:11-13). This was the kind of love Joseph had for his brothers. It was unshaken by the twists and turns of troubles in his later life or the ingratitude his brothers showed him early on in life (Genesis 14:5-8). This was the kind of love Ruth showed to her desolate mother-in-law, Naomi (Ruth 1:16,17). It was the friendship of Jonathan and David in life-threatening times (1 Samuel 18:3; 19:2; 23:16). This was the love John showed to the mother of Jesus in the dark hours of the crucifixion (John 19:27), and that Paul's friends showed to him when he was in prison (Aquila and Priscilla, Romans 14:3,4; Epaphroditus, Philippians 2:25,26; and the Philippian church, Philippians 4:15).

We must not look for perfection in our friend's love to us. We don't exercise that quality of love ourselves. The disciples were certainly sincere, though Jesus warned them about their weaknesses. That reality should humble, warn, and teach us about our own nature and strengths and weaknesses of true friendship (see Matthew 26:40,41). It was weakness, not willfulness or hypocrisy, on the disciples' parts that led to their abandonment of the Lord. Jesus recognized it as such and predicted it in Luke 22:28 and Matthew 26:56, but he still loved them as a *brother*.

But—ah! It is to him that we must look as the perfect example. He, the Son of Man, took our nature that he might be our *friend* and *brother* (see Hebrews 2:14). He is not ashamed to call us "brothers," the writer of Hebrews states (Hebrews 2:11-13). This is deep, mysterious *friendship!* He alone is truly worthy of our unlimited confidence. His love is so consistent. He loves at all times (see John 13:1), even to the point of his death (John 15:13) and the most unfaithful responses by his disciples, such as Peter's (see Luke 22:61). Jesus' love was *born for adversity*. He is united to us as the *friend* and *brother* we need. He is nearest to us in the lowest depths of our troubles. Though our glorified *brother* is now in heaven, yet he is still able to "sympathize with our weaknesses" (Hebrews 4:15). He is still "afflicted" in all our "afflictions" (Isaiah 63:9). He presents us to the Father as his own chosen ones, purchased by his blood, members of his body, of his flesh, of his bones (Ephesians 5:30). Here is true compassion in all its fullness and in all its helpfulness. Here, truly, is a *Brother born for adversity*. Trust him at all times and in all places, you struggling believers. You will then be possessed with the truly happy art of living beyond the reach of all disappointment.[17]

To Help You Meditate:

1. Can you recall a time when someone was truly a "brother" to you? How did he or she show brotherly love to you?

2. Describe a situation where you could have shown brotherly love but held yourself back because you were too tired, too comfortable, or too busy with some personal matter to get involved.

3. What is one way you can be a brother to a needy family member, school, or work friend?

---

[17] Bridges quotes from a sermon by a Pastor Howell: "Though solitary and unsupported, and oppressed by sorrows unknown and undivided, I am not without joyful expectations. There is one *friend who loveth at all times: a Brother born for adversity*—the help of the helpless; the hope of the hopeless; the strength of the weak; the riches of the poor; the peace of the disquieted; the companion of the desolate; the friend of the friendless. To him alone will I call, and he will raise me above my fears."

19:8 How to Rightly Love Your Own Soul

ESV
8 Whoever gets sense loves his own soul; he who keeps understanding will discover good.

NIV
8 He who gets wisdom loves his own soul; he who cherishes understanding prospers.

Wisdom Lived Out Today:

God has built many good patterns of cause and effect into life. They usually work for believers and unbelievers. It's just the way life is, by God's design. The book of Proverbs is full of them—over 300 by my count. They say, "If you live this way…then this will be the positive outcome." There are over 300 negative warnings in Proverbs, too, but this current proverb is one of the positive ones.

Aunt Kahee *discovered good* later in her life by *getting sense* earlier in her life. Her life is a testimony to the soundness of the wisdom in Proverbs. Her life experience points to the even more important spiritual wisdom of *getting sense* and *discovering good.*

When she was younger and living in Korea, Kahee had a successful photography business, but some very difficult times came her way. First, her father, to whom she was close, died. Shortly after that, Kahee was the victim of a violent robbery that nearly took her life.

She was deeply affected by these events and wisely sought help. She was open to *getting sense* about the things that had been happening to her. She knew she needed to look outside of herself for some guidance. In God's goodness, she found some skillful helpers and opened herself up to them, seeking to *understand* how to live in light of the losses and trauma she experienced.

The people she sought out were wonderfully helpful. Over time, talking to them led her to reconsider her life goals. The healing she began to experience planted some new thoughts into her heart and mind. "I've been helped," she thought. "Maybe I can use my photography to help others and not just use it to pay my bills. Maybe I can use my talent in photography to give others the kind of support I found." With that in mind, she moved to the U.S. and began her studies in psychology.

None of this would have happened if Aunt Kahee was not open to it. She aimed at *getting sense* and *keeping understanding.* The result: she *discovered* a meaningfully *good* path to pursue.

God has designed life to work like this. This is a sinful and broken world, so there will be bumps along the way for all of us, but generally, if one *gets sense* about her situation and *keeps understanding* about it, she *discovers good.*

The experiences in our lives are not without purpose. Even the painful ones. The Bible is full of difficult, even tragic, events through which God unfolded his beautiful plans for the very people who were suffering. Joseph was rejected and abused by his brothers and later slandered by a woman in Egypt, resulting in his imprisonment. Jeremiah was rejected and imprisoned in a dry well and left near starvation by people who didn't like his message from God for them. Jesus himself was crucified, but afterward, with the resurrection, was empowered to raise others from their spiritual deaths to spiritual lives of promise.

All these were *seeking* God's *sense* and his *understanding* about their situations. Even Jesus cried out, "My God, my God, why have you forsaken me?" He's the right one to turn to. After all, he is the architect, the "master workman" (Proverbs 8:30) or "master craftsman" (NIV) who makes life work. Aunt Kahee's example of thoughtful openness about her life continues to yield *good* in her life planning. Allow the hard times that come your way to drive you with openness to God. *Seek* his diagnosis for your situation and his wise counsel. This will lead you to "prosper," to *discover good*, produced by God's wise craftsmanship.

> **Prayer:**
>   Father, help me to have the humility in difficult situations to look to you for your wisdom about my circumstances and about how you want to use them in my life and in the lives of others. Help me to see that all that happens to me is under your loving and wise control for my good and your glory. Give me the eyes to *get* the *sense, keep the understanding,* and *discover the good* you have for me. In Jesus' name, Amen.

Bridges' Comments:

From this verse, by itself, it might seem that self-interest might win us to religious living. "Act religious and you will *discover good.*" What a shallow thought! One with such an idea does not know the solid happiness he is forfeiting by truly seeking what is of real value—*good sense (*or *wisdom)* and *understanding.*

> Get wisdom; get insight; do not forget, and do not turn away from the words of my mouth. Do not forsake her, and she will keep you; love her, and she guard you. The beginning of wisdom is this: Get wisdom, and whatever you get, get insight (Proverbs 4:5-7).

How are we to get this blessing? Solomon explained it earlier in detail in Proverbs 2:1-6. He said to focus your attention seriously and diligently on the search, then bring your heart to God for his light and his teaching. This effort will make this rich treasure your own. Yet it requires as much to *keep* the blessing as to *get* it in the first place. It may slip away from someone who is not making the effort to hold onto it. "Only take care, and keep your soul diligently…" (Deuteronomy 4:9). Then you will keep your treasure like the man Jesus spoke about who found hidden treasure in the field and bought the field to secure his possession of it (Matthew 13:44).

This is not just a worldly set of values that Solomon presents here. For the Christian to get possession of this *good* he must be willing to sacrifice everything (Luke 14:26,33), but the reward he will receive is far beyond the price he pays for it. It is real, infinite, and heavenly. To get this *good sense,* or wisdom, by paying the price for it, which Jesus spoke plainly about, is to *love our own soul*. "…whoever finds me finds life…" (Proverbs 8:35). Wisdom is saying that "all of life is in me and all of life is with me."

Isn't this the chief *good*, above every earthly good (see Psalm 4:6,7)? It is the eternal *good* when every earthly *good* shall have passed away (Psalm 73:25,26). Who should have our highest love, our supreme trust, the top priority of our time, and our best talents? Does the question even need to be asked? Asking it makes the answer obvious, doesn't it? It's like comparing pebbles with pearls, dust with diamonds, dross with gold. To follow our own way is to destroy, not *love our own souls*. "…he who fails to find me injures himself; all who hate me love death" (Proverbs 8:36).

To Help You Meditate:

1. We live in a world that stresses that we should love ourselves. How is this proverb different from the world's counsel?

2. What are two ways you can get sense as this verse urges?

3. Tell about someone who has made sensible good sense decisions and experienced a good outcome for themselves and others.

20:4   Video Games and Zombie Movies

ESV
4 The sluggard does not plow in the autumn; he will seek at harvest and have nothing.

NIV
4 A sluggard does not plow in season; so at harvest time he looks but finds nothing.

Wisdom Lived Out Today:

Sage lived with his mother until he was 42. There was nothing wrong with his body—he was strong and healthy. There was nothing wrong with his brain—he was smart. But he just didn't do anything—except play video games and lie on his mom's couch and watch zombie movies.

He had been a business major at a local community college and got his Associates Degree in Management. He's had part-time jobs every year since college, but he never held a full-time job long enough to learn a business or earn his way into a position to use his management training. He took no continuing education courses, attended no professional seminars, attended some job fairs, but never followed through on things that looked good to him. He would just lounge at home, play video games, and watch zombie movies.

Sage was a *sluggard*. He wasn't a nasty or evil guy toward others. He wasn't a drunk or druggie. He didn't carouse. He just didn't really do anything productive with his life. He was a lazy teen, a lazy 20-something, and now a lazy, unmotivated, middle-aged man. There were offers for him to get involved and move into leadership roles at some of his jobs, but he didn't want the hassle of people complaining or of having to compete with anyone. He didn't want to have to keep someone else's schedule, so now all he has is someone else's schedule—his low-end, part-time employee schedule. He's earned no freedom because he's shown no initiative, commitment, self-discipline, interest in others, or self-denial. He only does what he "feels" like doing.

His *autumns* or cold-weather seasons of opportunity have come and gone, one after another. Now offers for some kind of professional future are few and far between. He couldn't be bothered or inconvenienced in younger years, and now employers and people of influence don't trust him enough to be bothered to take a chance on him. He had no track record of maturity and responsibility. His mom, with whom he lived, felt sorry for him and supported his lazy lifestyle by allowing him to live with her and pay no rent, assume no household responsibilities, or even supervise others whom she had to pay to do the lawn, paint the railing, or shovel snow. He was too busy or too tired to do those things, he said.

When his mom had to move to an assisted-living facility, she had to sell the house to pay for her care. Sage was indigent. "But what about me!" he declared.

She tried to reason with him about work, maturity, being a man, and accepting responsibility, but this was all a foreign language to Sage. "The sluggard is wiser in his own eyes than seven men who can answer sensibly" (Proverbs 26:16). Sage had all the reasons ready to give for why he couldn't do any of what his mom urged. The problem: her counsel was about 30 years too late. He had grown accustomed to doing only what he felt like doing when he felt like doing it for as long as he wanted to do it and as long as it interested him.

Solomon knew that such slothfulness would have a barren outcome. *At harvest* such a person would *have nothing.* The time for preparing the soil, doing the work of planting, cultivating, watering or irrigating, figuratively speaking, was largely past for Sage, so he had no *harvest.* He had nothing to show for all those years. Now he was reaping other unsatisfying outcomes from his slothfulness.

"...with the measure you use it will be measured to you."

This is so different from Kaitlyn. Even in middle school she was in the orchestra, was always constructing an art project, rented craft fair spaces to sell some of her work, took extra art lessons, took violin lessons, developed her own website, played basketball with a community team, and assisted with the technology needs of the Sunday School teachers in her church. On top of all of this, she studied in one of the most demanding public schools in the district and excelled. That was her pattern. She had her parents' encouragement, but they didn't push these things on her. She was motivated to be all that God had created her to be. These were her dad's and mom's patterns too. Harvest for Katie yielded much in those years and continues to do so into young adulthood! Great opportunities opened for her. She is no *sluggard.*

Academically, athletically, socially, leadership-wise, and spiritually, youth is a season to plow. It's a season to get lots of experience and not to use excuses like "it's too cold," "it gets dark too early," "nobody cares," "nothing I do is good enough," "it's too much work," or "it's just not fun." Growth and fruitfulness occur because people decide to plow during such times of "cold" or *autumn* when others make excuses. This is hard to do because other friends may be partying, sleeping, making excuses, or blaming others for why they can't _____ (you fill in the blank).

On two or three different occasions Jesus said, "...with the measure you use it will be measured to you" (Matthew 7:2; Mark 4:24; Luke 6:38). The sense is that if you want scant outcomes in any area, give scant effort to that area. If you want fruitfulness, give the attention that will yield fruitfulness. Another way that Paul said it was, "what you sow, you reap" (Galatians 6:7; see also 2 Corinthians 9:6). He was talking about moral and spiritual choices. Using your talents, *plowing in autumn,* or making excuses for not using them are moral and spiritual choices. Faithful *plowing* and sowing will reap an amazing harvest. "...more than you can ask or think" (Ephesians 3:20), Paul said. This is true in just about any area, but especially in your relationship to Christ. Don't be *slothful* there. A focus on your spiritual opportunities in this season of your life will yield a fruitful *harvest* that is for now and for eternity. Spiritual neglect, though, leads to barrenness in this life and the next—forever.

Prayer:

Father, please don't allow me just to do what I feel like doing. Help me to keep your goal for me to be faithful and to plant and sow energetically, creatively, selflessly, and lovingly. Bring events into my life, even pain if necessary, to keep me from becoming a sluggard like Sage. Instead, bring glory to yourself by my sacrificial initiative in every area, especially in seeking to know you and your Word. Motivate me more and more with the desire to see the glory of Christ in my life and to show it to others. In Jesus' name, Amen.

Bridges' Comments:

Solomon teaches us about the lazy person with a vivid picture of what brings him to ruin (compare Proverbs 19:15,24). The *sluggard*, or lazy person, has his reasons ready to excuse himself from any work that would require him to make an effort. He will *not plow in the autumn,* when the weather is "cold" (KJV) and could be rainy. Autumn was the usual time for this work. The cooler weather and the intermittent rains were also the usual weather patterns for that season. If his heart would be in the work, nothing would keep him from doing it.

The smallest obstacle can hinder someone whose heart is cold in the service of God when it is *autumn*, their season of opportunity. They can't be bothered when it is not convenient for them at the time. Christian, ask yourself, have you used your energy for even one hour of *plowing* in your praying? One with a hollow profession of faith will only show a shallow effort in such disciplines as prayer, Bible reading, and sitting under the Word with the church. In contrast, the world gives itself fully to its pursuits. The flesh, our sinful nature, wants to avoid inconvenience and suffering (Matthew 19:21,22). Shrinking from the cold, *autumn*, as the Reformer Melanchthon observes, is the same as avoiding the cross. Even when some are convicted of sin and become "sorrowful" (Matthew 19:22) or sad, they may still not turn to Christ. They may still run after the convenience or pleasure of their sin (Matthew 25:3-9; Luke 16: 24).

If wishing could get someone to heaven, nobody would miss it.

The *sluggard* will reap the tragic fruit of his sin. If he *does not plow in autumn,* in the fall, the time he has for planting, he will end up *having nothing... in harvest.* That's the usual time for celebration, but this *sluggard...will seek and have nothing.*

People do not have much sympathy for a lazy person whose own sloth has brought him to poverty or homelessness. What else does this spiritual *sluggard* have to look forward to? The *autumn* cold, its unpleasantness, keeps him from being with God's people on the Lord's Day, so his soul shrivels and dies because it has no good spiritual food.

If wishing could get someone to heaven, nobody would miss it, but heartless and lazy wishes without crucifying the flesh, which means turning from doing what is easy and comfortable and turning to Christ, will miss the promise every time. Millions have perished because of spiritual laziness, even though they've been part of serious Christian churches.

Religious connections are not helpful if one lacks the diligence, commitment, and devotedness to seek Christ by faith in their *autumn,* while they have the opportunity. They may beg God's mercy in the great harvest, the time of God's judgment, but their pleas will be in vain. They will be condemned as the "worthless servant" (Matthew 25:26-30).

Younger or older professing Christians, is it time to live idly, lazily, or carelessly? You are standing at the door of eternity. Is it wise to be slack when you are so near our great salvation (Romans 13:11)? One old saint has said,

> Blessed are those who have sown much for God in their lifetime. Oh, the glorious harvest that those shall have! The very angels shall help them take in their harvest at the great day. And oh! The joy that there shall be in that harvest! The angels will help to sing the harvest-song, that they shall sing, who have been sowers of righteousness! (Jeremiah Burroughs cited by Bridges on Hosea 10:12.)

To Help You Meditate:

1. What excuses have you heard others use when they want to avoid working on a project, helping someone in need, or being part of a church youth group or work team?

2. When are you most tempted to use excuses not to spend time reading God's Word or worshiping with God's people?

3. Consider Mark 4:24, to which Bridges makes reference in this section. Read it in its context (the verses around it). What is one way you might be wise to think about this verse?

21:1 **There Are No Accidents**

ESV
1 The king's heart is a stream of water in the hand of the LORD; he turns it wherever he will.

NIV
1 The king's heart is in the hand of the LORD; he directs it like a watercourse wherever he pleases.

Wisdom Lived Out Today:

When I was 14 years old, my father decided that our family should move from our city home in Harrisburg to a farm in a small country township about half an hour away. He was not a Christian and didn't make the move for any conscious spiritual reason. Instead, we moved because it seemed like a move that would provide better for the family. It did in lots of ways.

Until that time, my mother had taken me and my two brothers and sister to a church in the Harrisburg area that did not teach the Bible clearly or urge people to trust Christ for their salvation. It was being good that mattered.

Prayer:
Father, help me never to give up hope in the face of unpromising situations or unfriendly people. You are in charge and will always have my back. You *turn* the *streams of water*, the events and people in my life, to be just what I need and what will glorify you. Thank you for being in charge. Teach me to trust you at every *turn* in my life, knowing that you control all the *turns*. In Jesus' name, Amen.

When we moved into the country, a friend and I began to attend the youth group of a small start-up church because of their interesting youth activities. In the course of the next year, the Lord used that small gathering to change the trajectory of my entire life. Jack and I became Christians and both of us chose other friends, colleges, and made future plans because of our conscious desire to do the will of God. The Lord had turned the *king's heart*, my father's, in the case of our move to the country, so that his will in my life would be fulfilled.

Aunt Kahee saw God's hand of providence work out in a different, life-shaping way. She made a post on Facebook, which was unusual for her in the first place. She said she needed help or a tutor with a Spanish class.

A young man at the college responded and offered to help. It was Ben Horne. That connection was the beginning of what would become their relationship and result in their marriage about a year later.

God controls every event in our lives, the lives of others, and all the circumstances of those who are used to shape our lives. That's why believers can be assured that there are no "accidents" in their lives—in the most literal sense. The Lord turns the *streams of water*, the experiences that affect our lives, precisely to produce the good he wants to be in our lives.

Sometimes the people and experiences God designs for us do not feel good or look promising. Feelings and looks, though, are deceiving. The Lord *turns* the *streams.* He's in charge—all the time. *Kings,* and everyone else, are under his control for his good purposes—even the ones that look confusing and out of control.

Bridges' Comments:

Most people believe that, in some way, God is in control of everything. He forces things to move that have no strength in themselves, like mountains or stars or oceans. He causes animals to move by instinct and people by their inborn natural abilities, intelligence, or desires. Similarly, he moves Christians by his grace and love.

In this verse, Solomon reminds us of the powerful truth that God's influence is unstoppable by even the most powerful people—including the kings of biblical times. We are totally dependent upon him. Even the most powerful ruler, with access to almost unlimited resources, is dependent upon God's choices. The *king's heart is…in the hand of the Lord.*

A *stream of water* shows how our freedom and God's sovereign influence are related to each other. The *stream* begins to flow as a trickle in the spring, not enough water to irrigate any field seriously for a farmer, but as more trickles flow together the stream strengthens and flows. It can be easily redirected to irrigate different rows of crops. In the same way, God redirects the intentions and decisions of even the most powerful authorities to accomplish his purpose.

God's influence is unstoppable by even the most powerful people...

The thoughts in the *king's heart* may begin in humility and be for the benefit of his subjects, but his heart can swell because of his great advantages, resources, and freedom. He may begin to accomplish much for the benefit of his people or he can become despotic and tyrannical. But God, the Great Sovereign, turns the worst and most oppressive ruler, notwithstanding all his political ambitions, to his own purposes with the same ease that *streams of water* are *turned* by a farmer wishing to irrigate different rows of crops. Though the farmer plans the path of irrigation, the waters flow naturally according to their nature as water. Similarly, God directs *the king's* heart who, nevertheless, acts naturally as an accountable human being for all his decisions. All the while he fulfills his unseen and unacknowledged Sovereign's will.

Nehemiah fully acknowledged God's authority when he wanted to make a request of the king. He "prayed to the God of heaven" (Nehemiah 2:4,5). God prevented Abimelech from sinning by taking Abraham's wife Sarah as his own wife or mistress. "It was I who kept you from sinning against me" (Genesis 20:6), the Lord said to Abimelech. Pharaoh's heart was turned in favor toward Joseph (Genesis 50:4-6). The Babylonian king showed kindness to Daniel and his three friends (Daniel 1:19; 2:48; 3:30; 6:1-3,28). The Persian king approved and helped the Jews rebuild the temple (Ezra 1:1; 6:22; 7:27; 9:9; Nehemiah 1:11).

The hearts of wicked kings are also in the *hand of the Lord* (Revelation 17:16,17), yet God has no part in their wickedness (Exodus 1:8 - chapter 2; Psalm 105:25). The hand of Pharaoh and the ambitions of Sennacherib and Nebuchadnezzar (Isaiah 10:7; Jeremiah 25) were God's instruments for his own purposes. Ahab's murderous heart was held in check and even used to accomplish the downfall of Baal in Israel (1 Kings 18:10,40). The councils of the kings of the earth against Christ were under God's control (Acts 4:25-28; compare also John 19:10,11). As the Psalmist says, he makes the "wrath of man to praise him" (Psalm 76:10). God's almighty rule is visible by the ways he controls even the smallest affairs. Consider Ahasuerus's sleepless nights (Esther 6:1,2), Nebuchadnezzar's appeal to the occult (Ezekiel 21:21), the government tax that led Joseph and Mary to Bethlehem (Luke 2:1)—these seemingly unimportant events were turning points with hugely significant roles in God's providence.

The history of the Reformation shows the same sovereign control over kings' hearts. Henry VIII did not intend to advance God's work, but had a godly son, Edward VI, who willingly advanced the cause of Christ by giving prominence to the gospel in his realm. This reflection on history encourages us to refer all our anxiety for the success of the gospel and Christ's church to the Head of the Church. We do not rejoice in any particular earthly king's or leader's rule, but that the King of Kings does reign (Isaiah 9:6).

We must be stirred up to pray earnestly for our earthly rulers (1 Timothy 2:1-3). We must pray that, as their hearts are *in the hand of the Lord as streams of water,* they may desire to lead and rule for his glory. Pray that they would care as a nursing mother for the church (Isaiah 49:23) and be a blessing to her people.

To Help You Meditate:

1. What is an event in your life that seemed little, but that put you in a situation that God has used in a big way?

2. Look up the examples in the fifth and sixth paragraphs in "Bridges' Comments." Select one that is especially meaningful to you about God's wise control.

3. What are some twists and turns, some unexpected, challenging events, of God's control in your life concerning which you can't see where they are leading? How can his sovereign oversight still enable a trusting believer to thank him for his wise control in the midst of uncertainty?

21:16　How to Stray from Excellent Coaching

ESV
16 One who wanders from the way of good sense will rest in the assembly of the dead.

NIV
16 A man who strays from the path of understanding comes to rest in the company of the dead.

Wisdom Lived Out Today:

Imagine what would happen if Evan, though a good basketball player, chose to stop listening to the instruction his middle school and high school coaches had given him over his school career. Maybe some of his classmates pressured him to spend more time with them and take it easy his senior year. Maybe he just got the idea in his head that he had practiced hard every year and now it's time just to have fun. "I've played hard for the team over the years, but now it's time for me just to enjoy myself."

Over the years, in this fictional story, his coaches repeatedly stressed, "Fundamentals! It's fundamentals, Evan. Practice the fundamentals!" Evan followed their wise guidance and became a terrific player. But in this last year of high school, he decides he just wants to shoot baskets and not work so hard in practice. "It's more fun," he says to himself, "just shoot the hoops."

He stops dribbling with his left hand. Stops dribbling without looking at the ball. Stops shuffling his feet or shooting foul shots without bending his knees. He stops wind sprints and stops the hard, painful drills. He *wanders from the way of good sense*. What would the result be?

Solomon was the second wisest man who ever lived, second only to Jesus, Scripture says. He wrote thousands of proverbs, was blessed by God with wealth beyond imagination in that age, ruled in Israel for many years with peace and prosperity, and was used by God to write three books of wisdom included in the Bible. Yet at the end of his life, he seemed to forget everything he had learned throughout his years. He married literally hundreds of women, many of whom he married to form political alliances for Israel. These often worshipped other gods from their countries. He even built temples for them for their gods. He gradually *wandered from the way of good sense.*"

How could this be? How could he turn from the Lord who had given him so much, including a world-wide reputation as a wise king over a glorious kingdom? This verse gives us a clue to what happened. *He wandered.* He "stopped listening to instruction," God's counsel, that Proverbs 19:27 says will have a similar outcome: you will stray from the words of knowledge."

No matter how much growth you have, how mature and gifted you are, no matter how much success you have serving the Lord, if you cease or stop listening to instruction from God's Word you will stray, or wander, from his wise counsel for living. The past is no guarantee of future security—only continuous attention to God's Word offers that assurance. In fact, becoming part of a group that is *dead* is Solomon's prediction. *Dead* people have nothing to offer. No future to look forward to. No hope for success, happiness, or usefulness.

Now back to our fictional story about Evan. What would be the outcome for Evan if he turned a deaf ear to his coaches and refused to pay attention to any more coaching? If they even allowed him to continue on the team, his usefulness to the team would disappear. He'd lose ball-handling sharpness, any real ability to flow with the team, and soon, the privilege to play and shoot altogether. He's strayed or *wandered* from the *way of good sense*—not just from knowing it, but from doing what is wise to be an effective player.

Wandering doesn't usually happen with one big, horrible decision.

That's what Solomon is warning about in this verse, but his warning is about something more important than basketball. It's about life—eternal life. If I *wander from the way of good* spiritual *sense*, or as Proverbs 19:27 says, *"cease to hear instruction,"* God's words of wisdom about living, I will *rest* among *the* spiritually *dead.* Sadly, Solomon did not seem to heed his own warning for a number of his final years of life. He stopped listening to his coaches: his parents, the prophets, the Levites and priests, and the Word that he had been given from God.

And he *wandered.* He didn't make one big, horrible decision to turn his back on the Lord. He strayed gradually, over time, because he stopped listening. You can avoid *wandering* or straying by praying regularly as you read and hear God's instruction: "Lord, teach me about the way my heart is leaning. Teach me how to apply your wise counsel to my desires, my hopes, my words and actions."

Make your decision now not to turn your back on the wise instructors of God's Word that he has placed in your life: parents, pastors, wise teachers, godly friends, and most importantly, God's direct counsel to you in his Word.

A rocket needs only to be slightly off course at the beginning of its launch to miss a target as huge as the moon. As you continue to pay attention to God's wise counsel, you will stay on course. You will not *wander or* stray from the most important "words of knowledge" about life and living now and for eternity. You will remain on the playing floor and get to shoot the hoops that matter.

For other verses in Proverbs stressing the critical nature of listening to wise counsel, see 1:8,10,15; 2:1; 3:1,11,21; 4:10,20; 5:1,20; 6:1,3,20; 7:1; see also 2 Peter 2:21. Many of these verses are best understood by reading the verses before and after them.

Bridges' Comments:

This verse seems to describe the dreadful and irreversible eternal condition of lost people (see Psalm 125:5). God had opened a way of *good sense* for them but they *wandered* from it. This implies that they were once in the *way* and had been taught it and even claimed to walk in it for a time.

Prayer:

Father, don't allow me to be so wise in my own eyes that I begin to think that I don't need the wisdom of others. Keep me from such pride and *wandering*, please. Especially help me to heed your counsel from those in my life you have directed to bring your guidance to me. Even Jesus listened to the wisdom of his earthly parents (Luke 2:51,52). Help me to imitate him and not stray from the words of knowledge. If he needed to receive the wisdom of his teachers and parents, how much more do I. In Jesus' name, I pray, Amen.

The end of willful *wandering* is eternal death. This was what happened to the wicked son of Jehoshaphat (see 2 Chronicles 21:1,4-6,18,19), and the rebellious children of godly Josiah (see 2 Chronicles 36:1-17; Jeremiah 22:17-19,28-30).

But we don't have to go to these biblical times to see this happen. It is not rare to see children of godly parents cast off the privileges they've had by being born into a strong Christian home. Though they have been taught the "sacred writings which are able to make you wise for salvation" and though they know "...from whom you learned it..." (2 Timothy 3:14,15), they have *wandered* (Jeremiah 14:10).

They show that they never really grasped the fullness of the truths of the gospel or its value. The *way of good sense* appeared too demanding and too humbling for them. They prefer the popular trends of the day. Their pride, self-gratifying dreams of the future, and lack of sincere spiritual care about the path they are taking (Matthew 6:23) has blinded them, so *they wander from the way of good sense.*

Coming to *rest in the assembly of the dead* can be easily connected to people who practice religious and moral things outwardly but have no heart connection with Christ. They may display emotions of sincerity and deep feelings about their beliefs because of a sense of guilt or something that stirs their religious feelings for the moment, but all this is without humble submission to the Lord Jesus for the forgiveness of their sins. In all this, they forget his loving, moment by moment lordship in their lives.

This is like the remorse of Saul. He became quieted and controlled when David played his harp for him (1 Samuel 16:14-23), but his heart was not changed toward God. The true cause of *resting in the assembly of the dead* is that in the full blaze of gospel knowledge, a living faith is absent. Therefore, prayer is not real, desire for the Lord and his will are not genuine, and there is no real effort and endurance for godliness. With all this knowledge and these spiritual privileges, such people still *wander from the way of good sense.*

Wandering is consistent with our sinful human nature (see Isaiah 53:6). The understanding that we've gained over the years, the times of conviction from the Holy Spirit, and the benefits that we've gained by being taught God's Word increase our level of responsibility before God (see Isaiah 58:12,13; Zephaniah 1:4-6). Be on guard for that first *wandering* step--whether it is ignoring truths of Scripture or in careless living. One step may determine the path you follow into error and spiritual tragedy like Bunyan's blinded *wanderers* (in *The Pilgrim's Progress*). They *wandered* out of the straight path and into the tombs of the *assembly of the dead*. It will be a special mercy of God if a *wanderer* is rescued and does not find himself at the end of life among *the assembly of the dead* for whom the "...gloom of utter darkness has been reserved forever" (Jude 12,13).

"It would have been better for them never to have known the way of righteousness than after knowing it to turn back from the holy commandment delivered to them" (2 Peter 2:21). Those who are comfortable *among the assembly of the* spiritually *dead* in this life reveal their true character and their destiny. Even with a Christian home background, one who *wanders* from the way of *good sense* takes himself off the path that leads to life.

Wandering is consistent with our sinful human nature

Watching the sad self-destructiveness that Faithful and Hopeful witnessed (in *The Pilgrim's Progress)* makes us do serious thinking about life. Such wanderers are warnings to us that should make us fear for them and ourselves and "rejoice with trembling" (Psalm 2:11). While we "stand fast through faith" in our relationship to God, we must "not become proud, but fear" (Romans 11:20). We are made of the same thing these *wanderers* are made of. We must always combine a healthy suspicion about ourselves with Christian confidence. We need to fear "lest any of you seem to have failed to reach it" (Hebrews 4:1). Likewise, we need to be thankful for the warnings that make us fear and for the encouragements to keep us from discouragement.

But in this proverb, the greater mass of people is described. They never professed to have known the way of life. They know that "wisdom cries aloud in the street" (Proverbs 1:20), yet they "...hated knowledge and did not choose the fear of the Lord" (Proverbs 1:29). Such a one will occasionally listen to the message of wisdom, but then he goes "away and at once forgets what he was like" (James 1:24). Noah's generation was like this. They literally remained in *the assembly of the dead* (see 1 Peter 3:19,20; 2 Peter 2:5; Genesis 6:4). This is the destiny of everyone with the opportunities to gain God's wisdom and yet who refuse it, turn away from it, and will be found, finally and forever "...dead in..." their "...trespasses and sins" (Ephesians 2:1).

To Help You Meditate:

1. Have you ever witnessed a friend who seemed to begin his spiritual journey well but then wandered from it? What are some of the factors that seemed to tempt him or her to wander from a spiritually healthy condition?

2. What temptations could invite you and maybe persuade you to wander from giving serious attention to spiritual concerns?

3. What have you witnessed others do that has made them grow stronger spiritually?

21:17,20   Do You Own Your Possessions or Do They Own You?

ESV

17 Whoever loves pleasure will be a poor man; he who loves wine and oil will not be rich.
20 Precious treasure and oil are in a wise man's dwelling, but a foolish man devours it.

NIV

17 He who loves pleasure will become poor; whoever loves wine and oil will never be rich.
20 In the house of the wise are stores of choice food and oil, but a foolish man devours all he has.

Wisdom Lived Out Today:

Few things motivate people, both young and old, more than money!

Remember when I offered to pay all the grandkids five cents for every log they would carry from where I cut them in the woods at the cabin to the woodpile where we would split them and stack them? Some of you made out like bandits. You worked really hard and earned quite a bit.

Uncle Brandon will never forget my $10 offer to him to get in the pond in late March to pull the jar out of the pipe that drains the pond. The water had to be in the upper 30s or low 40s, just above freezing (this may have been more about love for Julie and to impress me as his future father-in-law than about the $10). I think he still shivers when he tells this story about something that took place more than 20 years ago. People will do remarkable things for money.

Proverbs says financial payoffs can be wonderful incentives for wise living, careful saving, and thoughtful spending. *Wine, oil,* and *treasures* in these verses represent good and valuable possessions that can be used wisely—or squandered (wasted). What makes the difference? God has created you with the choices to keep wealth, pleasure, and possessions in a right balance in your life or to *love* them and *foolishly devour* them. It's not the possessions that are the problem, in Solomon's mind, it's how much we love them that is the issue.

Do you own your possessions or do your possessions own you? One test of who or what owns whom is how generous you are with your things and money. Nearly all of you and your moms and some of your dads have been part of ministry teams to very poor Haitian villages in the Dominican Republic. At the end of many of these trips, team members gave a lot of their clothes to the missionaries to distribute to the needy villagers among whom their team worked.

Some of you have served in other ways too. Katie, as a pre-teen, served as part of a ministry to orphans when Compassion International came to her church. She continues also as a technology supervisor for all the children's Sunday School teachers in her church. Others of you have earned money in various events to donate to important causes and charities. You were not just concerned about yourselves. Aunt Linda gives her time during the holidays to host people who have no place to go for dinner. She serves in her church during

Bible School in the summer and has begun a toy give-away ministry with her church for poor single moms so the moms can select gifts for their children for Christmas.

In Proverbs, Solomon speaks about that kind of generosity with time and money. For example, he says, "Whoever is generous to the poor lends to the LORD, and he will repay him for his deed" (Proverbs 19:17; see also 11:25; 21:13; 28:22). Wise young and older people are not focused on themselves and what they can get or buy. People who are focused on stuff, in the words of these proverbs, become *poor* because of their *foolish* values and desires. They *devour* what they have, and, in the end, what they have *devours* them. In other words, their possessions take possession or control of them.

> **Prayer:**
>
> Father, help me to keep my priorities in the right order; to keep my things submitted to you. Help me to be generous and hold my stuff loosely; to live like I know that it won't last forever. Help me to seek first your kingdom and not be distracted by what the world prizes most. Help me to give my life to "*buy*" Jesus who is the "pearl of great value" (Matthew 13:45,46) and the "hidden treasure" (Matthew 13:44). In Jesus' name, Amen.

Real *treasure, precious treasure,* comes by prizing what God prizes: a relationship with the One who is the real "*treasure*" (Matthew 13:44)—the Lord Jesus. That *treasure* will never spoil, fade, rot, be stolen, or be out of date. No new version will ever be needed. And his value in your life, if you love him, will motivate you more and more to serve others with what you have and not simply use this world and its possessions for yourself. Jesus said, "But seek first the Kingdom of God and his righteousness and all these things will be added to you" (Matthew 6:33). His rule in your life is the true riches to seek, prize, and love. Don't be easily seduced by the world's passionate *love* of its *wine* and *oil,* symbols of the stuff it *treasures* too much. This only results in bringing one to *poverty* in this life and in the life to come.

Bridges' Comments on 21:17:

19 Whoever loves pleasure will be a poor man; he who loves wine and oil will not be rich.

Is God against *pleasure*? If that were the case, it would truly drive people away from wanting anything to do with Him. *Pleasure* is his idea. As it is, *pleasure* is in the very character of God. "Her ways (speaking of 'wisdom') are ways of pleasantness..." (Proverbs 3:17). Solomon presents "wisdom" in a figure of speech in Proverbs that represents God. The *pleasure s*he offers is infinitely more satisfying than even the greatest material prosperity (Proverbs 4:6-9).

Doesn't God want us to enjoy our earthly comforts? Yes. "For everything created by God is good, and nothing is to be rejected if it is received with thanksgiving, for it is made holy by the word of God and prayer" (1 Timothy 4:4,5). Yet, strange as it may seem, the way to enjoy *pleasure* is not to *love* it but to live above it. "The greatest pleasure is to have conquered pleasure; nor is there any greater victory than that which is gained over our own appetites" (a quotation from Cyprian by Bridges). One who conquers his desires in this way, whether young or old, is like one who buys something as if it were not his to keep. He uses the things of the world but doesn't get engrossed in them. "For the present form of this world is passing away" (1 Corinthians 7:30,31). We are never to be pursuing this world as our true inheritance, our "portion" (Psalm 16:5), as though it could be the source of the permanent happiness for which we were created.

The one who gives his whole heart and time to love *pleasure* and who sacrifices his prudence and foresight to get it is on the certain road to being a *poor man* or woman (see also Proverbs 21:20; the life of Samson, Judges 16:1-21; and the prodigal son, Luke 15:13-16).

The one who *loves wine and oil*, symbols of the "stuff" people look to for a good time and personal security, is on this same self-destructive road. In biblical times, people would measure prosperity by abundant corn and *wine*. *Wine*, especially, if it has such an important place in one's life, is a "mocker" (see Proverbs 20:1; 23:21). It deludes people into a false sense of security. *Oil* was one of the most valuable commodities in Canaan, but to *love* it was also deceitful. Bridges quotes Matthew Henry, saying, "Those who could not live without their delicacies come to be in desperate lack of necessities" (author's paraphrase).

Pleasure is God's idea.

The saddest sight in the universe is to see someone who is locked in the prison-house of his selfishness. He sacrifices his everlasting soul's serious need of Christ's forgiveness and presence in his life for the *love of pleasure*. Salvation is thrown away as a worthless thing. This is the kind of *poverty* to dread. Utter eternal ruin is the end of such attraction and infatuation. Jesus spoke to the rich man in Luke 16:25: "Child, remember that you in your lifetime received your good things, and Lazarus in like manner bad things, but now he is comforted here, and you are in anguish." Earlier Jesus said, "...but woe to you who are rich, for you have received your consolation. Woe to you who are full now, for you shall be hungry. Woe to you who laugh now, for you shall mourn and weep" (Luke 6:24-25).

Youth often dream of uninterrupted *pleasure*. Older folks imagine retirement as a permanent vacation. Neither usually see the illusions and the false hopes that their dreams create. Earthly joys are empty in any long view. They may attract us during our lifetimes, but we will certainly leave them behind. To place our happiness in *pleasure* is to try to build our lives upon a wave of the sea. It rolls from under us and then plunges us into the depths of hopelessness, emptiness, and despair.

But some young or older people are divided in their minds about whether to pay the price to follow Christ. Jesus said, "You cannot serve God and money" (Matthew 6:24). They try to live with the material *pleasures* of this world and claim the spiritual benefits of the next. They ask, "Do we have to be that different from the world?" But this question misunderstands how true faith changes us. When he saves us, God creates a hunger and thirst in us to please him. We want to satisfy a new, holy appetite that he gives us. With these desires, one who gives his life to Christ knows he must separate himself from the pleasures the world lives for. They don't support the growth and life in Christ that I now want. They quench it.

Is it surprising that those who do not know heaven's Christ should be absorbed with earth's *pleasures*? Shouldn't the heirs of heaven live above the *love* of earth? Believers will not be impressed by one who is controlled by his desire for pleasure any more than being impressed by a pig that rolls around in its own filth.

Guard yourself carefully. Watch out for the danger and temptation—the lure of this world's promises of *pleasure*. Keep alert constantly. Though you must use this world's things in your daily living, allow your heart only to have a light grip on them and a tight grip on the things above (Luke 21:34). If you grow in your *love* for *wine* and *oil,* symbols of prosperity, you will be a *poor man.* You will become indifferent to prayer, heartless, and dead to God. You will value shadows as though they are real and interpret truly solid substance as mere shadow. Heavenly pleasures will lose their sweetness to your taste as you prize earthly *pleasures* more highly. One writer said, "For sure, the more a man drinks of the world, the more it intoxicates him."

Spiritual character is our glory. God links personal holiness and spiritual enjoyment. You cannot have the second without the first. Keep the emptiness (Ecclesiastes 2:11) and bitterness (Proverbs 14:13) of this world's *pleasures* and the all-sufficient, fully satisfying pleasures in Christ (Psalm 16:5,6; 17:15; 73:25,26) before you at all times. Shall we let anyone's flawed desires and infected taste buds overpower our wise and sound thinking about what really matters? God forbid!

Bridges' Comments on 21:20:

20 Precious treasure and oil are in a wise man's dwelling, but a foolish man devours it.

Loving what the world thinks is true wealth or *treasure* is the road to poverty in every kind of way (Proverbs 21:17). God does enable us to enjoy wealth as the fruit of work and of his blessing (Proverbs 10:22). He provides comforts and advantages like the way valued *oil* was used in biblical times for cosmetic, medicinal, cooking, heat, and light purposes.

Loving what the world thinks is true wealth or *treasure* is the road to poverty in every kind of way.

Jesus was not forbidding comfort and pleasure to his people when he said "do not lay up for yourselves treasures on earth" (Matthew 6:19). Rather, he was speaking about hoarding wealth for personal security, selfishness, and distrust of God (Luke 12:16-22). *Precious treasure* is in *a wise man's dwelling.* It comes by prudence, discretion, thoughtfulness, and hard work. Such an accumulation of *treasures* is not the same as worldliness

(Proverbs 10:5; Genesis 41:48). Being thoughtless and careless about likely future needs or challenges is not an act of faith. On the contrary, such attitudes are foolish acts of recklessness and negligence (Proverbs 22:3).

The *dwelling* of a godly poor person often contains true valuables. They are the reward of his responsible Christian living and zeal. In contrast, one's palace is truly poverty-stricken where the Bible, with its riches, is not prized or respected, and where the oil of gladness, the Spirit's gracious fruit of joy, is not highly valued. Whoever prizes these *treasures* will have a *wise man's dwelling* regardless of his social position.

A *foolish man*, though, however great his treasure, *devours* what he has. He gulps it down in one way or another: with drugs, alcohol, wastefulness, laziness, gambling, and a variety of other self-indulgent and self-destructive patterns. He serves a master who will leave him with nothing at the end of the year and the end of his life. Drudgery and utter loss await him.

> **Bridges' Suggested Prayer:**
> O God! Please do not leave me to my own foolishness or I'll spend and waste all my *treasure*, the wealth of life you've entrusted to me, instead of investing it and increasing it for your glory and my spiritual and eternal advantage. In Jesus' name, Amen.

This was the prodigal son's experience, but when his Father got involved, the mercy he showed changed his son from being foolish, wasteful, and self-indulgent to being wise, humble, and thoughtful. The Father's love brought him into *a wise man's dwelling* where he became the owner of *precious treasure and oil,* much more desirable than the things he yearned for when he abandoned his father in the first place (Luke 15:13-24).

The Bible speaks of other foolish people besides the addict or spendthrift. Many waste the *treasures* of *desirable* opportunities. One is especially *foolish* who squanders the opportunity to grow in the knowledge of God and in personal holiness (Proverbs 13:20). What riches would be in the hands of a fool if he had a heart for it, but he loses his golden moment! The *treasure and oil* are *devoured* or squandered.

Time and life may be wasted in reckless, thoughtless entertainment and amusement. There are many culturally appealing ways to waste life. One can become numb to a sense of responsibility and wise living if he has little or no desire to live his life devoted to God's purpose in every daily routine. He can become comfortable with living for the present moment, for what feels good, without any thought about eternity.

To Help You Meditate:

1. What treasures can you be most tempted to love too much?

2. Describe someone in your life who seems to have the right balance of having possessions but not being controlled by them.

3. What do generous people believe about their possessions and wealth that gives them joy?

22:11   How to Become a Person of Influence

ESV
11 He who loves purity of heart, and whose speech is gracious, will have the king for his friend.

NIV
11 He who loves a pure heart and whose speech is gracious will have the king for his friend.

Wisdom Lived Out Today:

How would you like to have important people as your friends? People like pastors, employers, teachers that you respect, a mayor, a governor, or even the President? Solomon seems to be saying that this can be a good thing. This proverb tells us one way those connections can happen.

First, he says *pure hearts* and *gracious speech* go together. That's the way God designed life to work, and when they do go together, they can create respectful friendships with influential people that can have a lifelong effect on us.

One of the older deacons in our church told of his remarkable rise in rank in the U.S. Air Force. He said when he was a junior officer, his senior officer would ask his and other men's opinions about a decision he needed to make. Many would tell their superior what they thought he wanted to hear. They'd never disagree with him. They would not show the weaknesses of his decision-making. But Jack did not do that. He would always tell him the truth—especially if his superior was going down the wrong path. Many times his superior would get angry at Jack because it seemed like he was always finding weaknesses in what he was saying, but over time, as his superior was promoted in rank over and over, he made sure he took Jack along with him with each move. He told Jack, "It's because I know you'll tell me the truth, not what you think I want to hear." Jack had a *pure* or true *heart* and spoke respectfully, but frankly, to his commanding officer. Such a person *will have the king,* or in this case, his superior officer, *for his friend.*

Jack had a *pure* or true *heart* and spoke respectfully, but frankly, to his commanding officer.

It's possible to pretend to have a *pure* heart by using words that sound respectable and sincere in order to impress someone. The religious leaders of Jesus' day were this way. He called them "whitewashed tombs." They looked and sounded good on the outside but were full of dead people's bones (Matthew 23:27). Jesus also made that clear when he said a wide range of evil things come from the heart: evil thoughts, sexual immorality, theft, murder, adultery, coveting, wickedness, deceit, sensuality, envy, slander, pride, foolishness (Mark 7:21-23; see also Luke 6:43-45). Sometimes people fake it, so Jesus said, "Either make the tree good and its fruit good, or make the tree bad and its fruit bad, for the tree is known by its fruit" (Matthew 12:33). Sooner or later, usually sooner, one's real nature shows up by the fruit he bears. It's a natural connection. "Even a child makes himself known by his acts, by whether his conduct is pure and upright" (Proverbs 20:11). Even an unsophisticated child soon shows the kind of person he is by his words and attitudes. It's a normal, inevitable connection—character is revealed by what one says and how he says it.

As an encouragement, Solomon says this kind of link, words and character, can help you create a strong, positive relationship with someone. This can affect your whole future. If you link a *pure heart,* your godly wants, motives and goals, with *gracious* or respectable *speech,* the way God wants you to, you will have people of influence, like *a king,* as your friends. They will trust you. They will make the connection between your respectable speech and the kind of person they think you are. They will depend upon you and respect you. Character and *gracious speech* can open many doors of genuine friendship with people the Lord may use in your life for your good, his glory, and your useful, wide-ranging influence.

Prayer:

Father, I need always to keep in mind the connection between my words and the character I display to others. Help me to guard my heart so that my reputation as a respectful and truthful person, in the things I say, gives me connections with people with whom I can speak about your love and grace, wisdom and power.

Let these features in my life position me to influence others for your Kingdom. In Jesus' name, Amen.

Bridges' Comments:

"Purity of heart" describes spiritually renewed people, not the natural, unconverted ones. This is not simply surface varnish. It's not pretension or show or affected appearance of holiness that marks the Christian. Rather sincerity, humility, avoidance of sin, and conformity to the image and character of God describe the child of God. The one who has come to bear this *purity* fully in his character is one who lives in the presence of God. He who loves this *purity* is the child of God on earth. He longs for more and more of it in this life. He wants to grow toward this "goal." This "goal" is Paul's word for his striving ambition in Philippians 3:12-15.

When the fountain or spring is pure, it yields clean, refreshing water. When the "tree is good..." it produces fruit that is good. "For out of the abundance of the heart the mouth speaks" (Matthew 12:33-35).

Purity of heart is not simply surface varnish!

Purity of heart refines one's whole character. It pours grace on one's "speech" so that it attracts the attention and admiration of others who may not even understand where it has come from. The values that motivate such *purity* are a mystery to many (Proverbs 31:10, 26). This was the character of our Savior's *gracious speech.* "And all spoke well of him and marveled at the *gracious* words that were coming from his mouth" (Luke 4:22;

compare Luke 19:48, Psalm 14:2,7). The moral influence of this *purity of heart* or godly character shines a righteous light on disgraceful behavior and makes us ashamed of it.

Solomon spoke of his strong belief that the king should be the "friend" of a gracious servant. This had been his father's conviction (Psalm 101:6; 119:63). Godly character smoothed the way to royal favor for Joseph (Genesis 41:37-45), Ezra (Ezra 7:6,21-25), and Daniel (Daniel 6:1-3,28). We also find godly Obadiah having the trust of wicked Ahab (1 Kings 18:3,12). Ahab's conscience was so sensitive that even though he hated God and wanted no part of holy living, he sought godly Obadiah's advice.

The choice to have *gracious speech* ought to be more true of us than it is (Proverbs 16:12,13). It goes well for a kingdom when the sovereign ruler's choice is to follow this rule (Proverbs 25:5; 28:2). The Great *King* marks this kind of person as his *friend*. He embraces him with his fatherly love (Proverbs 15:9). He welcomes him into his heavenly kingdom (Psalm 15:1,2; 24:3,4). "Blessed are the pure in heart, for they shall see God" (Matthew 5:8). What greater *friend* could one ask for?

To Help You Meditate:

1. What was one time when someone told you something truthful that you didn't want to hear at first, but later appreciated his honesty?

2. Can you think of a time when you were tempted to NOT speak truthfully to someone about something he was doing that you thought was wrong or could be harmful to someone?

3. How do you think one develops the pure heart and gracious speech that this proverb urges you to have?

22:29   How to Stand Before Kings!

ESV

29 Do you see a man skillful in his work? He will stand before kings; he will not stand before obscure men.

NIV

29 Do you see a man skilled in his work? He will serve before kings; he will not serve before obscure men.

Wisdom Lived Out Today:

Uncle Ben worked hard in high school, in college, in the military, in his part-time jobs, and finally in his full-time job. He struggled with most of the school work he did and his part-time jobs were not his first love while he was in college. But he was friendly and had good attitudes. He showed up regularly for work, was trustworthy, and tried to learn the businesses, but nothing really clicked. Nothing became a real love.

Then Uncle Brandon introduced him to one of his business executives in a division that made crash dummies. Uncle Ben had always been good with his hands. He was creative even as a young child, making weapons and clothes for superhero toy models. Then later in his teen years he created shirts, pants, shoes and other clothing by taking clothes apart and sewing them into different designs and patterns. His hands were always busy and his mind creative, so the dummies job was something he liked, but that detail work led him into exploring detail work in other divisions of the company. This exposed him to computer engineering technology-related things. The bug bit. He took courses at Drexel and Penn State while continuing his full-time job and interviewed for an engineering tech job. The people liked him and the recommendation he had as a hard worker. His interviewers saw his positive spirit and liked his initiative and teachability. He got the job.

He'd been with his company less than two years when his general supervisor told him he wanted him to be his replacement when he retired in two more years. To get him ready for more of that, the company sent him on trips to learn more in Japan, Hawaii, and other states of the U.S. Ben loves his work and his supervisors love him. He's *skillful in his work* and he *stands before kings...* (figuratively speaking) *...not...obscure men.*

Your diligence will set you apart from many of your peers. Christians have a much more serious reason to serve and work *diligently* or *skillfully.* They have a Savior who takes notice and blesses such qualities. Sadly, a wide proportion of young adults today have little motivation, display a poor track record of dependability, show little initiative, little respect for authority,

Prayer:

Father, the pressure to be mediocre is all around me. Help me to be diligent and trust you to put me in the right places in your time. Help me to be faithful with the talents and bear the character of respect and responsibility as your servant in whatever I do. Help me to use all that you've entrusted to me and every platform of recognition and advancement for your glory. In Jesus' name, Amen.

have big appetites for pleasure, little self-discipline, and a crippling sense of entitlement. People of influence and authority, like *kings,* will generally see *skillfulness* and diligence in workers. These are the people they want in their presence. They will make an impact.

Bridges' Comments:

Do you see? This proverb marks someone out for special notice. Who? One who is *skillful in his work.* This is one who is quick, alert, and efficiently and wisely using his time, talents and opportunity in his work. He is like the great missionary Henry Martyn who, when in college, was known as a man who "had not lost (or wasted) an hour."

An *obscure,* insignificant position or work role is much too low for such a person. *He will stand before kings...not...obscure men.* This was the case for Joseph (Genesis 39:3-6; 41:42), Nehemiah (Nehemiah 1:11; 2:1), and Daniel (Daniel 6:1-3,28)—all were diligent in their different service roles and ended up *standing before kings.*

Even though this promise may not always be fulfilled in its most literal sense, the *skillful* man will have standing and exercise authority in his own spheres of life. This was the honor that was conferred upon Eliezer by Abraham (Genesis 24). He was committed to careful thinking and decision-making on behalf of his master.

> The noble character of a person doesn't depend on the position he holds. One's more humble, though not famous, life may be just as rich in character and influence as people in more public and visible positions. Faithfulness in the unspectacular routine of one's work will display one's dignity just as much as the good work of another who is entrusted with the fortunes of an empire (Author's paraphrase of a quotation from Dr. Chalmers cited by Bridges).

Skillfulness, even without godliness, is often the way to worldly advancement. Pharaoh chose some of Joseph's brothers for supervisory roles because of their ability (Genesis 47:6). Jeroboam owed his rise to a position of leadership in Solomon's realm to his skillful and "industrious" work and character (1 Kings 11:28). But when a man is "fervent in spirit, serving the Lord" (Romans 12:11), faithfully using his own talents for the Lord in view of his accountability to him (Luke 19:13), both the *obscure* and the more notable people of influence in this world will be below him. *He will stand before* the King of Kings with unimaginable honor and unquestioned acceptance. He will hear, "Well done, good and faithful servant. You have been faithful over a little; I will set you over much. Enter into the joy of your master" (Matthew 25:21-23).

When the Queen of Sheba witnessed Solomon's wisdom, she exclaimed, "Happy are your men! Happy are your servants, who continually stand before you and hear your wisdom" (I Kings 10:8)! If those who stood before the wise King Solomon were as happy as the Queen of Sheba imagined, what must it be like to stand before the great King for those who see his face and serve him forever (Revelation 7:15; 22:4,5)? "This is honor for all his godly ones. Praise the LORD" (Psalm 149:9)! "If anyone serves me, he must follow me; and where I am, there will my servant be also. If anyone serves me, the Father will honor him" (John 12:26).

To Help You Meditate:

1. Tell of a time you were advanced or saw someone else get advanced or given a privilege by someone in authority because they liked the faithful hard work they saw.

2. If you were a boss or business manager, describe someone (without naming him or her) that you would not hire or promote. Why would you not hire or promote him or her?

3. Bridges highlights several biblical characters in his comments on this verse. Select one you think you can learn from the most because of the character's skillfulness.

23:1-3 Not Everything Is What It Seems to Be

ESV
1 When you sit down to eat with a ruler, observe carefully what is before you,
2 and put a knife to your throat if you are given to appetite.
3 Do not desire his delicacies, for they are deceptive food.

NIV
1 When you sit to dine with a ruler, note well what is before you,
2 and put a knife to your throat if you are given to gluttony.
3 Do not crave his delicacies, for that food is deceptive.

Wisdom Lived Out Today:

Not everything is what it appears to be!

This is especially true when it comes to the favors, offers, and promises from someone who has a higher authority and is over you. He may be up to something, not necessarily for your benefit, but surely for his benefit.

I used to play the game Risk with your moms and dads when they were kids. I usually won. I won because I was always giving advice to the other players—advice that was always good for them AND always good for me. That meant I had all of them fighting against each other in the game and leaving me alone. This worked for many years until they began to catch on. Then no one listened to me and I usually ended up losing. The point is that advice, counsel, and gifts that someone offers to you may be ways he is trying to get control of you—to get you to do what he wants, even at your expense.

These verses don't mean *everyone* is out to get you, but the wisdom of Proverbs is from the eternal God who made us and knows what is in peoples' hearts. He warns us to be very careful. When there are gifts, meals, privileges, approval, acceptance, and opportunities offered by someone who is an authority in our lives, there is often more to the offer than first meets the eye. Someone has said, "If it looks too good to be true, it usually is!" and "There are no free lunches." That last saying dates back to the 19th century when saloons offered free lunches to people to get them to come into the bar and get them to buy drinks. Someone is paying for whatever they offer to give away free, and it usually ends up being the person receiving the "freebee."

More positively, another use of generous gifts and offers by wise leaders is to test people. Dining with someone in authority or hearing his offer of generosity may be a test of your self-control and wisdom. Does he see a greedy streak in his guest? How self-controlled is he in the face of generosity? Is he out to get anything he can get or does he show restraint and carefulness and interest in others? Is he interested in serving or in simply looking out for himself? You may be tested to see if you have the ability to say "no, thank you" to opportunities that may not be opportunities at all, but tests or traps. Such a wise young adult will be trusted because he or she is seen to be thoughtful, not easily influenced.

This may show that one is a person worth the risk of hiring or using in a responsible position as a decision-maker. She may be seen as one who can't be bought or easily influenced. She's not only thinking about herself and what may be to her advantage.

The spiritual application for this is easy to make, too, isn't it? The Evil One waves all kinds of "lavish meals" in the form of opportunities to get ahead, get the approval or acceptance of the in-group and gain popularity. College fraternity and sorority houses (special in-groups in college) have hazing parties that have often been ugly reminders that there may be a serious cost to wanting to be part of a group or frat house. Hazing is a ritual of acts someone must do or conditions someone must meet to become part of the house. In some cases, these have been so dangerous that pledges (the students who want to be part of a frat or sorority) have died trying to meet the group's conditions for membership. Hazing has even been outlawed in some states and by many colleges and universities.

Prayer:

Father, make me alert to the offers and invitations that I receive—especially the temptations Satan waves in front of me. Help me to exercise the kind of maturity and self-control in the face of people's generosity that helps me to see situations clearly and not feel flattered to the point that I'm not thinking wisely. I want you to be my Lord to whom I give all my allegiance. In Jesus' name, Amen.

Satan "prowls around like a roaring lion, seeking someone to devour" (1 Peter 5:8). He promises much, but he is a liar and the father of lies. "Sin takes you where you don't want to go, keeps you longer than you want to stay, and costs you more than you want to pay" (Tony Evans). "*Observe carefully what is before you!*"

Bridges' Comments

God's Word is our rule for faith and living. It brings God's claim to direct all of our spiritual and natural actions. "So, whether you eat or drink, or whatever you do, do all to the glory of God" (1 Corinthians 10:31). All of the daily details of life fit under God's oversight.

Suppose you are invited, in God's providence, to eat with an important person. The caution offered here is wise: "*observe carefully what is before you.*" Think where you are; what temptation could be lurking here? What impression is your participation likely to make? If you follow your cravings or show light-heartedness or lack of a caution in such a situation you may give unbelievers reason to make excuses for their unbelief or criticism of you and of Christians in general. Such attitudes could tempt weak believers to follow your example and fall into a trap or temptation they were not expecting (see 1 Corinthians 8:9; Romans 14:21).

But these verses are mainly concerned with the effect of such an offer of generosity on our own selves. Is it not possible for generous offers to stir up our desires and interests too much? So the caution is clear and serious: "*When you sit down...if you are given to appetite...,*" that is, if you tend to give in and go overboard when someone makes a generous offer to you, "*...put a knife to your throat.*" If they make an offer to you of something that you really want, handle that desire as seriously as you would a threat of violence: "*...put a knife to your throat.*" Be stern and determined with yourself (see Proverbs 23:31).

The writer of Psalm 141 prayed, "Do not let my heart incline to any evil, to busy myself with wicked deeds in company with men who work iniquity, and let me not eat of their delicacies!" (Psalm 141:4). Don't give an inch to your desires. Resist the second, third, or fourth appeal to give in. The "*delicacies...are deceptive food.*" Sometimes they come from your host's insincerity and misleading interests, but in the final analysis, even if they don't, the gifts and offers of generosity in this life can never be fulfilling. They will be disappointing. They won't give the lasting pleasure that you may have hoped for. Solomon found that out and wrote about it in Ecclesiastes.

> And whatever my eyes desired I did not keep from them. I kept my heart from no pleasure, for my heart found pleasure in all my toil, and this was my reward for all my toil. Then I considered all that my hands had done and the toil I had expended in doing it, and behold, all was vanity and a striving after wind, and there was nothing to be gained under the sun (Ecclesiastes 2:10,11).

To accept the offers that come your way may be okay, but to crave them and deeply *desire* them is fearfully dangerous.

The young person who knows his own weaknesses will know that he must be cautious. Watch out! Wasn't it the "desires of the flesh" that allowed sin to enter the human race and overwhelm us all (Genesis 3:6)? Giving in to the offers before us and desires we have for them has often tarnished a Christian's testimony (1 Corinthians 11:21,22; Philippians 3:18,19; Jude 12,13) and dampened his spiritual liveliness and enjoyment (see Gen-

---

God gives us that which satisfies our needs, not our greeds.

---

esis 25:28; and compare Genesis 27:1-4 with Genesis 27:26-29). If Jesus' disciples, who were used to simple and sparse living, needed the caution to "take heed" (meaning, watch yourselves) when he sent them out to serve and to follow him (Luke 21:34), such a warning seems to apply to us even more if someone in authority over us makes offers to us. These can be strong, appealing temptations.

We were created with the high honor to have dominion over all creatures (Genesis1:26,28; 9:2). It is our shame, though, if any form of creature should have dominion over us. God gives us our bodies to feed and strengthen us, not to pamper and soften us. He gives us bodies for us to use as his servants, not to master us. He gives food to us for our necessities (Matthew 6:11, 25-33), not to satisfy any feeling or desire that captures us (Psalm 78:18). God gives us that which satisfies "our needs, not our greeds." We are to plan to take care of what we need, not the desires of the flesh. "But put on the Lord Jesus Christ, and make no provision for the flesh, to gratify its desires" (Romans 13:14).

One who puts on the Lord Jesus Christ can never degrade himself to promote the desires of his human nature, his flesh. If an unbelieving Roman philosopher (Seneca) could say, "I am greater and born to greater things than to be the servant of my body," wouldn't it be more shameful for a Christian, now reborn as an heir with an everlasting crown and inheritance, to be the slave of his old desires?

To get as close as we can to going overboard with any pleasure by using the freedom we have in Christ can place us in serious temptation. Be on guard at this weak point. You will find great benefit by being cautious. Remember Paul's determination in 1 Corinthians 9:27: "I discipline my body and keep it under control, lest after preaching to others I myself should be disqualified." He was conscious that he could lose control and seriously weaken his influence and the reputation of the gospel. Peter said it a little differently:

> ...supplement your faith with virtue, and virtue with knowledge, and knowledge with self-control, and self-control with steadfastness, and steadfastness with godliness, and godliness with brotherly affection, and brotherly affection with love. For if these qualities are yours and are increasing, they keep you from being ineffective or unfruitful in the knowledge of our Lord Jesus Christ (2 Peter 1:5–8).

This practical approach to our spiritual warfare will break the power of many strong temptations and give us wonderful victory over our old nature's desires.

To Help You Meditate:

1. Tell of a time when you saw someone accept an offer from another but later ended up regretting it.

2. What are some things people may offer you to test your loyalty or faithfulness or self-control?

3. What are pleasurable things that test your self-control? When are those tests most likely to come at you?

23:4,5   Capturing or Being Captured

ESV

4 Do not toil to acquire wealth; be discerning enough to desist.
5 When your eyes light on it, it is gone, for suddenly it sprouts wings, flying like an eagle toward heaven.

NIV

4 Do not wear yourself out to get rich; have the wisdom to show restraint.
5 Cast but a glance at riches, and they are gone, for they will surely sprout wings and fly off to the sky like an eagle.

Wisdom Lived Out Today

Nothing in this world lasts! Everything wears out, breaks, dies, gets stolen, or becomes out of date. That's true of the designer shoes you wear, the cool shirt or pants you bought, and the music and technology you own. The computer you get will be outdated in the first year you get it, and you'll begin to think about another upgrade. This is such a tough lesson to learn. We live in a world that is obsessed, maybe addicted, to getting the newest things or the most things. "If I just have that _____ (you fill in the blank), it will make all of life worthwhile." But you've already lived long enough to know that if the things don't wear out or break, you will get tired of them soon enough and want something else to replace them. They "fly" away, as the Hebrew word in this verse literally predicts. So, it urges, don't let your *eyes light on* (or literally, the Hebrew says "don't let your eyes 'fly' after") the stuff in the first place. Don't be seduced by a lie.

Jesus urged us to lay up treasures in heaven. Earth is where moths and rust take their toll on things. You know that your keys for your house, car, or locker, and your passwords for your computer, phone, and internet sites exist because thieves exist and search for ways to steal things. Nothing in this world is secure and nothing here lasts, so "seek first the kingdom of God," Jesus said, and all the things of real worth, especially relationships, will be added to you (Matthew 6:33). This is a promise about wealth that will never "fly" away.

Prayer:

Father, I can be attracted to the newest gadget, style, or sound. Help me to keep these things in the right balance in my priorities. Help me not to lose my focus by being captivated or intrigued by things in ways that get control of me. I want you to be in control of me—nothing and no one else. In Jesus' name, Amen.

Bridges' Comments:

Here we have a warning against covetousness, wanting something too much. Wanting stuff isn't always wrong. Wanting it too much is. If riches come from the blessing of God, receive them thankfully (Proverbs 10:22; Genesis 31:9). Then dedicate them wisely and freely to do his will. But what comes more naturally to us is to labor or *toil to acquire wealth* and turn what we want into a kind of idol. That is what the language in these verses implies. This desire emerges from a worldly kind of wisdom that comes out of us naturally. This is not the wisdom "from above" that James wants us to pursue (James 3:15). Wealth may be acquired, with God's blessing, in a way that does not involve covetousness (see Proverbs 28:19,20,22; Ezekiel 28:4,5; Luke 16:4-8), but that is not the focus in these verses.

The wise man uses a beautiful word-play to describe the true nature of riches. It is foolishness at one moment to let your *eyes light on* (literally fly or glance on) riches like a ravenous bird of prey (Jeremiah 22:17; Hosea 9:11), and the next moment have them escape your grasp (also literally fly) as they *sprout wings flying like an eagle.*

If we are eager to get earthly treasure and neglect heavenly eternal treasure, we are either deluded or insane.

We do not learn this lesson quickly. God's school of discipline is usually needed to convince us of the emptiness of such *toil* as well as the nature of what is really *wealth.* If we are eager to get earthly treasure and neglect the heavenly eternal treasure in the process, we are either deluded or insane. If we truly believed that eternal things were real, our hearts would be devoted and our minds would be focused upon them. If we really believed what God says about what is real and important, wouldn't that belief keep us from giving so much time and effort getting the empty things of this life that attract us?

As to the natural, intrinsic value of this world's things, Luther declared that the wealthiest nation in his day, the Ottoman Empire, "...was only a crust, which the Great Father of the family casts to the dogs." The United States should take heed! The West's values and riches are only a crust that will get stale and be eaten up and plundered by others over time. History is a good tutor for us.

As to the lasting nature of earthly *wealth* on a personal level, there is no need to invent *wings,* for *suddenly it sprouts wings.* The person who concentrates his wisdom, talents, and energy, who sacrifices his peace, rising up early and going to bed late (Psalm 127:2), to *toil to acquire wealth,* has often lost it all in an instant, just when he thought he was secure. God's discipline (Genesis 13:5-11; 14:12), or laziness (Proverbs 6:9-11), extravagance (Luke 15:12-16), injustice (Proverbs 20:21; 21:6; James 5:2,3), and robbery may bring one to the deepest poverty (Job 1:14-17). The longest wealthy streak one can have can disappear in a moment in God's economy. Eternity is at the door (Luke 12:20). Naked shall we go out of the world, as we came into it (Job 1:21).

Even this obvious truth does not make most of us *discerning enough to desist* (turn) from our earthly obsessions. Just knowing these things won't make someone abandon his own wisdom, seek true wealth while living here (Proverbs 8:18-21), and make the decision to store up enduring "treasures in heaven" (Matthew 6:20). Grace is needed.

So, here is the contrast: The world thinks only what they see and feel is meaningful and real; the Christian knows it is the invisible that is dependable and lasts. So if you are convinced that the one is a shadow and the other is the real thing, shift the focus of your attention. Give only limited friendship to the things of earth. Give the passion of love to the things of eternity. Thank God for the "better possession and an abiding one"—one that lasts (Hebrews 10:34)!

Having said all of this, it is true that there are moments when believers do rest and indulge themselves in the *wealth* of this world in spite of the "uncertainty of riches" (1 Timothy 6:17). At such times, we need sharp lessons to remind us how *suddenly it sprouts wings, flying like an eagle toward heaven.* Oh! Think, Christian, of your birth from above, of your eternal expectations. Think of the kind of person you will be in a short time when this false promising world will be pushed aside to make way for the eternal realities of the Kingdom of the Son of God! With this future glory in mind, consider how you degrade yourself *when your eyes light* upon a "world [that] is passing away" (1 John 2:17).

To Help You Meditate:

1. What is one thing you wanted so badly for a while but after you got it, you got tired of it or just didn't want to use it very much like you thought you would at first?

2. What are some of the most attractive things your generation easily turns into idols? How can you avoid that temptation and keep good balance in your life?

3. What specific biblical truths can you remind yourself of to help you capture but not be captured by the world and to use it rightly?

24:1,2   Not Being Influenced by People of Influence

ESV

1 Be not envious of evil men, nor desire to be with them,
2 for their hearts devise violence, and their lips talk of trouble.

NIV

1 Do not envy wicked men, do not desire their company;
2 for their hearts plot violence, and their lips talk about making trouble.

Wisdom Lived Out Today:

It's easy to want to be with popular people, isn't it? That's true even when popular people aren't so good. That's what these two verses are about.

Popular people can have lots of influence, get lots of attention, and can have lots of privileges. Those are not bad things, but if the attention they are getting seems to give them a stage to have a bad influence on others, then the wise man's warning is good to heed: *Be not envious...nor desire to be with them.*

God's counselor in this proverb does not leave us in the dark about how to detect these people. He says you can tell if someone is a bad influence by her plans (she *devises violence*) or her talk (her *lips talk of trouble*). Keep your radar up. How do the "in crowd" friends, the kids others want to be with, talk about others? How do their plans affect people who are not so popular, the left out or just different ones? How do their conversations and maybe their gossip influence the way other kids look at the outsiders? Do their actions and intentions help or hurt, build up or tear down, support or undermine, encourage or discourage others?

When Uncle Ben turned 21, we had a birthday party for him. He was in a college near home at the time, so Grandma and I told him to invite some college friends to the celebration. About 30 friends came, but what we saw, quite plainly, was that most were Koreans, with some Chinese and African-Americans, a Hispanic guy, and one Caucasian.

During the party I asked one of the Korean fellows why so many Koreans like Ben. He said, "That's easy. Ben pays attention to us. He helps us. Most others don't spend time with us or seem to go out of their way to help us. Ben does!"

Uncle Ben was the kind of friend to seek out and spend time with. This proverb is a warning about the opposite kind of relationship and how to detect it.

Other proverbs, like Proverbs 13:20, warn that the "companion of fools will suffer harm." Paul said something similar in 1 Corinthians 15:33, "...bad company ruins good morals." Solomon also says that nastiness will end up falling back on their own heads. "Whoever digs a pit will fall into it, and a stone will come back on him who starts it rolling" (Proverbs 26:27), or, as commonly said today, "What goes around, comes around." That is often true in this life because of the way God makes life usually work, but not always. Sometimes these folks get away with their rock-rolling and pit-digging, but God is not asleep. He is not ignorant. "Do not be deceived; God is not mocked, for whatever one sows, that will he also reap" (Galatians 6:7).

Prayer:

Father, help me to be the kind of friend Jesus was to others. Help me not to be impressed or attracted to people who are hurtful to others and themselves. Their goals are different, their gods are different. They live for themselves. I want to live for you and use my life for the advantage of needy people, not to take advantage of them. Help me to care more about what you think and not so much about being accepted by people who don't know or seem to care about you. In Jesus' name, Amen.

Friendships are so important during young adult years, aren't they? It hurts to be left out, not invited, easily ignored, or even more painfully, to be mocked or laughed at. But the wise young adult will be careful to not be seduced, snared or trapped by the promises of attention, friendship, and popularity that come from the wrong kind of people—even if it means feeling alone or sad right now. These losses are temporary for the follower of Christ. Keep the long view, the big picture, in mind. It is the remedy, the "antidote to *envy*," says one excellent writer on Proverbs.

The first half of Proverbs 13:20 asserts that there is another alternative, and it has a different, rewarding outcome. It says, "Whoever walks with the wise, becomes wise..." Other Proverbs that speak about this same positive benefit for such good choices are Proverbs 1:10–15; 3:31–32; 23:17–18; 24:19. The wisest person to keep company with, of course, is the Lord Jesus—a friend who "sticks closer than a brother" (Proverbs 18:24). The identity he gives all his Kingdom citizens is as kings and priests. They have everlasting acceptance by him. What other friend can top that?

Bridges' Comments:

Solomon gave this advice earlier, "Let not your heart envy sinners, but continue in the fear of the LORD all the day" (Proverbs 23:17), but it's hard for young people to walk by faith (2 Corinthians 5:7) if the promises of God are about spiritual realities that we cannot see right now (Hebrews 11:1). What makes it especially hard is when we see and *envy* others who appear to be enjoying the glory of this world's "stuff." Our culture urges us to get all we can and enjoy whatever we get—now!

We can see our condition most clearly, not when we look at the outward effects, but our inward heart motives.

This makes it easy to live without giving any serious attention to God. The world does not accept the idea that "Man shall not live by bread alone" (Matthew 4:4). Those who think this way and have a spirit of *envy*, allow open sin to be honored and the blessings that flow from wise living to be called curses. In a believer, such *envy* withers godly character qualities, poisons our peace, clouds our confidence, and stains our Christian testimony.

The full cup or pleasure in the house of *evil men* stirs up others' *desires to be with them* (Psalm 73:10-14). If hearing God's warnings about the alarming end to which this way of life leads does not make them question their life-style, seeing the hard and hurtful character of these *evil men* should do it (see Proverbs 23:17,18). But it is Satan, poisoning the minds of people, who motivates them to *devise* or plot *violence* in their *hearts* and *talk of trouble* with their *lips* against unsuspecting people. If Satan's shroud of deception were lifted, no one would fall for it. When Haman was *devising* or plotting *violence* against the Jews, his own jealousy and *envy* were deceiving him (Esther 3:8,9; 5:13; Matthew 26:16; 27:3-5; Job 7:15). He ended up being hanged on the very gallows that he plotted and built for someone he hated.

Who would envy Judas? In his agony of remorse, he chose to hang himself rather than live. The psalmist pled, "...do not sweep my soul away with sinners, nor my life with blood-thirsty men..." (Psalm 26:9; 28:3). Let me, instead of studying how to hurt others, study how to reach and build up my fellow-sinners for Christ.

The Christian is the only enviable person in the world. What look like blessings that evil men experience are God's heavy curses. If they were humbled by them, the sting of such curses could really be a great benefit for a sufferer, leading him to Christ. We can see our condition most clearly, not when we look at the outward effects, but our inward heart motives. If we are right with God on the inside, every difficult trial is really a blessing and promise of future benefits. If, on the other hand, we are not in God's favor and don't have his smile upon our hearts and lives, every benefit and good that we experience is really a cause for a deeper level of our judgment—if we ignore the message these blessings tell us about God's goodness.

Instead of being *envious* of these people in their successful evil planning and speaking, rejoice that your Father never counted the empty attention and benefits of this world to be of such a high value that you should have them. They are beneath you as a child of the King. He only gives "good gifts" to his children (James 1:17; Luke 11:11-13).

To Help You Meditate:

1. What rewards or benefits do young adults think will come their way by hanging out with popular people (good or bad)?

2. How could keeping "the long view, the big picture, in mind" be helpful to you or another tempted to become close to popular but foolish people?

3. In what sense should the Christian be "the only enviable person in the world"?

24:19,20   Bold, Brash, and Busted

ESV
19 Fret not yourself because of evildoers, and be not envious of the wicked,
20 for the evil man has no future; the lamp of the wicked will be put out.

NIV
19 Do not fret because of evil men or be envious of the wicked,
20 for the evil man has no future hope, and the lamp of the wicked will be snuffed out.

Wisdom Lived Out Today:

"C'MON, YOU *****," Captain Billy Tyne defiantly yelled at the gigantic wave that was about to flip and destroy his ship and drown him and his crew of the Andrea Gail in the blockbuster movie *The Perfect Storm.* He was bold and brash. He had no fear of God and no thought of the eternity he was about to face, just the determination to face this wave with the courage of a fearless sailor.

Many years ago, when I was in college, I went to visit the sister of a good high school friend. Darlene was older than I was and received a fatal diagnosis of cancer. She had just a few months to live. I wanted to share the gospel with her. I had known her and her family for many years.

As I began to talk about Jesus and his love for sinners who would trust him, she interrupted me. "Rick, I'm glad you came, but you don't need to talk about this stuff. I'm OK. I've made my peace. I've been good enough for God to accept me in heaven. I'm sure I don't have anything to worry about. God will take care of me."

The problem was that Darlene had no trust in Christ as her Savior. She had no awareness that she was a sinner in need of salvation. She wasn't even willing to think about such truths or read about them in the Bible. Her boldness, her confidence, and her self-assurance came from her self-assessment—"I'm a good person, and I'll be OK to meet God."

I left her house literally shaking inside with fear for her. How could someone so near the edge of eternity be so complacent, so coolly confident, and so indifferent to the holy God she was about to meet?

Such people as Darlene and Captain Billy might seem like people to envy and maybe even imitate—bold and confident in the face of an enormous enemy such as death.

But Solomon shows the hollowness of this kind of foolish confidence. He counsels us not to *envy* such people or *fret* because of the way they proudly boast and live for themselves or even threaten us with some kind of harm or insults. They are shortsighted. They think only about this life. They are motivated only by what they can imagine and dream about for their future, but without any solid reasons for why their imaginations or dreams are true. They have talked themselves into believing their fantasies.

But believers in Christ have a surer hope. It's rooted in the sacrifice of Jesus for sinners. There is no other firm hope. Their hope is in his promise of forgiveness and acceptance for everyone who turns to the Lord Jesus for salvation.

Prayer:

Father, it's easy to feel embarrassed when I compare myself to some of my friends. They seem to be so confident in things they do and say even though they don't know you or care to know you. Help me to keep my mind on your promises and be confident in life not because of me, but because of what the Lord Jesus has done for me and because of the future he has for me. That is a hope that will never wear out, be spoiled, or be contaminated (1 Peter 1:4,5). Help me to be bold because of Christ being with me always (Matthew 28:20), not because of an imaginary picture of heroic strength in myself. In Jesus' name, Amen.

Don't feel threatened by any brash or proud attitude unbelievers may display. Like a popular style of pants, shirts, or shoes that they wear, their confidence will become very thin and wear out very soon. Allow your confidence to be because of Christ—not anything you've done, can do, or hope to do in the *future*. That *lamp* of hope will never be put out.

Bridges' Comments:

When someone needs repeated warnings because they are *fretting,* they reveal a deep-rooted disease in their hearts (see Proverbs 24:1,2 and 23:17,18). *Fretting* is worrying. It is playing something over and over in my anxious, fearful, or envious mind. When believers reflect on the mercies of God for even just a few moments, they will see how little reason they have for worry and envy. The mercy of God is infinitely greater than we can imagine. It will sweep the clouds from our sky and make us ashamed of any of our discouragement.

In comparison to God's goodness, we have no reason to *fret* or be *envious.* We have a future. Thinking about that future gives great hope to the righteous. "Surely there is a future, and your hope will not be cut off" (Proverbs 23:18). Such a focus in our thinking will keep our memory or envy of the ungodly in check. Our hope will not disappoint us. Theirs will disappoint them.

Leave the unbeliever with his false hopes. Leave him to his judge. His "lamp…will be put out" (Proverbs 13:9). Sometimes the ungodly person displays a boldness, even a determined fatalism to face the end of life. He puts out his "own lamp" with his rashness. Bridges tells of an unbeliever named Hobbes: "I give my body to the dust, and my soul to the Great Perhaps. I am going to take a leap in the dark." But it was not a leap "in the dark," as he thought, another old author noted, "but into the blackness of darkness forever."

Keep eternity in the balances as you assess life's threats. Don't put too much stock in the show of confidence and cockiness the unbeliever may show in this life. Don't envy his inheritance, and do not undervalue the richness of the future happiness stored up for you because of your hope in Christ. Don't bemoan what is in store for you. Our future is far beyond the unbeliever's imagination, and his future has nothing in it for us to envy. His lamp burns, his prosperity flourishes, but only until it kindles the fire of God's judgment. Then it is extinguished! But the lamp of the godly is only put out here and will be made to shine as a star of heaven for eternity.

To Help You Meditate:

1. Upon what kind of things do non-Christian people base their confidence about life and the future?

2. What keeps Christians from being bold and confident about God's priorities and plan for the future?

3. What reasons can you give not to "fret"?

25:2,3   How Does It Work?

ESV

2. It is the glory of God to conceal things, but the glory of kings is to search things out.
3. As the heavens for height, and the earth for depth, so the heart of kings is unsearchable.

NIV

2 It is the glory of God to conceal a matter; to search out a matter is the glory of kings.
3 As the heavens are high and the earth is deep, so the hearts of kings are unsearchable.

Wisdom Lived Out Today:

When Uncle Ben was still in high school he began to experiment with creating stylish shirts, pants, shoes, and t-shirts. He'd take apart clothes that he had or had purchased and redesign and alter legs, arms, zippers, pockets and logos. He'd often show up for a meal or be ready to go out with friends wearing clothes we'd never seen before—things he'd "made." Ben would sell some of his creations, give some away, and wear many. For his high school graduation present, Ben asked for his own sewing machine so he could continue his work with clothing. He still does some occasional sewing. But in those years, Uncle Ben gave serious attention to learning about style, the kinds of fabric he was working with, and developing the skills to do his creative work. Design and creativity fascinated him, but he had to give focused attention to his work and learn how God knitted the creation together in the first place. Which fabrics, colors, threads, and designs worked and which did not?

God doesn't make every kind of knowledge lie on the surface for people to discover like the colored eggs in plain sight for a young child's Easter egg hunt. God *conceals* features of his creation and the way life works so that people will study and not take things for granted or be careless with what they know. Uncle Ben had an interest in clothing, but he gave attention to fabric, styles, and techniques of sewing to learn how to separate and sew pieces to create unique designs. These are all features of God's creativity that he had *concealed* but still made available to someone who would *search things out.* Uncle Ben *searched.* He enjoyed the work and spent many hours doing it. Friends and customers honored him because of his work. His search for the way God made clothing "work" was a pleasure for him and others.

The mysteriousness of the plant, animal and mineral worlds we live in, the incomprehensibility of our personalities, our remarkable bodies, the universe beyond us and the micro worlds within us all speak of the *glory of God.* God gives knowledge and insight to those who, like *kings,* have the desire, time, and resources to *search things out.* Only the most blind and irrational can come away from such a study and not think of the awesomeness of the One who put all this together in the first place. Psalm 14:1 says, "The fool says in his heart 'There is no god.'"

Prayer:

Father, help me not to be so distracted by the things of life that I don't think about how you have put them together in the first place. Help me to be a zealous learner and explore your world and everything in it for your glory and the pleasure you make possible in the *search*. Deliver me from being the dull, complacent resident of your world who doesn't see your magnificence. Jesus created all our world and holds everything together (Colossians 1:16,17). Amazing! Help me to be captured by and humbly enjoy his glory as the glorious Creator and Savior with everything I learn. In Jesus' name, Amen.

Learning opens up so many worlds—God has designed life to work that way. Most importantly it helps us see our littleness in comparison to our amazing Creator. He is big! He is glorious! Who could put all this together? What kind of mind, creativity, and power must such a One have! *Search!* Enjoy the *glory,* respect and honor God grants to those who *search things out* successfully, but be sure to give him the glory he's due as the Creator of it all! Worship the Creator, not the creation.

Bridges' Comments:

Here Solomon contrasts the great King of Heaven and the comparatively insignificant kings of earth. The glory of each is opposite the other. God's glory is shown in the knowledge and wisdom he *conceals.* The glory of earthly kings is shown in what they can discover or learn when they *search...out* features of his creation. *It is the glory of God to conceal things,* whether he dwells in "clouds and thick darkness" (I Kings 8:12; Psalms 18:11; 97:2) or is "clothed with splendor and majesty, covering (himself) with light as with a garment...", "who dwells in unapproachable light" (Psalm 104:1,2; 1 Timothy 6:16).

How much more glory belongs to God because of what he has revealed about his being, works, and ways, than we can begin to understand because of our smallness and creatureliness! What he has brought to light shows a little of how much he *conceals.* We look at his works. These are just a small part of his ways. His revelation and his works allow us to get just a glimpse of him. "Behold, these are but the outskirts of his ways, and how small a whisper do we hear of him!" (Job 26.14).

We study the seasons of his sovereign rule and providence in the world and in our private affairs, but we sense that we need to pray about what we see over and over again so that we think about them rightly. "Your way was through the sea, your path through the great waters; yet your footprints were unseen" (Psalm 77:19).

We stand in awe of what God has gloriously *concealed* in his great work of forgiveness. John Owen observed that "if it were not somewhat beyond what men could imagine, no one could be saved." In other words, if we had to figure out the plan of salvation on our own, we would never experience it—he had to reveal it. It's a plan so far out of our sight that no one can take it all in. Many sincere believers forget how unsearchable God's forgiveness is and have only a glimpse of his wisdom. As a result, they forfeit confidence in their standing before God and their enjoyment of the peace of the Gospel. We think that we have to know more than he has revealed for this assurance, and it frustrates us.

The same applies to God's great purposes of grace. When we accept its unfathomableness, how far over our head his wisdom is, our hearts burst with reverent praise and adoration. "Oh, the depth of the riches and wisdom and knowledge of God! How unsearchable are his judgments and how inscrutable his ways!" (Romans 11:33). But if we don't accept the mysterious depths of his grace, we are like one standing on the shore and silently admiring the ocean rather than entering into it. To wade in those depths is the sure way to be overwhelmed by them.

Owen said, "…if it were not…beyond what men could imagine, no one could be saved."

In these verses Solomon educates his children in this mystery to encourage them in their lives of faith (John 13:7). He urges them to act upon and live by his deep truths; to come to God's eternal Word without preconceptions of their own to limit it. God, therefore, speaks in the boundless and bottomless works of his grace with a voice from the inner sanctuary: "Be still, and know that I am God" (Psalm 46:10). And this shade of mystery, beyond our ability to grasp it fully, is really the believer's highest joy. Mystery is the dwelling place of our adorable God and Savior. Do not the clouds that *conceal* him radiate the fullness of his glory (Habakkuk 3:4)?

Don't they display him as the simplest yet most incomprehensible Being? Even the greatest human intellect can never by searching "find out the limit of the Almighty" (Job 11:7). Bishop Hall said,

As there is a foolish wisdom, so there is a wise ignorance. I would be pleased, under the circumstances, to know all that I need to know and all that I may know. I leave, though, God's secrets to himself. I'm happy that God has made me part of his court to stand in his presence and worship and serve, though not part of his council in which he makes his decisions. O Lord, let me be blessed with the knowledge you have revealed. Let me be content to worship your divine wisdom in what you have revealed.

So, it is *the glory of God to conceal things*—to do many things, but only reveal a glimpse of their full knowledge that is far beyond our ability to grasp. The greatest glory in his creation is infinitely distant from us. *God conceals.* There is no way we could bear seeing the full brilliance of his glory in all he's made and done. Nevertheless, *it is the glory of kings* (and other people of privilege) *to search things out.* This doesn't mean they may try to play God. They are still creatures like the people they lead. Yet, since people depend upon these leaders in many ways, they must *seek things out* in the stores of wisdom in God's design of creation in order to lead wisely and judge fairly. They must keep the big picture of situations and individual cases for justice in mind. This is why God commanded leaders to write out a copy of the law for their daily study and guidance (Deuteronomy

17:18,19). Solomon displayed such discernment in searching out justice, even without evidence from other sources and despite conflicting testimony (1 Kings 3:16-28).

A leader, though, must guard his counsel and decision-making with caution and care. He sees the bigger picture better than most of those under his leadership. To them, his *heart...is unsearchable.* It may be as impossible for them to measure *the heavens for height and the earth for depth* as to figure him out. This doesn't mean such leaders are making bad decisions, but it does mean we need to be careful about jumping to conclusions and being critical of the decisions and judgments of political, church and other leaders (2 Peter 2:10,12; Jude 8,10). A more humble and fruitful practice for all of us is to offer "...supplications, prayers, intercessions, and thanksgivings...for all people...in high positions..." (1 Timothy 2:1-3).

To Help You Meditate:

1. What areas of knowledge intrigue and interest you?

2. If someone has no interest in "searching things out," what might that say about the way he is thinking about life? What could lead someone to adopt such attitudes of disinterest?

3. Identify three important reasons you can think of for one to "search things out."

26:1   When Honor Isn't Honorable

ESV

1 Like snow in summer or rain in harvest, so honor is not fitting for a fool.

NIV

1 Like snow in summer or rain in harvest, honor is not fitting for a fool.

Wisdom Lived Out Today:

Some things are really out of place. A toddler driving a car, a 275-pound woman in a bikini, a 70-year-old man trying to dress like a teenager, and as this Proverb states, snow in summer or rain in harvest.

These last two examples were not only out of place, they made life more difficult. Snow in summer means the temperature would be cold and the plants in a garden might freeze. A worker could also slip and fall more easily while trying to work. Rain in harvest meant that the work of harvesting would be slower and food could rot in the ground because it could be too wet. Warmth and fair weather in the summer were best for harvesting crops. The weather cited in this proverb was out of place and put a good harvest at risk. That's what honor does if it is given to the wrong people, people who clearly don't deserve it. It's out of place and, most seriously, can make life much harder.

Imagine Cami as president of her high school senior class. A major tradition in her high school has been for the senior class to put together an event for the Special Olympics special-needs children. She's going to need responsible, trusted classmates to take leadership roles to make this event successful. She'll want someone to plan the games, someone to plan the special awards, someone to plan food, someone to select students to run the activities, and, very importantly, someone to advertise the events for the whole school student body and the community.

Trevor, one of her classmates, comes to her and says, "Cami, I want to be put in charge of the making of the posters to hang up around the school and for producing the advertisements for the stores in the area." Cami knows this is a really important part of the planning. She's also been impressed with Trevor's artwork. She knows that a really reliable person is necessary for this role or the whole project will fall flat.

Trevor says, "I get really good grades in art, so I can do this. I've been in the Spanish club and was manager for the track team. I like to be involved in things."

"That's great, Trevor. You definitely have the right skills, but let me talk to a few of the teachers you've worked with and I'll get back to you." Cami was being cautious because she had gotten the sense from others that Trevor doesn't stick with important projects very long.

When Cami talks to the advisor for the Spanish Club, she found out that Trevor really didn't do anything. "He and his buddies just sat around in the meetings making fun of others in the club. They even missed about half the meetings," the advisor said.

And how about his role with the track team? "How helpful was he as a manager when he had that position?" She asked the coach. "He didn't even stay with the team through the season," the coach says. "He quit as manager after less than a month and left the team and me scrambling to find another manager to help out with the track meets."

Should Cami honor Trevor by giving him the advertising leadership position?

Trevor fits into the category of the undependable and even harmful "fool" that this proverb talks about. A fool in Proverbs is one who lives for himself, not considering others. He's not necessarily a mean or nasty person. He's not stupid, either. He simply does not consider God's wise counsel for how to live and how to relate to others. He's like snow in summer and rain in harvest—he makes work really much harder and doesn't help get the important tasks done. He hinders them. He's unreliable like the weather.

> **Prayer:**
> Father, I want to be worthy of your honor by being a faithful person. Help me not to be like *snow in summer or rain in harvest* that makes work harder, discouraging or drudgery for anyone. Especially don't allow me to have that effect on your work and your people. Help me not to be such a fool who will misuse attention that others give to me. Please make my life one that honors you. In Jesus' name, Amen.

Cami would be wise *not* to give Trevor the leading role with advertising and promotion for the Special Olympics events. She might allow him to help another student whom she really trusts to work faithfully in that kind of work, but to give the honor of leadership to someone who is not trustworthy, someone like Trevor, would be *"not fitting."* Or to say it another way: honoring Trevor would really put at risk the goal of serving these needy, challenged kids.

Solomon's counsel here is to urge young adults to be wise leaders. To honor wise leaders and not fools—to recognize people who have a track record of dependability and faithfulness. Giving honorable attention to someone with a foolish pattern of self-centered, careless, irresponsible living will usually slow the work down and may even be harmful.

Solomon is not only giving you a caution about who to honor and not honor. He's also encouraging you to be a responsible, trustworthy person. He wants you to be one who can be honored because you show a wise pattern of care for others and take responsibilities seriously.

The most important task any of us can fulfill is to live faithfully for Jesus—to do his work. God himself honors that kind of living with his blessing and care in such people's lives. In fact, such faithfulness leads him to multiply blessing upon blessing for these people. That's what the Matthew 25:14-30 parable of the talents emphasizes. Jesus speaks praise to a faithful worker when he says, "Well done, good and faithful servant. You have been faithful over a little; I will set you over much. Enter into the joy of your master" (Matthew 25:21). Jesus says the opposite to the unfaithful servant whom he held accountable in this parable. That servant lost all his privileges and received God's judgment for his foolishness. Because of his folly he is called "wicked and slothful" by Jesus (Matthew 25:26).

May your Master and others in need find you "good and faithful" and so *honor* you as a wise servant of his.

Bridges' Comments:

The richest blessings or honors lose their value when given to the wrong people. *Snow* is a beautiful wintry covering. It also has the functional value of preparing the soil and plants for springtime and keeping them from deep freezing and killing temperatures, but *in summer* it is out of season. Similarly, *rain* in its season is a valuable gift, but *in harvest* it can interrupt a farmer's work and, if too much falls, can destroy a crop for the season and create widespread community loss.

This is why *honor* that is unwisely conferred upon or granted to a *fool...is not fitting* for him. He doesn't deserve it and doesn't know how to use it (see Proverbs 30:21,22 and Ecclesiastes 10:5–7).

Honor given to Joseph and Daniel because of their wise counsel and character was a compliment to them and a benefit to the others over whom they were appointed (Genesis 41:38-40; Daniel 6:1-3), but when a *fool* or a mocker of spiritual things is promoted or *honored* publicly, sooner or later his foolishness will be the source of his own disgrace. For Haman, the second in command to Ahasuarus, King of Persia, public honor gave him a platform for his own pride and abuse of his power. He tried to use his position for his own glory. In short order, this led to his and his family's disgrace (read the book of Esther, chapters 3-7).

Let us learn, then, to make our own profession of faith *honorable* with consistency and faithfulness. We ought to seek that heavenly wisdom (James 3:17,18) that will make us worthy of any *honor* that may be given to us. "One who is faithful in a very little is also faithful in much, and one who is dishonest in a very little is also dishonest in much" (Luke 16:10).

To Help You Meditate:

1. Describe a situation where a wrong person or the wrong people were put in charge of something. What led to their failure or negative impact?

2. What qualities would make you a person to be honored to lead or be in charge of a great responsibility or project?

3. Read the brief sections of verses cited about Joseph and Daniel in "Bridges' Comments." What character qualities seem to stand out about each? How could you practice these qualities at home? In school? With friends?

27:1 It Ain't Over 'Til It's Over

ESV
1 Do not boast about tomorrow for you do not know what a day may bring.

NIV
1 Do not boast about tomorrow, for you do not know what a day may bring forth.

Wisdom Lived Out Today:

"We've got this game!" That's what I thought when Penn State was three touchdowns ahead of Michigan at halftime. I called my son-in-law Paul, an ardent Michigan fan, to gloat. All he said was, "It ain't over 'til it's over." He was right. Michigan came back in the second half to smother Penn State and win the game.

We don't know *what a day may bring*. We can only bank on a prediction about the future when God tells us what will happen. His knowledge of the future is certain. He controls it!

But this verse isn't just talking about knowing the future. It's about *boasting* about it. It's declaring that I'm going to succeed, win, get a promotion, gain some benefit, enjoy a victory or honor in something that will happen in the near future. I think Shaun, Nate, Becca, Lesley and Luke have wisely learned not to do this. They've seen what overconfidence in many athletic competitions can do to individual players and teams. They've seen players brag about the outcome of a game before they played it—and lose. The point of this verse is that such boasting is foolish. We *"do not know what a day may bring."*

The better thing, James teaches us, is to respond more humbly. James writes about this in his New Testament book:

> Come now, you who say, "Today or tomorrow we will go into such and such a town and spend a year there and trade and make a profit"— yet you do not know what tomorrow will bring. What is your life? For you are a mist that appears for a little time and then vanishes. Instead you ought to say, *"If the Lord wills, we will live and do this or that"* (emphasis mine). As it is, you boast in your arrogance. All such boasting is evil (James 4:13-16).

"All such boasting is evil," James concludes. Why? Because when we boast we put ourselves in the place of the only One who knows the beginning from the end—God. We are stating that we have control of life, and we don't. A key player may be sick or injured or a tragedy in the family may occur that takes the wind out of everyone's sails. It may be one of those days when nothing goes right, and there are lots of errors or penalties, lots of missed baskets, bad passes, or missed goals. Any of hundreds of things can happen to interrupt our braggadocious assertions. We're not in control. That's Solomon's message! Humbly recognize that you are dependent upon God and his control of all of history—the big picture of all life and the smaller pictures of your life right now.

There are future things we can *boast* about, though, things the Lord Jesus has promised for all who know him. Their future includes his love, forgiveness, and eternal life. It includes the promise of his presence here and now throughout this life and the soundness of his wise counsel in his Word for all the decisions of this life. He guarantees the fruit of the Spirit to be enjoyed more and more in this life, the future judgment to be avoided because of Jesus' death in their place, a very real heaven that is guaranteed for eternity, and much more.

We can *boast* about these because they are God's doing, not ours. They are his promises and determined will, not our hollow bragging or optimism. He knows and guarantees a future of hope, strength, victory, and happiness for all his children.

Boast about what he is up to. Not what you hope will happen but can't guarantee. "All such boasting is evil."

Bridges' Comments:

The Apostle James says something similar to this: "Come now, you who say, 'Today or tomorrow we will go into such and such a town and spend a year there and trade and make a profit'— yet you do not know what tomorrow will bring. What is your life? For you are a mist that appears for a little time and then vanishes" (James 4:13,14). Both Solomon and James have the same rebuke for someone who boasts that he or she has tomorrow to look forward to. *...you do not know what a day may bring* (Solomon in this proverb), and "you do not know what tomorrow will bring" (James 4:13).

To provide for tomorrow is a biblical duty (see also Proverbs 6:6-8; 10:5; 24:27). After a farmer has brought in his harvest, he plants his seed for the next season. The Christian who is conscious of living out God's will for his life, who rests on God's daily care and provision, walks with God by working daily in dependence upon him. But to *boast about tomorrow*... "all such boasting is evil" (James 4:16).

It is truly illogical, even crazy, to *boast* of what is not our own. *Tomorrow* may be described as an unknown birth. One may wake up in eternity *tomorrow*, or *tomorrow* may give birth to other challenges or opportunities. Yet the one living for his pleasure or for what the world values, he who *boasts* as if *tomorrow* were his own, puts God out of his own thoughts about his life. Others like Isaiah and Luke illustrate how crazy this kind of living is in Isaiah 56:12 and Luke 12:16-21.

Some who live with this kind of over-confidence may tell themselves that they will take spiritual things more seriously *tomorrow*. They may put off turning away from sin and committing themselves to the Lord Jesus today because they believe they can take care of such spiritual matters in some future day. Such a one may say to himself, "I'll turn from the world and its promises and live for eternity *tomorrow*" (Acts 24:25). Would anyone be so foolish as to put off such a decision like this if he believed he would not have a *tomorrow*? Most likely not. We naturally look forward to what we think the future holds for us. Yet, taking *tomorrow* for granted makes many forgetful or ignorant of the enemy's deceitful "designs" (2 Corinthians 2:11). He gets people thinking like this to make them forgetful about God and the uncertainty of *tomorrow*.

Having expressed this caution, we still must live as if *tomorrow* will come. Otherwise, if we thought there would be no *tomorrow*, no one would be motivated to do anything. We would neglect the day-by-day responsibilities for living and forget to prepare urgently for eternity. But we normally forget about the uncertainty of life. We begin to do some

---

It is truly illogical, even crazy, to boast about what is not our own.

---

thinking about eternity when someone's death startles us in some way by showing up unexpectedly or interrupting our regular daily living. How little do we "die daily" (1 Corinthians 15:31).

We can even be so dull as not to think about death with careful personal reflection. Our thoughts can speed ahead to an inheritance we may receive or the way another's death may be for our professional or social benefit. Our deep anxiety about earthly matters and carelessness or disinterest about heavenly ones says much about us. The young look to middle age and middle-aged people look to the last stages of life. We all tend to have our ways to *boast about tomorrow.*

Biblical and world history put these *boasts,* this over-confidence, to shame. In the days of Noah, "...they were eating and drinking and marrying and being given in marriage, until the day when Noah entered the ark, and the flood came and destroyed them all" (Luke 17:27). Abner intended to betray Ishbosheth, Saul's son, and go over to David's side and deliver the kingdom to David because he was insulted by Ishbosheth. He was killed before he could deliver much of anything (2 Samuel 3:9,10,27). Haman had a great sense of pride, self-satisfaction and confidence about his future career when Queen Esther invited him to her banquet. He was hanged like a dog before nightfall (Esther 5:12; 7:1-10). The man who built bigger barns, named "Fool" by Jesus, would give an unexpected account of his soul to God "this night." "This night your soul is required of you, and the things you have prepared, whose will they be? So is the one who lays up treasure for himself and is not rich toward God" (Luke 12:19-21). *...you do not know what a day may bring.*

It is natural for a young adult to be looking forward in hope for *tomorrow*, but a beautiful flower can be cut early or may fade shortly after blossoming. The strong and the weak may be cut down in the prime of life (Job 21:23-26). Do any have a lease or title of ownership on their lives? Though there is a promise of forgiveness for any who repent and believe the gospel, where is the promise of *tomorrow* for repentance?

Does growing older help you to give more serious thought about these matters? It can, but long-drawn-out years of ungodliness and putting off this kind of serious thought can harden someone into a person who is indifferent, too busy right now, or one with the habit of procrastination for this kind of thinking.

What if in the middle of a life of such self-confident *boasting* and self-assurance you face an altogether unexpected day of judgment, one that surprises you and one for which you are unprepared, one that leaves you to grieve forever over your false confidence of security and long life while you are in the lake of everlasting fire (Matthew 24:48-51)? Stop! Consider! Weep! Pray! Believe now, while your conscience speaks to you. Trust in Christ as your security. He is the only guarantee for *tomorrow* that you can have. "…now is the favorable time; behold, now is the day of salvation" (2 Corinthians 6:2). Enthrone the Savior in your heart.

There is no more moving sight than an unbelieving older person, with one foot in the grave, losing all he has had in the world and infinitely more in eternity. One moment he's in this world. The next, he is gone. Heaven and hell are no small matters, no child's playthings. *Tomorrow* presumed and today neglected ruins all. If one stands on the brink of eternity's edge, he has a privileged moment for prayer before the door of mercy is closed forever.

Tomorrow presumed and today neglected ruins all.

Has the child of God any more reason to *boast about tomorrow* than the unbeliever? What a change his humility will make in his worldly circumstances (Job 1:21) or his Christian experience (Psalm 30:7)! Never will you feel more secure than when you live with the sense that you have no security for a single hour in this life. Leave your cares with God. Rest in his love (Psalm 37:4). Let your disappointments prepare you for your heavenly rest. Bind all your wishes and pleasures to his gracious will. Say, "if the Lord wills…" (James 4:15).

You also need to heed God's warnings. Our hearts readily listen to the world's appeal to satisfy our desires for earthly enjoyment. If we truly believed that "…the appointed time has grown very short…for the present form of the world is passing away" (1 Corinthians 7:29-31), we would not "…rejoice as though [we] were not rejoicing." In other words, we would always be reserved in our joys in the things in this life—they aren't to be depended upon. We would not prize the pleasures of earth so highly if we had a secret confidence that we have a *tomorrow* to look forward to.

As we give up the hope of acquiring the treasures of this world or the likelihood of receiving them later in life, we can be assured that we are only giving up a shadow. The real substance of my happiness remains immovable. To see things as temporary, that is, to "look not to the things that are seen but to the things that are unseen," is true spiritual reality. "For the things that are seen are transient, but the things that are unseen are eternal" (2 Corinthians 4:18). Remember, as one has said, that this world is a wonderful laboratory for perfecting our souls for the next, so "stay dressed for action," Jesus said. Live so as not to be surprised by his coming, "…for the Son of Man is coming at an hour you do not expect". Be ready to "open the door to him at once when he comes and knocks." This is our happiness. "Blessed are those servants whom the master finds awake when he comes..." (Luke 12:35-40).

To Help You Meditate:

1. Describe a time when you or someone you've heard about was embarrassed by a humbling defeat that you or the other person had boasted about beforehand as a sure victory.

2. What does James' counsel to say "if the Lord wills" show about one who follows it?

3. How does biblical hope for the Christian differ from the false optimism of an unbeliever who boasts about his future?

27:5,6   False Friendship Says, "But It Won't Do Any Good!"

ESV
5 Better is open rebuke than hidden love.
6 Faithful are the wounds of a friend; profuse are the kisses of an enemy.

NIV
5 Better is open rebuke than hidden love.
6 Wounds from a friend can be trusted, but an enemy multiplies kisses.

Wisdom Lived Out Today:

It was a senior Bible class. One of the girls with whom I thought I had a good student-teacher relationship had just returned from a trip to Paris with her family. I asked if she had gone up the towers of Notre Dame Cathedral.

"Yes, we saw the gargoyles stationed all along the top of the Cathedral."

"Did you see any that looked like you?" I asked, trying to be funny. She laughed— a little, as did I and a few other students. I didn't give it another thought. Then I went on with the class.

A day later her dad came into my office. He was polite but very serious. "Do you know how hurtful you have been to my daughter?"

"I'm sorry. I don't know what you mean," I said.

"You made fun of my daughter in class yesterday."

I didn't remember anything I had done to make fun of her. "I don't believe I did that," I said. "I respect your daughter very highly."

"You asked if she saw any gargoyles that looked like her," he reminded me.

I was shocked. He was right. I saw that in my effort to inject humor into the conversation, I made a comment that deeply affected his daughter. I had completely dismissed the comment and didn't think of it a second more. I had no idea how hurtful I was to her.

"My daughter is already sensitive about her looks, as a young lady. Your comment greatly embarrassed her. Other students said they couldn't believe you'd said that in class." His *open rebuke was better than hidden love.*

It dawned on me what I had done. I was ashamed. "You are right," I said. "I did say that. I had no idea how hurtful such a comment would be to her. I have only the highest regard for her. I am truly sorry." I asked his forgiveness for speaking like that to his daughter.

"I will ask the forgiveness of the class in general and ask her forgiveness in a way that will not embarrass her further," I said. "I was totally out of line to be so thoughtless. I am so sorry for my carelessness."

This faithful father was not only faithful to support his daughter, but he was a faithful friend to *wound* me with his reproof. His faithfulness was first to obey the Lord and talk directly to me, then to seek protection for his daughter, and finally to *faithfully wound* me as a friend.

They both forgave me. Consistent with their love for the Lord, the father and daughter and I shared some positive moments throughout the balance of the school year. But his stinging rebuke, his *wound,* has been a lifelong reminder of how thoughtless words could hurt without any intention to be hurtful. His faithful *wound* has been a powerful and positive message to my heart for many years.

Too often we won't *wound* a *friend* by talking to him openly about something he's wrongly done or said. We rationalize that "he'll just think I'm saying I'm better than he is," or, "it won't do any good any- way; he won't listen to me." Both of these may be true, of course, but *faithfulness* as a *friend* means risking that friendship and maybe being accused of not really being a good friend. It may mean you suffer from his angry reaction. Being *faithful,* though, is caring enough for your friend not to let him keep on hurting himself or others by his foolish behaviors, words, or attitudes. It's *love* as God describes it. It's what God tells me wise and *faithful* friendship involves. The *kisses* of an enemy are what may feel good or sound good at the moment, but they are not helpful, caring, evidence of true *loving friendship.* Other proverbs tell us *how* to speak wisely; this one just tells us to speak *lovingly!*

> **Prayer:**
> Father, help me to be faithful to you to bring wounds into the lives of others and not just offer *kisses* like some *deceitful enemy* might do. Help me not to pretend to *love* people, to offer *kisses* (patronizing or flattering words) to them, by ignoring hurtful sin and pretending everything is all right when it's not—especially when I see their wrong-doing affecting others. Help me to be a true friend, even if it means risking that friendship for his benefit. Help me to care what you think more than what anyone else thinks and to be a *faithful friend.* Help me, also, to be willing to receive the loving corrections from people who care about me, to be humble enough to recognize when I step over the line with my words or actions. In Jesus' name, Amen.

Bridges' Comments:

What is a friend like, in the deepest sense? Is he one who will just say things to make me feel good? Is he one who will say things that flatter me? Is he one who just enjoys being with me? This is very shallow friendship. It's not what I value in a friend. Friendship like this falls far short of what I need!

I am a poor, straying sinner with a wandering and blind heart. I go wrong with every step. The friend I need is one who will watch over me with *open rebuke.* He is one who will correct me when it is needed and not flatter me with shallow praise or false words of encouragement. If someone isn't willing to confront me when I'm in the wrong, his genuine friendship is doubtful. It's a friendship that is useless. It's a paralyzed friendship.

Secret or *hidden love* that keeps me from saying needed but painful things to a friend, inflicting painful *wounds* by *open rebuke,* is not *love* at all. By God's standard this is "hatred" (Leviticus 19:17), not love. It is far better to *wound* a friend by probing around a wound with pressure, cutting out an area of infection like a surgeon might do, or trying to remove dirt or a splinter with a needle in a friend's foot or hand, than simply covering it over with a bandage. *Rebuke* that is kindly, thoughtfully, and prayerfully given cements friendship. It does not threaten or weaken it. It heals. If such caring conversation does result in resentment or anger, it only proves that the friendship was never that strong to begin with. Many people insist that they are true friends, yet by avoiding this loving, vital responsibility, they treat their friend as "an enemy." That was the Apostle Paul's conclusion in Galatians 4:16. "Have I then become your enemy by telling you the truth?" he asked.

Some evade this kind of open conversation by telling themselves that true friendship "always pleases" a friend, but God's counsel shows that true friendship requires us to "please [our] neighbor for his good, to build him up" (Romans 15:2). Christian faithfulness is the only way to live rightly in relation to a *friend*. Many shy away from this kind of friendship and live with a guilty conscience because of their neglect. They know in their hearts that they have not been *faithful*.

Open rebuke, however, must not contradict the rule of love that is to shape all our interactions. We are to "go and tell him his fault, between you and him alone" (Matthew 18:15). Too often, instead of speaking privately to our brother, one's offense is proclaimed through the church or other small group before it ever reaches the proper destination. *Open rebuke* describes a sincere personal conversation, not public exposure of an offender. There are exceptions to this, of course, as when the nature of the offense is very serious or when the welfare of others may be at risk (1 Timothy 5:20), but never let a shallow version of *love* replace or dilute the genuine *love* that may need to *wound*.

Christian faithfulness is the only way to live rightly in relation to a friend.

Would it have been possible for Paul to stand blameless before his Lord by shrinking in *hidden love* from confronting a brother apostle who had compromised a basic principle of the gospel (Galatians 2:11-14)? Peter's sin required *open rebuke*. Such sin must be obvious before we bring it to public view. Likewise, thoughtless slips of the tongue should not elicit our strong reproof, but when needed, we must not forget the spirit of love and gentleness that should control our approach and our words. Leighton, a brother to whom Bridges refers, exhibited such gentleness in his character. When he did reprove offenders, it was correction to a believer who repeated his behavior. The mark of true godliness is an eagerness to have our faults pointed out and a spirit of thankfulness to those who are willing to give themselves to such a self-denying act of *love*.

Having a *friend* who will faithfully reprove us is a very great help in our Christian walk. Such a friend is to be valued above the greatest treasure. One old-time bishop Bridges quotes said that "he who would be safe must have a faithful friend or a bitter enemy to keep him from evil by the corrections of the one or the condemnation of the other." This kind of *faithfulness* is much more valuable than the smooth politeness of the world's manner. In fact, believers should still appreciate and thank those who practice this kind of love because of the benefit that comes from it—even if their friends may lack some of the graciousness or artfulness that would make it easier to receive.

The truest *friend* of man is one whose *wounds are faithful*. He will not pass by a single fault in his people. He applies this principle out of his holy character and the deep regard for his friend's welfare. Who would not prefer such a *faithful wound*, however painful, in the place of the deceitful *kisses of an enemy* (See Proverbs 26:23-26 and Nehemiah 6:2)? The *kiss* of Judas was a bitter ingredient in the Savior's cup of suffering (Matthew 26:48,49 compared to Psalm 41:9 and 55:12,13). His foreknowledge of Judas' treachery (John 6:70; 13:18-26) did not make his betrayal any more bearable or weaken the intensity of his incalculable suffering on behalf of those he loved.

To Help You Meditate:

1. Describe a time when, out of fear, you backed away from talking to a friend about a wrong act or attitude he or she displayed. What could you tell yourself the next time a situation like that occurs to help you speak truthfully and compassionately to someone?

2. How is such openness by a friend who lovingly speaks with a word of rebuke or correction truly loving?

3. What are reasons a true friend may give himself or herself to speak with loving, open rebuke to a friend? What if the friend doesn't respond well to the conversation?

28:1   Jesus Has Your Back!

ESV

1 The wicked flee when no one pursues, but the righteous are bold as a lion.

NIV

1 The wicked man flees though no one pursues, but the righteous are as bold as a lion.

Wisdom Lived Out Today

When you are sure someone's got your back, you don't have to be looking over your shoulder!

Every human being comes hardwired with the inward sense: "There is a God to whom I must answer." This is what the Apostle Paul means when he says, "For what can be known about God is plain to them, because God has shown it to them" (Romans 1:19). It's "plain," but they don't want to see it.

A few verses later Paul refers to that knowledge again and says, "...they know God's decree that those who practice such things deserve to die..." (Romans 1:32). In other words, everyone not only has a sense of right and wrong, but also has a sense that wrong will be judged by God.

So, *the wicked flee when no one pursues,* or chases them, because they have a sense that "God is going to get me for the wrong I am doing or have done or plan to do."

Aunt Kahee is studying both art and psychology in order to help children and others with a form of art therapy. One feature of her approach to people plagued with guilt that can truly help them will be to direct them to the "Wonderful Counselor," the Lord Jesus. Jesus forgives sin. He's the only one who can do that—sin of any kind. He totally paid for it by his death. For the person, young or old, who trusts in Jesus for forgiveness (John 3:16), "the blood of Jesus...cleanses us from all sin" (1 John 1:7). His forgiveness alone will "...purify our conscience...," and more than that, it sets us on the path to "...serve the living God" (Hebrews 9:14). None of our guilty behavior needs to be paralyzing. Christ came to heal such effects of sin.

A person whose trust is in the Lord Jesus, the Good Shepherd, can *be bold as a lion*. His Good Shepherd is his cover from every accusing thought—even the ones that are accurate. His mind and conscience are just as active and accurate as the unbeliever's—even more so because of the Holy Spirit's influence in his life—but the finger of guilt has no power over the believer because Jesus took it all with his blood. As stated above, the "blood of Jesus...cleanses us from all sin".

Psychologists know that this sense of a guilty conscience and the thought that "I'm going to be judged by God" is real. Much of non-Christian psychology is devoted to wrongly helping people get rid of both of those senses: "I've done wrong" and "God is going to get me because of it."

The world, and maybe some of your friends, may try to cancel out these thoughts in their heads and hearts by telling themselves that a guilty conscience is only something you feel bad about because of how your parents or a preacher treated you. Your parents punished you and threatened to punish you for "bad" behaviors. Your preacher warned you about Hell and God's judgment and "bad" behaviors. So, you grew up feeling guilty about crossing the boundaries *they* drew for you.

The real problem, non-Christian therapists and counselors insist, is not with you, but with your idea of bad behaviors or false boundaries. There really aren't any bad behaviors, and God... well... he is irrelevant or doesn't exist the way the Bible describes him, so get past these two faulty ways of thinking and you'll be fine—guilt free. You can live any way you want to.

Prayer:

Father, help me to live boldly and confidently because Jesus has my back. Thank you for the blood of Christ cleansing me down to the depths of my conscience—the part of me that wants to remind me of my sin and weakness. Thank you for the completeness of his sacrifice for me. Thank you that all past, future and daily sins are covered by his blood. If I confess my sins, he is faithful and just to forgive them all (1 John 1:9). Help me to live with confidence because eternity is full of promise for me—all because of Christ—and help me to hold out this hope to friends who don't know you. Help me to rescue them from *fleeing* in foolish directions in life to escape their guilt. In Jesus' name, Amen.

But therapy and medications galore still don't cancel out what God has built into us—a conscience. We all have a sense that there really is right and wrong and there is a God to whom we're accountable. But the *wicked,* people who say they really don't care about God's law or his will for righteous and just living toward others, still *flee.* It's true that some can persuade themselves that God is a myth and that there really are no rights and wrongs, but like the rust on a car that has been painted over, this knowledge stamped on our hearts by God will bleed into our consciousness over time. Maybe dimly or maybe more frighteningly—no matter what we try to cover it with. Such people almost always will *flee* somewhere for help: alcohol, drugs, sex, food, TV, music, academics, sports, even suicide. They *flee* even though no one on the outside of them is chasing them. It's their hearts and minds that are dogging them. Francis Thompson described this consciousness as *The Hound of Heaven* in his famous poem by the same name in 1893.

Believers may live confidently—because of Christ and his righteousness, not their own innocence or perfections. They don't have any—except in Christ—and they may know "surely" that "goodness and mercy shall follow me all the days of my life..." (Psalm 23:6). He's got your back!

There is no reason for fear for the Christian, even when we fail to follow him perfectly, which will be our normal weak form of obedience, because Jesus' death covers the believer's sin completely. His blood purifies us to the depths of our "conscience," our deepest psychological part (Hebrews 9:14). This is the part that drives others to *flee* in fear, but we may live *bold as a lion* and "serve" (Hebrews 9:14)—all because "...the blood of Jesus his Son cleanses us from all sin" (1 John 1:7). Amazing grace!!!!

Live boldly because of trust in your Savior. He's got your back! Paradoxically, the *wicked* who reject God's authority *flee* from so many other fearful things that aren't real threats in the eternal scope of things, but the *righteous* who submit to him are free from every threat and *bold as a lion* as they approach life.

Bridges' Comments:

The wicked, the name for any who defy, resist, or disregard God, may appear *bold* when they face a threat. They may appear *bold as a lion* if they do not think seriously about any danger or uncertainties in life or if they can ignore their troubled consciences because of wrongs they've done, but if one's guilty conscience is aroused, fear can sound an alarm about the God he or she doesn't want to acknowledge. Then he may *flee though no one is chasing him.* All of us have a deep inner awareness of God and his law. When a guilty conscience is roused, fear results. Guilt is the parent of fear.

Adam knew no fear until he broke God's commandment and became a guilty creature. Then, when he heard the searching question, "Where are you?" he replied, "...I heard the sound of you in the garden, and I was afraid, because I was naked, and I hid myself" (Genesis 3:9-10). But *the wicked flee,* not only when their enemies pursue them (Deuteronomy 28:25), but *when no one pursues* (Leviticus 26:17; Psalm 53:5). Conscience is an invisible pursuer. It stalks its victim closely. It is the messenger warning of the coming wrath of God. There are times when the "...sound of a driven leaf shall put them to flight" (Leviticus 26:36; Job 15:21) and when the "...shadow of the mountains..." (Judges. 9:36) will terrify them. Cain was in fear for his life because he murdered his brother, even though there were no others on earth to fear but his father (Genesis. 4:13,14). Many bold unbelievers have wilted in the face of sudden danger. When the uncomfortable thoughts of judgment come to mind, many a conscience has turned pale at the question, "...what will become of the ungodly and the sinner?" (1 Peter 4:18).

Conscience is an invisible pursuer.

But if guilt brings fear, its removal gives confidence (Hebrews 10:22; 1 John 3:21). *The wicked flee...but the righteous are bold as a lion.* Fearless as the King of Beasts, the child of God fears nothing but offending his Father. The fear of him, the loving attitude of respect and desire to do his will alone, drowns out every other fear. "Though an army encamp against me, my heart shall not fear..." (Psalm 27:3). Moses didn't fear the king's wrath (Hebrews 11:27). Caleb and Joshua stood firmly against the peer pressure of the other spies (Numbers 13:30). Elijah challenged Ahab's anger to his face (1 Kings 18:10,17,18). Nehemiah, in a time of threat and danger exclaimed, "Should such a man as I run away?" (Nehemiah 6:11). Shadrach, Meshach, and Abednego stood undaunted before the furious Nebuchadnezzar (Daniel 3:16). The Apostles' "boldness" astonished their enemies (Acts 4:13). Paul before the Roman governor (Acts 24) and even before Nero, the Roman Emperor, had a courageous testimony (2 Timothy 4:16,17).

In early church history, Athanasius before the Imperial Council of Heresy and Luther at the Diet of Worms were *bold as lions.*

But this is not just true of a few believers. Faithful and steadfast Christians will be *bold* to walk contrary to the course of this world. They will not be intimidated by the scorn of other people because of their values or shaken by those who despise or mock the Word of God. Instead they will "glory" or "boast" in being worthy to be persecuted because of Christ. They will not be afraid of other people, for "If God is for us, who can be against us?" (Romans 8:31). Likewise, believers need not be afraid of Satan. Though he is a "roaring" lion (1 Peter 5:8), he is a chained one! "Resist the Devil…," and coward-like, "…he will flee from you" (James 4:7).

If there is any lack of *boldness* in us, it springs from a wounded conscience, prayerlessness, or a lack of trust. On the other hand, our *boldness* comes from a sense of our own weakness. God's "power is made perfect in weakness" (2 Corinthians 12:9). When God intends us to do great things, he makes us feel, that "…apart from me you can do nothing" (John 15:5). Thus, pride receives its death-blow and God receives all the glory to himself.

Charles Bridges cites a prominent pastor of his day, Bishop Hall, who had expanded on this contrast between the *wicked* who *flee,* and the *righteous* who are *bold as a lion:*

> The *wicked* is a coward, and is afraid of everything; of God, because he is his enemy; of Satan, because he is his tormentor; of God's creatures, because they, joining with their Maker, fight against him; of himself, because he bears about with him his own accuser and executioner. The godly man, contrarily, is afraid of nothing; not of God, because he knows him as his best friend, and will not hurt him; not of Satan, because he cannot hurt him; not of afflictions, because he knows they come from a loving God, and end in his good; not of the creatures, since "the very stones in the field are in league with him;" not of himself, since his conscience is at peace.

To Help You Meditate:

1. Why can imperfect Christians still live and serve Christ with confidence?

2. Why do people who reject God's relevance for life still look for ways to feel good about themselves and their lives? What are some of the ways they try to eliminate their fears?

3. Who are some of the biblical characters you admire who were bold as a lion? Why do you have such deep respect for them?

29:1   The Point of No Return

ESV

1 He who is often reproved, yet stiffens his neck, will suddenly be broken beyond healing.

NIV

1 A man who remains stiff-necked after many rebukes will suddenly be destroyed—without remedy.

Wisdom Lived Out Today:

He was only 60!

He was just told that he would only have months, maybe a year to live. He had killed his liver, and other organs were now in the process of dying.

My brother Bob, your great-uncle, had been an alcoholic for years. His drinking ruined two marriages and other relationships, cost him many jobs, and left him penniless and with lots of life-wreckage in his past. When he died, he owned a truck, a computer tablet that he had never opened, a Bible, a few changes of clothes, and lots of shoes.

About two years before he died, Bob had some warning signs in his body that something was very wrong inside of him. Doctors warned that he may have gone too far but tried to offer him hope. He stopped drinking and moved into a mission in Harrisburg, PA. (He had been sleeping in his truck for some time before that. No one would rent him an apartment.) He became the laundry specialist at the mission and worked at that faithfully to earn his keep there.

Bob was friendly and funny. He could leave any visitor laughing to tears by his stories. In those two years at the mission he gave his heart to the Lord and became a servant to many, but the warnings from doctors and family members he had ignored over and over for years were now coming to pass. He was dying. He was beyond the point of no return. No transplants or medical treatments could significantly delay his death.

Bob had been *often reproved, stiffened his neck,* and was soon *broken beyond healing.*

Not all stubbornness ends like Bob's, of course. Some is more serious than others, but it is true that willfulness and refusing to live wisely, as God directs, does have a cost—sometimes one that will last a lifetime.

This is true of believers and unbelievers. Sin and foolishness, when I stick to it, will cause

Prayer:

Father, I can be stubborn. I can want my way and no one else's sometimes. Forgive me. Help me to have a spirit that is willing to hear correction and *reproof* from others—even my parents, teachers, pastor, and good friends. Help me to listen to you when you speak in your Word and through other wise people you put in my life. In Jesus' name, Amen.

something to die—to some degree. It might be a relationship, trust of a friend or employer, a reputation of dependability and faithfulness, a marriage, or respect by children and other family members. Bob's death illustrates this in a dramatic way.

Be wise. If you are corrected or *reproved* by parents, teachers, or others, don't *stiffen your neck* or "harden your heart" as other passages in the Bible describe this response. Humbly ask God to teach you the way you should go and to give you the strength to change and follow his wise counsel.

Bridges' Comments:

What a terrifying warning! The stubborn ox that stiffens his neck against a yoke (Jeremiah 31:18) is a vivid picture of one who refuses God's invitations and warnings. This was God's chronic complaint against Israel (Exodus 32:9) and a true picture of many unbelievers.

A person can ignore a sense of guilt followed by a plagued conscience, followed by even more guilt. He may even ignore the warning messages of God's disciplining hand in his health, circumstances, failures, hurts, and conscience. Yet the rebel *stiffens his neck*, plugs his ears against the voice of God, and invites the judgment that God threatens.

Sometimes God speaks with "the rod of correction" (Proverbs 22:15) in the form of pain. He intends this to produce "wisdom."

Sadly, this is often a pattern among children of godly parents and those who hear the Word of God faithfully preached (Proverbs 5:12,13; 1 Samuel 2:12). They ignore or even mock every form of communication God has used to offer his gracious invitation to them. God's righteous judgment may become clearer as such stubborn ones become more determined to rebel against God's will for them. Painful consequences often follow. The more informed such a one is of God's wise counsel for his life, the *stiffer* he may make his resistance. Every heartbeat seems to be an objection and a rebellion against God's love.

Sometimes God speaks with "the rod of correction" (Proverbs 22:15) in the form of pain. He intends this to produce "wisdom." This pain could be by illness, an accident, or the death of a friend doing some of the same things he is doing and that he knows to be wrong. But if the fool (one who ignores God's wise counsel for living and goes his own way) continues to despise all God's reproof, his *destruction* will come *suddenly* (1Thessalonians 5:3) and be *without remedy* (Proverbs 1:22-31; 6:15; 28:14,18).

This was why God destroyed the old world by Noah's flood and the cities of Sodom and Gomorrah (Luke 17:22-29) by fire from heaven. Pharaoh also grew more stubborn under God's rod and rushed madly to his own ruin (Exodus 9:21,34; 10:27,28; 14:28). Eli's sons did not listen to their father's rebuke. As a direct result of their stubbornness, both died in one day (1 Samuel. 2:25,34; 4:11). Ahab, after *many rebukes* by Elijah the prophet, *hardened his neck* and went to battle in disguise so he could not be identified by the enemy, but "someone drew his bow at random and hit the king of Israel between the sections of his armor" (1 Kings 22:34). Judas, too, must have made his heart hard against the Lord's warning (John 6:70; 13:10,11,18-27). He'd been with Jesus for three years, but he rushed onward "to go to his own place" (Acts 1:25) with his betrayal of Jesus. The desperation he felt led him to commit suicide.

God is longsuffering, but God's patience does have an end. Once this fearful moment comes for those he endures "with much patience," they are shown to be "vessels of wrath prepared for destruction" (Romans 9:22).

No *remedy*, not even the Gospel, for they reject it, can save them. As they lived, so they die and stand before God *without remedy*. No blood and no advocate is there to plead for them. As they sink into the burning lake, every wave of fire, as it rolls over them, seems to resound with the chorus: "There is no remedy, you are *beyond healing!*"

Sinner—Oh! that you would be wise and consider your guilt, your condition without Christ, your future hopelessness. Consider it now, while final judgment is still in the future. Do you not feel the Spirit of grace pleading with your heart? Will he not save you now from your sins? Would you not obey his call to trust him? You are standing upon mercy's ground, between heaven and hell. O, God of almighty sovereign grace, show this sinner reading these words your longsuffering (1 Timothy 1:16). Let him sing your everlasting praise as a "brand plucked from the fire" (Zechariah 3:2), a monument of your over-abounding grace.

To Help You Meditate:

1. Can you think of an area of stubbornness in your life that would be wise to turn away from? Imagine that area of stubbornness taking deep root in your life so that you never change from it. What could be the long-term outcomes from such a pattern?

2. Some stubbornness is good—not the ones this proverb is speaking about, of course. Can you think of some patterns of stubbornness that would be good to cultivate?

3. How does God, in love, often use pain as a warning to turn from stubborn patterns—for the unbeliever and the believer?

29:20   Don't Sign It!

ESV
20 Do you see a man who is hasty in his words? There is more hope for a fool than for him.

NIV
20 Do you see a man who speaks in haste? There is more hope for a fool than for him.

Wisdom Lived Out Today:

In my first year of teaching at a Christian school, a group of young teachers and a few veterans became upset at an administrative policy announced by the headmaster and principal. These angry teachers talked to others of us who were in our rookie year of teaching and urged us to sign a petition, a complaint. They wanted to send their appeal immediately to the Board of the school—going over the heads of the administrators.

I was young and new. I explained the situation to my senior pastor and asked for his advice. He referred to the wisdom of this verse and urged me *not* to sign the petition. He said, "Slow down. There were probably things about the situation that the teachers didn't understand." He said this hasty action was probably going to affect their testimony and maybe their future ministry at the school.

He was right! By God's good wise counsel through him, I did not sign the petition.

That was the last year several of them taught in the school, and signing did tarnish the reputation of the signers among the administration, Board and some parents. Could they be trusted to handle future differences with the grace and wisdom God wants to be true of his people? Their actions created some doubt. They were *hasty* with their words.

The Bible says justice and fairness issues should be very important for Christians. You will have opportunities to complain, criticize, and even petition people in authority for the rest of your life about wrongs you observe. Be sure to get the facts before you join such causes. "The one who states his case first seems right, until the other comes and examines him" (Proverbs 18:17). There is usually more to a story than first appears. Get the facts and then pursue justice and righteousness with the character God wants you to bear—"the wisdom from above" (James 3:17).

> **Prayer:**
> Father, don't allow me to jump to conclusions and blurt out my first impressions of things. Help me to be wise and humble in my reactions to things that don't seem right when they crop up. Help me not just to "shoot from the hip" and put myself in a more hopeless or irretrievable spot than the *fool* has by his responses. Help me to be like Jesus, who was humble and gentle, even when he rightly understood the wrongs that were being done to him. He didn't lash out at his accusers and abusers. He loved them. Help me in my pursuit of righteousness and fairness to take action, but to be like Christ. In Jesus' name, Amen.

Bridges' Comments:

In Proverbs 29:19, just before our present verse, Solomon says that words alone don't always get people to cooperate.

In this verse, Solomon says that *hastily* spoken words can also make matters worse. *Words* are *hasty* when someone speaks without thinking. The words are just blurted out without forethought (see also Proverbs 18:13). They are *hasty* when one gives his opinion about something without asking others for their thoughts because he thinks that would take too much time and he's in a hurry to get what he wants. *Hastiness* shows up in someone who pushes his thoughts and his opinions forward in front of others who are more mature, knowledgeable, or wiser than he is. This is the fool who "gives full vent to his spirit" (Proverbs 29:11). It is the person marked out for the warning in Proverbs 26:12 who is "wise in his own eyes..." Solomon says "there is more hope for a fool than for him."

It is difficult to reason with this person. Until his stronghold of pride is shaken, no one will be able to talk sensibly to him. The one who is conscious of his weaknesses distrusts himself and is open to ask and receive the thoughts and advice of others. He is more likely to be guided wisely than the one who is convinced that he is right from the start.

It is God's goodness that holds us back from *hasty* judgments or from expressing quick opinions. If we had a perfect mind, our first thoughts would be correct, but we are imperfect. We must think carefully before we speak. It is sound wisdom to admit that our judgment may be mistaken. Self-control and humility will produce solid maturity in the way we express ourselves. This way of thinking is especially important when we discuss spiritual or religious things. Be careful to defend or oppose nothing in a discussion until you have tested it by the true standard—God's Word. Moses postponed his judgment on what looked like sin until he had brought the matter to God (Leviticus 24:10-12). Be "...quick to hear, slow to speak..." (James 1:19).

To Help You Meditate:

1. Have there been times when you made a quick judgment about what someone did and later regretted it because you didn't have all the facts? What could you have done differently?

2. Describe someone you've seen who has handled a difficult matter wisely—without "being hasty in his words."

3. What could be the motivations in a person who quickly jumps into a conversation with his judgments and opinions? What kind of thinking could help him slow down?

30:1-3   Too Stupid to Be a Man

ESV

1 The Words of Agur son of Jakeh. The oracle. The man declares, I am weary, O God; I am weary, O God, and worn out.
2 Surely I am too stupid to be a man. I have not the understanding of a man.
3 I have not learned wisdom, nor have I knowledge of the Holy One.

NIV

1 The sayings of Agur son of Jakeh—an oracle: This man declared to Ithiel, to Ithiel and to Ucal:
2 "I am the most ignorant of men; I do not have a man's understanding.
3 I have not learned wisdom, nor have I knowledge of the Holy One."

Wisdom Lived Out Today:

This is one of the most amazing passages in Proverbs for me. Agur is a sage—a man of wisdom whom others highly respect and to whom they look for counsel. In verse seven we learn he's pretty well up in years. He's been around for a while. In the first verse, he, or his teaching, is given the title *oracle*. This points to him or his teaching as special or as having special authority. Only seasoned, deeply respected community fathers received this recognition. Even more significantly, his authority is certified by God, being included here as Scripture.

Prayer:

Father, I am often blind to my weaknesses. I need to be realistic like Agur but also faithful like he was. I have had such privileges from my family, my church, and others. Help me not to waste them. Help me to become more and more consistent and wise in following the counsel in your Word and from others you've put in my life. Deliver me from discouragement by just looking at myself and then becoming hopeless and useless to you or others. Help me to look to you like Agur did and serve others as he did even while conscious of his weaknesses. You be my strength, please. In Jesus' name, Amen.

Agur was an amazingly wise man, but struggled to think and act rightly and to resist following sinful desires "common" to all people (1 Corinthians 10:13). "But how could I have these struggles?" he seemed to be asking himself. "When I consider the privileges I've had to study, learn, teach, lead, and even mentor other young people over many years, how can I still battle with sin as I do?" This struggle humbled him. "How could I be so weak, battle so long and hard, when I've had such great spiritual privileges and advantages?" This internal spiritual war was wearing him out. The battle was exhausting! So he confesses, *I am weary...and worn out.* (The ESV translates words in the first verse as being *weary and ..worn out.* Other translations interpret the words as names for two of Agur's students, Ithiel and Ucal. I'm following recent authorities who use the words to mean Agur's humble admission that he knows he hasn't "arrived" yet.)

All of you grandkids have had some wonderful privileges too. Some have been in Christian school, some have been home-schooled, while others have been in strong public school settings. Most of your parents have made your family be part of a good gospel preaching and teaching church. You've been part of Sunday Schools, Awana groups, and youth groups. Some of you have even traveled with some ministry teams of your church and have been to Christian camps and on church youth retreats. What spiritual advantages you've had!

Do you ever struggle with the same contradictions in your own life that Agur seemed to have? Maybe you struggle against the tendency of your heart to be negative, impatient, or disrespectful. Do you ever battle within yourself over your attitude when you are with your family in church gatherings to hear the Word of God? How about the way you talk to your mom when she asks you to clean up your room or change your shirt? How about the battle of being content without the latest technology or the most popular style of clothes?

Agur's battles with his sinful tendencies were real challenges to him, too. However, he must have won many battles with sinful temptations over the years in order to earn the respect he received and to be thought of as a sage or wise man.

But he knew what it was to lose many battles too. This happened enough for him to feel like he was *too stupid to be a man.* The word for *stupid* that he uses is a word that is related to being a dumb animal. He's saying, "I am so ignorant and low with the things I battle with that it's like I'm a dumb beast of the field." He goes on to say he even feels sub-human: *I don't have the understanding of a man.*

Do you ever struggle with the same contradictions in your life that Agur seemed to have?

Part of what makes him feel less than human, like a beast, is his awareness of all the experiences, privileges, and opportunities he's had with the Lord. Given these, and seeing the personal battles he has, he feels he doesn't know the first thing about being wise or truly knowing God. "If I really knew the Lord with the maturity people think I have," he's saying, "my life and battles would be so much more victorious! With all my years to interact with God and others, I should be so much farther along in my growth and maturity than I am."

Do you ever feel like that in your efforts to do the right thing when the overpowering temptation to do or say or think the wrong thing seems to win out? You are in good company.

This could seem really discouraging if this was Agur's last word about his life, but it's not. It's clear that Agur is a humble servant who is wise enough to know that he hasn't arrived! In the words of the *hood,* he knows "He ain't all that!" But the balance of this chapter of wise counsel shows him to be a careful observer of life and a recognized good counselor to young people who are beginning their journey to adulthood. His title as an *oracle* shows him to be someone who has struggled with temptations but has won significant victories. He, by God's grace, has been growing—one step at a time. He is respected for his life example even though he is a flawed person. His openness and his humility raised him to a great pinnacle of respect among his peers and the younger generations. His wisdom is for young adults facing their battles too. Wise young people will listen to him because he is in the trenches of spiritual warfare with them.

Agur begins with these humble admissions to his family and others in the community of faith. He wants them to know they must be humble about their own view of themselves. You live in a world that wants you to have a very different view of yourself. It's a world that wants you to think that you need no one else, that you are the captain of your own destiny. Agur knew better. He knew that the best route to wisdom, freedom, and maturity would be to learn God's wisdom.

The rest of this chapter is his counsel to young adults to let them know that their own self-sufficiency isn't all that self-sufficient. Their privileges and spiritual knowledge won't keep them safe from temptation and failure. He's saying, "If you fool yourself into thinking you are OK and need no help from God, your self-confidence will leave you *stupid...and without the understanding* human beings were created to have in the first place. You will be way short of being all that God intended you to be." There is always more to learn about how to live and be the man or woman God wants you to be. None of us will make progress toward maturity by ourselves. All of us need the humility and counsel of an Agur in our lives. All of us need to learn from the One who put us together and who holds life together (Colossians 1:17)—Jesus Christ. He is true wisdom (1 Corinthians 1:30) for people who 'mess up' and are messed up—that would be all of us!

Bridges' Comments:

The two concluding chapters of Proverbs are an appendix to the rest of the book. Nothing certain is known of the writers in these two chapters. It is pointless to speculate about matters like this where God is silent. It is far better to give our full attention and heart to the writer's instruction. Not knowing the writers of many of the Psalms does not limit their profit to us. We know their author even though their writers' names are hidden. It is enough for us to know that they were men who "...spoke from God as they were carried along by the Holy Spirit" (2 Peter 1:21) and that the community of believers in their age recognized their writings as the Word of God.

Agur was recognized as one of the wise men from among the Old Testament people of God. His "words" were an *oracle* or "prophecy," a divine instruction given "unto Ithiel and Ucal." (The King James Version translates as men's names the words the ESV interprets and translates as *weary* and *worn out*). These men were probably two of his disciples. Except for their names, they also are unknown to us.

Ithiel and Ucal may have come to Agur for instruction. He was led to express himself with the most humbling sense of his own ignorance. "You come to me for instruction. But...*surely I am too stupid to be a man. I have not learned wisdom.*"

Later in Israel's history, Amos shows the same spirit of humility. He said, "I was no prophet, nor a prophet's son, but I was a herdsman and a dresser of sycamore figs. But the LORD took me from following the flock, and the LORD said to me, 'Go, prophesy to my people Israel'" (Amos 7:14,15).

Agur went on to state that he did not "…have…knowledge of the Holy One." His language is very strong. He could hardly have stressed his point more emphatically. He confesses himself to be "stupid" or "brutish," as we all are by nature, but because the Holy Spirit awakened his self-consciousness, he considers himself to be "more" ignorant than any others. Is he speaking truthfully or is he exaggerating his spiritual condition with artificial modesty or false humility? If he is being overly demeaning, wouldn't he be dishonoring and denying the work of God in his life?

Agur spoke the truth as he sensed it from his own self-reflection and from God's teaching. Let any of us take "the lamp of the LORD" to search "his innermost parts" (Proverbs 20:27). What we will find with such self-examination is a mass of foolishness and sin as well as the Spirit's working inside of us! Such folly mixed with such wisdom! Such ignorance with such knowledge! Instead of standing tall above others with all the privileges of his wisdom and knowledge, he can only bow low and cry out in shame, "I am too stupid to be a man." Any of us who reflects on his own heart knows that this is true of us as well. We may even think that no one else is as bad as we are.[18]

Such folly mixed with such wisdom! Such ignorance with such knowledge!

Even with his awareness of his own shortcomings, the most discerning, clear-sighted person, seeing God's law clearly and feeling sorry for his sins, will feel that he could never humble himself enough to impress God. He could lie low, lower still, infinitely lower in the dust, yet none of that would be enough humility to earn God's favor.

Holy Paul, comparing himself with the spirituality of the perfect law, exclaims, "…I am of the flesh, sold under sin" (Romans 7:14).

Isaiah, in the presence of a holy God, cries out, "…woe is me! For I am lost; for I am a man of unclean lips…" (Isaiah 6:5).

Job, when he sees God's power, sinks into a sense of absolute nothingness and unworthiness. "Behold, I am of small account…" (Job 40:4). "I had heard of you by the

---

[18] Compare Proverbs 14:10, "The heart knows its own bitterness, and no stranger shares its joy." The following comments from Jonathan Edwards' *Religious Affections* Part III, Section vi, illustrate this subject: "He that has much grace, grasps, much more than others, the great height to which his love ought to rise. He sees better than others how little a way he has risen towards that height. Therefore, when comparing his love to how far he has come in his life, he is astonished to see that he has not made much progress at all. The nature of true grace is that the more a person has of it, seeing the corruption that still lives in him, the less he seems to be where he should be in growth of goodness and holiness. He sees the past and present sinful deformity of his heart as well as sin's hateful defects in his highest spiritual desires." (Author's paraphrase of Edwards' comments.)

hearing of the ear, but now my eye sees you; therefore I despise myself, and repent in dust and ashes" (Job 42:5,6). Asaph, too, one of the Psalms' writers, was conscious of God's spotlight of wisdom shining on him. It revealed how twisted his own foolishness was, so he calls himself a "beast" (Psalm 73:22).

The more personal our thinking is about God and the closer our communion is with him, the deeper will be our humility and self-abasement before him, like the winged seraphim before the throne in Isaiah 6:2 who used two of their wings to cover their faces and two to cover their feet. It is fitting, therefore, that the wisest and holiest of men, though "...renewed in knowledge after the image of [the] creator..." (Colossians 3:10), should confess with Agur, *"surely I am too stupid to be a man..."* Genuine humility is the only path of wisdom. Unless a man stoops, he can never enter the door—he must "...become a fool that he may become wise" (1 Corinthians 3:18)[19] but when he is humbled in his shame, then let him see the house of his God in its breadth and length (Ezekiel 44:5; Ephesians 3:18,19). Let him enjoy more and more clear displays of his incomprehensible God.

How we must approach God's presence with reverence! We must have no careless, light or presumptuous spirit. He who knows our hearts and sees our deep desires for more knowledge of him will generously answer us above and beyond what we even know to seek.

To Help You Meditate:

1. What did Agur seem to know that kept him going, even though he was conscious of the failures of his life? How can that knowledge be helpful to you when you feel like you can do nothing right?

2. Why do the world's popular teachers try to get young people to think they are okay, no matter what failures they've had?

3. "Genuine humility is the only path of wisdom," Bridges states. Why is that true? From Agur's experience, what can we learn about our sin and the true nature of how to gain wisdom?

---

[19] There is a fine ray of wisdom in that consciousness of ignorance that led Socrates to confess—"I only know one thing--that I know nothing." Compare 1 Corinthians 8:2.

30:4   **Where Are the Answers I Need?**

ESV

4 Who has ascended to heaven and come down? Who has gathered the wind in his fists? Who has wrapped up the waters in a garment? Who has established all the ends of the earth? What is his name, and what is his son's name? Surely you know!

NIV

4 Who has gone up to heaven and come down? Who has gathered up the wind in the hollow of his hands? Who has wrapped up the waters in his cloak? Who has established all the ends of the earth? What is his name, and the name of his son? Tell me if you know!

Wisdom Lived Out Today:

Imagine Silas coming to me for computer advice! (I know very little about computers except how to use one.) Imagine Joey coming to me for advice about basketball! (I was cut from the only basketball team I was close to becoming a part of in high school before the season started.) Imagine Luke coming to me for advice about using the electric tools in his dad's shop! (Crazy! I have very little in the realm of building experience!) Imagine Cami coming to me for medical advice! (I've had very little training in healthcare—and that was about four decades ago.) Silas would be wise to talk to Uncle Jeremy, his dad, who knows lots about computers. Joey would be wise to talk to Uncle Jed, his dad, who played varsity basketball in high school. Luke would be wise to ask Uncle Eric, his dad, about their tools—he built their house. And Cami would be wise to talk to Aunt Julie, her mom, a registered nurse.

Whom can I go to for answers? Whom can I trust to know enough, have enough life experience, and speak truthfully to me about my questions? Who can give me good answers to questions I have about my life, my parents' rules, my future if my parents split up, my friends, these zits on my face, my future in this dangerous world, or what to do if nobody likes me?

Agur was a recognized sage or wise man in his community. He knew what it was like not to have all the answers that he wanted—especially about his own life problems. In Proverbs 30:1-3, he's confessed his own lack of wisdom about life and the Lord. In fact, he felt totally at a loss. This was in spite of the fact that many in his day thought he had it all together. He was an older man with a known and respected record of helpfulness. That even made him feel more desperate! He probably thought, "People think I can give wise answers to their problems and questions, and I don't even have all the answers for my own challenges."

But, though he didn't think he was all that special, he did know one important thing. Agur knew the kind of person to look to for help. He knew a good helper would be someone...

1.   *...who has ascended to heaven and come down.* Someone who **knows about worldwide life** and not only about his own little neighborhood.

2. *...who has gathered the wind in his fists.* Someone **who points out invisible, hard to see things that matter.** These may be life-shaping attitudes, motives, and goals (like the kind of attitudes I should look for in my friends). They might not be visible, but they still affect me.

3. *...who has wrapped up the waters in a garment.* Someone **who controls all the unstable,** changeable things in my world, things that seem to flow and change and be out of control, things inside of me (like my moods) and outside of me (like other people's trustworthiness).

> **Prayer:**
> Father, give me the humility to look to you and keep looking to you for wisdom about all my decisions. You are the only one who sees the beginning and the end, the visible and the invisible, the permanent and the changeable. You alone have truth that doesn't change. Give me the wisdom to seek it, depend upon it, and practice it. Give me the wisdom to hide your counsel in my heart so that when I need it, it is right at hand for me to apply.
> Help me to watch Jesus' acts and listen to his counsel and to imitate him. In Jesus' name, Amen.

4. *...who has established all the ends of the earth.* Someone **who really is in charge of everything** and is not surprised by anything, anywhere, at any time (like terrorists, earthquakes, sickness, or my dad's job). One whom I can trust for his control.

5. *...with a name, and a son with a name.* Someone **who is personal,** relates to people well, and listens, loves, and cares. One who understands family matters and can help me in all my relationships.

Who is the person whom Agur trusts in all these ways? It is the God who has spoken in his Word. Agur knew he could count on God and look to him for answers to any and every life matter. After all, he has put everything together in the first place. Colossians 1:15-17 says this is true about Jesus, *his son.*

> He is the image of the invisible God, the firstborn of all creation. For by him all things were created, in heaven and on earth, visible and invisible, whether thrones or dominions or rulers or authorities—all things were created through him and for him. And he is before all things, and in him all things hold together.

Bridges' Comments:

It is no surprise that Agur admitted his own beastly and animal-like ignorance in the first three verses of this chapter. His thinking about the majesty of God only increased his awareness of his smallness. God's works and nature were beyond amazing. It's like Agur's eyes were blinded by the blaze of the sun. For anyone to see YHWH (God's personal and saving name of promise in the Old Testament) as one who has *ascended...and come down* in his creative and saving power and glory (Genesis 11:1,8; 17:21; Exodus 3:8), and then, later, to see him in his Son, the Lord Jesus (John 1:51; 3:13; 6:62; Ephesians 4:9,10), would be amazing. To see him hold the loose winds *in his fists* (Job 28:25, KJV), have control of the *waters* (Job 26:8; 38:8-11; Isaiah 40:12; Jeremiah 5:22), and rule over the *ends of the earth* (Job 26:7; 38:5; Psalm 93:1; 119:90) would be astounding. These sights would cause the most powerful people to shrink to nothingness in their own eyes. The identity of the only one *who has* done this is not in doubt. It is God alone. What human being can make such claims about himself?

The works of our great Maker are overwhelming to view. So, *what is his name...surely you know!* Who is this One? In other words, can anyone completely figure him out? Does anyone know all that goes on within him? Job had these same questions and came to similar conclusions about God.

Can you find out the deep things of God? Can you find out the limit of the Almighty? It is higher than heaven—what can you do? Deeper than Sheol (a name for the grave)—what can you know? Its measure is longer than the earth and broader than the sea (Job 11:7-9).

The Psalmist says it this way: "Be still, and know that I am God" (Psalm 46:10). Don't try to figure him out. Trust him! Humble yourself before the nature and character that he paints of himself in his Word. "I lay my hand on my mouth" (Job 40:4b). Figuratively speaking, lie in the dust before him. Confess with the apostle Paul,

Oh, the depth of the riches and wisdom and knowledge of God! How unsearchable are his judgments and how inscrutable his ways! (Romans 11:33).

The works of our great Maker are overwhelming to view.

Agur increases the mystery of God when he asks, *"What is his name, and what is his son's name?"* Names in the Bible are significant. As in Jesus' case, they often refer to one's character or work. Agur is asking about God's Son's identity. It will reveal more of God's amazing nature.

"No one knows the Son except the Father..." Jesus said in Matthew 11:27, yet what we do know about the Son is revealed to us. He is a Son in the Godhead (an old term used for the mystery of God's nature as three separate persons yet one divine being or essence—the Trinity). The Son is from eternity (see Proverbs 8:22-30). He exists co-eternally with the Father and has the Father's nature and yet is a distinct person. The Son is sovereign, omniscient (all-knowing), omnipresent (everywhere), and omnipotent (all-powerful). He controls the winds and waters (Matthew 8:26; 14:32). He establishes the earth (Hebrews 1:3). He is one who is "in the form of God [and] did not count equality with God a thing to be grasped" like some special prize he could lose. Equality is his by nature (Philippians 2:6).

What is his name? His name is known only to himself (Revelation 19:12). The completeness of who he is, is way beyond our ability to grasp. In that sense it is mysterious.

We must not go beyond what Scripture affirms about him (Genesis 32:29; Judges 13:18). We must stop where God's revelation stops. If we go beyond this boundary, we begin to speculate and guess about things that are not revealed. The temptation, then, is easily to be lifted up in pride (Colossians 2:8)—thinking we know a whole lot more about God or his Son than others know. Sadly, many have gone this route. They think they understand more than others do about God. They give explanations for things about God, heaven, spirit beings, and other matters that go beyond information that God has revealed, but the genuine follower of Jesus knows that the fullness of Jesus' character is just as incomprehensible and mysterious as the Father's. The believer humbly lies at the Lord Jesus' feet and thankfully adores the mystery that he cannot "find out" (Job 11:7).

As much as our Teacher expands our awareness of himself, let us drink in his teachings.

Yet the truths God has revealed to us, from the depths of who he is and who his Son is, are truly pearls of great price. Let us reverently gather these truths to enrich our souls. As much as our Teacher expands our awareness of himself, let us drink in his teachings. Within the boundaries of his revelation, let us examine the length and breadth of the land. The righteous do not care to "go beyond what is written" (1 Corinthians 4:6). The desire to know more than what God has revealed must not dampen our passion to be wise by what he has written for us. To seek to know him beyond his revealed boundaries is rashness. To believe what is revealed is holiness, and to know him as he has revealed himself is life eternal. Unsearchable as he is in his greatness, he is nevertheless near enough to dwell in us. Yours, Christian, is the unspeakable privilege to be one with him who is One with the Father. (Read John chapters 15-17 for the wonderful and mysterious interplay of him "in us" and we "in him".) Therefore, if you *know his name,* as much as he's revealed about it, you won't be able to keep it to yourself.

To Help You Meditate:

1. What are some of the invisible, changeable forces that affect you? How can Agur's source for stability and confidence become yours?

2. Can you think of invisible, changeable forces that affected Jesus? How did he respond? Was he surprised by them? Where did his strength lie?

3. Jesus said, "Whoever has seen me has seen the Father" (John 14:9). What character qualities did Jesus' life reveal about the Father that Agur could trust?

30:5-6   How Do I Get the Answers I Need?

ESV
5 Every word of God proves true; he is a shield to those who take refuge in him.
6 Do not add to his words, lest he rebuke you and you be found a liar.

NIV
5 Every word of God is flawless; he is a shield to those who take refuge in him.
6 Do not add to his words, or he will rebuke you and prove you a liar.

Wisdom Lived Out Today:

Shaun and his dad took me golfing. It was my first golf outing. They both explained the differences between the clubs, how to stand, how to hold the clubs and many other important pointers for staying on the fairway and out of the sand traps, woods, and ponds. I avoided most of these most of the time, but when I didn't follow their advice carefully, my ball landed in all of them. I enjoyed the game and didn't make it too painful for them to have me along, but that was because I paid attention to the people who knew more than I did.

The God of Scripture knows more than you and I—about everything in every category of life. That's what Agur goes on to speak about in verses five and six. God has spoken and given us specific counsel and practical principles to apply; all the guiding principles we need for this life and the next. The Apostle Peter said this, too, about 900 years later. He has given "...us all things that pertain to life and godliness, through the knowledge of him who called us..." (2 Peter 1:3).

In Proverbs 30:5 he says that *every word of God proves true* and is adequate for all my life situations, so I don't need to *add to his words.* His words of counsel are trustworthy. They give safety, *a refuge,* and *shield* of protection to whomever pays attention to them. After all, consider what he knows about life, his ability to see even the invisible things that can affect me. Consider his control of things that seem out of control, his awareness of everything everywhere, and his understanding about relationships. Who else has that kind of knowledge? How foolish it would be to try to improve on or *add to his words*—especially with *words* from someone without his knowledge! Any such ignorant *words* will only end up distorting the truths he's written in his Word for us about life.

So, do you want answers? Maybe not today, but times will come when you do. Look to the same source Agur did—to God's Word! It's a "lamp to my feet and a light to my path," the Psalmist wrote (Psalm 119:105). It will give light to you, too.

Read his wise counsel, his Word, every day. Maybe just a few verses or paragraphs a day. Ask, "What is there about me and my life that makes the wisdom of God in this verse or paragraph important for me to think about?" "What tendency or pattern is God warning or encouraging me to think about?" "How did Jesus show this wise pattern of living?" Make a daily habit of asking wisdom-seeking questions about what you read in his Word.

Are there changes in your attitudes, actions, motives, or thoughts and words that would be wise for you to practice? Agur was looking for just such counsel. The examples, commands, illustrations, and the character of God and the Lord Jesus are sources for that wisdom. The important questions that you will have about life won't happen on some planned schedule. They don't make appointments or announce when they are going to show up. They just show up unexpectedly, but if you are exposing yourself to God's wide range of wisdom about life, day by day, by reading and thinking about God's wise counsel in his Word, you will position yourself for the *refuge* and *shield* he provides for every need you have.

Prayer:

Father, the temptation is to look everywhere else for answers and to you last of all. Help me to reverse that—to come to you first—and then give me the humility to follow your wise counsel, regardless of where it takes me or what it may cost. There is no situation or condition in my life about which you do not speak wisely. Help me to be humble enough to look to you for it. Likewise, help me to have the pattern of looking to you every day to store up wisdom for the times questions and challenges will come. Give me the consistency every day to be in your Word and to meditate upon truths you have laid out for me. In Jesus' name, Amen.

In our golf game, by following Shaun's and his dad's advice about my angle, my stance, my grip, and how hard to hit the ball, I was able to chip the ball over a sand trap and only a few feet from the hole. It only happened once like that, but it did happen, and it was because I was humble enough to believe what they told me to do and then do it. Likewise, following God's wisdom, like Agur, will give you a refuge and shield in your decision-making. It will spare you the frustration and loss that come with listening to counsel that tries to *add to his words.*

Bridges' Comments:

Compare Deuteronomy 29:29 to these verses in Proverbs 30: "The secret things belong to the LORD our God, but the things that are revealed belong to us and to our children forever, that we may do all the words of this law."

Nothing can be learned with certainty about God by abstract speculation. Go to his Word. Here is where there is light and purity. Though there are mysterious, unrevealed truths about God that he has not opened up to our understanding, there are things he has revealed. They are for us to learn and follow.

Everything he's given us God intends us to use to influence our hearts and our behavior. This contrasts seriously with the heart affections to which other religious writings want to take us. There is no permission or encouragement to sin in God's Word. His Word exposes all our hidden sins, all the attitudes and behaviors that we privately hold within ourselves. *Every word of God proves true.* This cannot be said of any other book in the world. Where else is such gold found without any impurities? His Word is "pure...like silver refined in a furnace on the ground, purified seven times" (Psalm 12:6; see also Psalm 119:140).

So, if *every word of God proves true*, be careful not to minimize or make light of any one of them. Very few people read all of his Word. To view the universe of truth that the Scriptures reveal, we must embrace the fruitful gardens (the enjoyable, story, action-oriented sections) as well as the more thought-challenging and less action-packed sections (the detailed, descriptive, and lecture sections). Both come from God's hand and everything in them is of value. Meat can be gained from the details in the books of law and from the history in the lives of kings with their wars and conflicts. There are even many benefits that come by observing people who followed their sinful desires. All of Scripture is Scripture and "all Scripture is breathed out by God and profitable..." (2 Timothy 3:16).

A common Bible-reading trap is to read mostly favorite passages of Scripture. It's easy to miss what God is truly saying by not considering the whole of what Scripture says, the wider passage around a particular word or verse, its context. It is possible to focus on opinions about doctrinal teachings, practical directions, prophetic predictions, or deeper personal experiences. By not keeping the context in view it's possible to miss the true intent God is revealing. Doctrine can become misleading. The practical teachings can lead to a sense of self-righteousness. The prophetic can become imaginative and speculative and miss practical godliness. The one looking for deeper personal experiences can mistake excitement and good feelings for down-to-earth gospel faith, fruitfulness, and holiness. Jesus rebuked the Jews for just such distortions of the Scriptures, saying, "You are wrong, because you know neither the Scriptures nor the power of God" (Matthew 22:29).

Nothing can be learned with certainty about God by abstract speculation.

The great goal of reading Scripture, therefore, is to bring out the whole mass of solid truth with all its implications and glory. God has wisely knit Scripture together so intricately that we cannot grasp any one portion fully unless we think of it in connection with the big picture of all of Scripture. Any interpretation is suspicious if it seems to be forced, to be out of sync with its larger context, or to throw important truths to the side. When a statement of Scripture seems to contradict another, the conflict is usually a balancing truth. Each differing teaching keeps us from imbalance—like the muscles in our body, some are designed to help us move in one direction and others are to help us move back again.

Every heresy or false teaching probably has been built upon some text of Scripture taken out of context—exaggerated or pressed past the boundaries of the whole counsel of God. False teachings cannot stand upon the wider scope of God's revelation. Likewise, the whole of Scripture contains no error. *Every word of God proves true.* Some of us may err because a verse is familiar and we do not search the context carefully. Others may simply not delve into Scripture in any depth at all. If one's heart is right as he approaches Scripture, God will help him become aware of his error and correct it.

The most foundational truth for the Christian is that the Word of God is God's truth. Though it is not all of equal importance, the believer will regard it with equal reverence and respect. We recognize that God is the author of every letter of it. *Every word of God proves true.* To reject any one word of it shows that the whole of it is in question. Bridges quotes the English Reformed pastor, John Owen, as saying that to whatever message the title "...the word of YHWH refers, we must stoop and bow down our souls before it, and captivate our understandings unto the obedience of faith."

This kind of reverence grows out of trust in God. This is a faith that brings a *shield* of God's favor to his dependent child (Psalm 2:11,12; Isaiah 56:2). Sometimes God allows Satan to surround a believer with darkness and to imagine all kinds of troubles coming against him. What will the Christian do in such a time? Does he look to God as his *shield* and *refuge?* He will if he is trusting that *every word of God proves true.* As with Abraham (Genesis 15:1), God *is a shield to those who take refuge in him.* He says to himself, "In all my life circumstances, when troubles come at me from within or without, especially as I think about my guilt before God and the certainty of death and judgment, 'You are my hiding place and my shield'" (Psalm 119:114).

The great goal of reading Scripture, therefore, is to bring out the whole mass of solid truth with all its implications and glory.

Nothing honors God like turning to him in every time of need. If there is ever going to be a time and place for rest, peace and safety, it is in Him. Where else can these be found? Anyone who looks elsewhere is deluded and will only meet discouragement. Even the child of God can trace any sense of desperation to his weak trust in his Divine *shield,* but the *Word of God* not only proves true and dependable, it cannot deceive anyone. It is totally sufficient for all our needs. It is tested like gold in a refining kiln. It needs nothing to be *added* to it to make it more adequate for any of our situations, so to *add to his words,* *words* that have Divine authority, will earn God's *rebuke* and result in shame (Deuteronomy 4:2; 12:32; Revelation 22:18,19).

The Jews *added* their oral law and written traditions to God's Word (Mark 7:7-13). The Roman Catholic Church has done the same thing by adding books to the Old Testament that the early church never recognized as Scripture. Some authors and religious leaders have made similar attempts in our own day. They give religious traditions the same or nearly the same authority as Scripture. They are treading on spiritually dangerous ground. They are adding a new standard, besides Scripture, as an authority for us to be saved by and to live by.

If the "...sacred writings (Scriptures)...are able to make you wise for salvation" (2 Timothy 3:15), what more is needed? If "all Scripture is breathed out by God and profitable for teaching, for reproof, for correction, and for training in righteousness" (2 Timothy 3:16), and if it is sufficient to make "...the man of God...competent, equipped for every good work" (2 Timothy 3:17), what more needs to be said to assure us of Scripture's completeness? If someone questions the Scriptures' total sufficiency and truthfulness in order to undermine its authority, he is sowing deceitful seeds that will breed evil and contaminate God's truth.

It has never been as important as it is today to clarify what is and is not God's Word. God has carefully guarded his *pure* Word for more than 3,000 years from human error. May he prevent his pastors and teachers from "teaching for [true] doctrine the commandments of men," as they proclaim "The Lord has said" when he has not spoken what they are declaring! What reverence, humility, and godly jealousy should such spiritual leaders practice in order not to *add to his words* by their false interpretations or creative imaginations! May they rely on and teach God's mind alone as revealed in his *true* Word.

To Help You Meditate:

1. What are common sources others look to for counsel or advice about living? How do these sources compare with God's Word?

2. What cautions are wise for you to heed when you seek answers or counsel for life situations that you confront?

3. Why is the context (the verses, chapters and even other books of the Bible) of any verse or passage important to consider when trying to interpret and apply God's truth to your life?